Implementing
C# 11 and .NET 7.0

Learn how to build cross-platform
apps with .NET Core

Fiodar Sazanavets

www.bpbonline.com

First published: 2023

Published by BPB Online
WeWork
119 Marylebone Road
London NW1 5PU

UK | UAE | INDIA | SINGAPORE

ISBN 978-93-55513-281

www.bpbonline.com

Dedicated to

To my mother, **Liliya Sazanavets**, *and to the memory of my father,* **Dzmirty Sazanavets**, *who sadly isn't with us anymore. To my wife,* **Olga Sazanavets**

About the Author

Fiodar Sazanavets is a Microsoft MVP (Most Valuable Professional) and a senior software engineer with over a decade of professional experience. He primarily specializes in .NET and Microsoft stack. He is enthusiastic about creating well-crafted software that fully meets business needs. He enjoys teaching aspiring developers and sharing his knowledge with the developers' community.

Throughout his career, he has built software of various types and various levels of complexity in multiple industries. This includes a passenger information management system for a railway, distributed smart clusters of IoT devices, e-commerce systems, financial transaction processing systems, and more.

About the Reviewers

❖ **Vache Chek** is currently a senior software engineer with a specialization in backend and cloud computing.

Science and technology have been a constant source of fascination for him since his teenage years, when he began programming as a hobby on his Commodore 64 at the age of 13. Over time, his passion for programming grew, and he eventually pursued it as a career. Despite being self-taught, he has found that the most effective way to enhance his skills is by sharing his knowledge with others.

❖ **Kratika Jain** is an Enthusiastic Senior Software Developer eager to contribute to team success through hard work, attention to detail, and excellent organizational skills in leading and managing multiple projects while ensuring code quality, security, design pattern, and test cases with continuous integration build processes. She has participated in Agile project management and developed backend applications using Asp.NET, MVC, .NET CORE, Entity Framework, SQL server, and knowledge of software patterns and practices.

Acknowledgement

I want to thank all the people who have supported and mentored me throughout my career. This includes Dikaios Papadogkonas, Vache Chek, Ian Turner, Paul Eccleston, Frank Lawrence, and all the other people I have worked or collaborated with.

Preface

Welcome to this book about C# 11 and .NET 7! If you are a software developer, you have probably heard of C# and .NET, and you may have used them to create desktop, web, or mobile applications. C# is a modern, object-oriented programming language developed by Microsoft, while .NET is a powerful and flexible software framework for building applications for Windows, Linux, macOS, and other platforms.

This book is intended for developers who want to learn the latest features and enhancements in C# 11 and .NET 7. Whether you are a beginner or an experienced programmer, this book will provide you with the knowledge and skills you need to take advantage of the latest developments in C# and .NET.

In this book, you will learn about the new language features in C# 11, such as raw literal strings, improved date handling, and using generic maths. You will also discover the new APIs and improvements in .NET 7, such as a more intuitive command line interface, new functionality in the core libraries, and new project templates.

Moreover, this book will guide you through the development of practical applications using C# 11 and .NET 7. You will learn how to create web applications using ASP.NET Core, mobile applications using .NET MAUI, and compiled in-browser code by using Blazor. Although these technologies are not new, all of them have been enhanced quite significantly with the latest .NET update and this book will demonstrate these enhancements.

This book will also teach you how to use some more advanced .NET tools. You will learn how to build and run artificial intelligence models by using ML.NET. You will also learn how to build distributed applications by using the latest containerization capabilities of .NET.

I hope you will enjoy reading this book as much as I enjoyed writing it. Happy coding!

Chapter 1: Getting Familiar with .NET 7 Application Structure - introduces the reader to .NET 7 and provides a full set of instructions on how to get started, even if you have never used .NET before.

We will first set up our development environment. As you can build .NET apps on either Windows, Mac, or Linux, you will be shown what integrated development environments (IDEs) or a code editor you can install on the operating system of your choice.

We will then create a basic .NET application based on the Console Application template. Once the application has been created, we will examine the structure of a .NET project. Then we will write some code, which will enable us to get familiar with the basic C# syntax along with its inbuilt data types.

Chapter 2: Overview of C# 11 Features – demonstrates many exciting new features have been added to C# 11 to make the lives of developers easier and make the process of writing software more efficient. And this chapter will showcase all these features.

We will first cover struct auto-default, which allows struct-based objects to have their property values set to default values of their data types. This would prevent exceptions from being accidentally thrown. Next, we will cover generic attributes. This feature allows developers to use the generics feature of C# while defining attributes. This makes it easier to work with annotation in the code.

Afterwards, we will talk about sequence pattern matching. This feature gives developers more flexibility while comparing collections. Then we will move on to the new string-related features of the language. These include new raw string literals and multi-line interpolated strings. We will complete the chapter by looking at the required object members and static interface members.

Chapter 3: What is New in .NET 7? - focuses on the new features that have been added to the .NET platform itself, which consists of the SDK, build tools and the core libraries. We will start by going through the SDK and build tool improvements. The new features in these areas include the improvement to the command line interface, compiler optimization and so on.

Then we will cover various improvements to the core libraries, which come from Microsoft and System namespaces. The new features that have been added to these libraries include better observability improvements, new JSON features, improved RegEx, the ability to use TAR compression and several other improvements. Finally, we will go through the deprecated features of .NET 7 and breaking changes that have been introduced into the platform.

Chapter 4: MAUI and Cross-platform Native Applications - MAUI, which stands for Multi-platform App UI, is a framework that allows developers to build native applications that can be compiled to run on Windows, Mac OS, iOS, and Android. The intention behind this framework was that the same code base can be used to build an executable for any platform. And this includes both desktop computers and mobile devices.

In this chapter, you will learn how to use MAUI to build any type of a native application that the framework supports. You will learn how to set up your code base in such a way that you would then be able to compile your code into any type of executable. Some platforms supported by MAUI have some limitations in terms of what you can and can't do on them. And in this chapter, you will get to know those limitations.

Chapter 5: Database Access with Entity Framework 7 - the server-side components of web applications are often required to access a database of some sort. Usually, this is done via an object-relational mapper (ORM), which abstracts away the database access and make it possible to manipulate data directly in the code. ASP.NET Core comes with its own ORM, which is known as Entity Framework Core. In this chapter, we will have a look at the latest version of this ORM - Entity Framework 7.

In this chapter, we will first examine the fundamentals of relational databases that Entity Framework 7 was designed to work with. Then you will learn how to use the ORM itself. There are a few ways you can set up the ORM inside your ASP. NET Core application. And in this chapter, we will have a look at them all: code-first and database-first.

Chapter 6: Web Application Types on .NET - introduces the reader to ASP.NET Core - the main framework on .NET that is designed for building web applications. We will also have a look at various types of web applications that ASP.NET Core supports.

First, we will start with ASP.NET Core fundamentals that are common to all ASP. NET Core application types. Following this, we will have a look at Web API, which is a type of an application that provides REST API for incoming HTTP requests but doesn't have any web pages. We will then move on to model-view-controller (MVC) applications, which allow the web pages to be rendered dynamically depending on the controller actions and the data from models. Finally, we will cover Razor Pages, which is a type of ASP.NET Core application where each web page has a server-side object associated with it.

Chapter 7: Blazor and WebAssembly on .NET - Blazor is a framework that allows developers to write .NET code that can be executed in browsers. This can be achieved in two ways - either by using Blazor WebAssembly or Blazor Server.

Blazor WebAssembly application is compiled into an executable that can run directly in browsers. It can also be hosted inside a standard ASP.NET Core application. Blazor Server, on the other hand, runs all its code on the server. In this case, the component in the browser will be communicating with the code on the server in real time via SignalR. Each of these hosting models has its pros and cons, even though the code would be very similar. This chapter provides an overview of all these hosting models.

Chapter 8: SignalR and Two-way Communication - introduces SignalR - an inbuilt ASP.NET Core library that allows the client and the server to engage in two-way real-time communication. The chapter shows how to build server-side components of SignalR, as well as demonstrating how to set up various types of its clients.

We will cover two types of SignalR clients - JavaScript and .NET. Both client types can be either used in-browser or as stand-alone applications. For example, JavaScript is a language that is native to in-browser applications. However, with technologies like Node.js, it can also be used in stand-alone applications. .NET is primarily used in stand-alone applications. But with a technology like Blazor, it can be executed in the browser as well.

Chapter 9: gRPC on ASP.NET Core - gRPC is a wrapper protocol that relies on HTTP/2 and enables efficient exchange of messages. This chapter demonstrates how to enable gRPC communication on ASP.NET Core. We will cover all the fundamental concepts of gRPC. You will learn Protobuf, which is the messaging protocol that gRPC uses. You will learn how to use Protobuf to set up both server and client-side gRPC components.

You will learn all four call types that gRPC supports, which are unary, server-streaming, client-streaming, and bi-directional streaming. Finally, you will get familiar with all the data types that Protobuf supports.

Chapter 10: Machine Learning with ML.NET - ML.NET is a library that allows developers to build machine learning application on .NET with relative ease. For example, the library makes it possible to select an ML algorithm and generate model for it in C# code. This model can then be re-used for multiple scenarios.

In this chapter, you will learn how to use ML.NET. First, we will go through its most fundamental features. Then, we will create some sample ML models by using some of its most popular algorithms. You will then learn the fundamentals of training and evaluating your ML model. And you will also be shown how to use a low-code model builder to build an ML model in a graphical user interface.

Chapter 11: Microservices and Containerization on .NET 7 - Large-scale applications are often deployed as interconnected microservices that can be scaled out individually. And usually, the best way to deploy microservices is via containers. This will ensure that each service behaves consistently regardless of what environment it's deployed on. Because it runs in its own isolated environment, it won't be affected by any processes that happen on the operating system of the host machine, unless it has been explicitly exposed to such processes.

This chapter will show you how to apply orchestration to .NET 7 applications. It will walk your through .NET 7 Docker container images and the process of integrating Docker functionality with your .NET projects. Then you will learn the basics of container orchestration. For this purpose, we will have a look at Docker Swarm and Kubernetes.

Code Bundle and Coloured Images

Please follow the link to download the
Code Bundle and the *Coloured Images* of the book:

https://rebrand.ly/4xyu6op

The code bundle for the book is also hosted on GitHub at **https://github.com/bpbpublications/Implementing-C-Sharp-11-and-.NET-7.0**. In case there's an update to the code, it will be updated on the existing GitHub repository.

We have code bundles from our rich catalogue of books and videos available at **https://github.com/bpbpublications**. Check them out!

Errata

We take immense pride in our work at BPB Publications and follow best practices to ensure the accuracy of our content to provide with an indulging reading experience to our subscribers. Our readers are our mirrors, and we use their inputs to reflect and improve upon human errors, if any, that may have occurred during the publishing processes involved. To let us maintain the quality and help us reach out to any readers who might be having difficulties due to any unforeseen errors, please write to us at :

errata@bpbonline.com

Your support, suggestions and feedbacks are highly appreciated by the BPB Publications' Family.

Did you know that BPB offers eBook versions of every book published, with PDF and ePub files available? You can upgrade to the eBook version at www.bpbonline.com and as a print book customer, you are entitled to a discount on the eBook copy. Get in touch with us at :

business@bpbonline.com for more details.

At **www.bpbonline.com**, you can also read a collection of free technical articles, sign up for a range of free newsletters, and receive exclusive discounts and offers on BPB books and eBooks.

Piracy

If you come across any illegal copies of our works in any form on the internet, we would be grateful if you would provide us with the location address or website name. Please contact us at **business@bpbonline.com** with a link to the material.

If you are interested in becoming an author

If there is a topic that you have expertise in, and you are interested in either writing or contributing to a book, please visit **www.bpbonline.com**. We have worked with thousands of developers and tech professionals, just like you, to help them share their insights with the global tech community. You can make a general application, apply for a specific hot topic that we are recruiting an author for, or submit your own idea.

Reviews

Please leave a review. Once you have read and used this book, why not leave a review on the site that you purchased it from? Potential readers can then see and use your unbiased opinion to make purchase decisions. We at BPB can understand what you think about our products, and our authors can see your feedback on their book. Thank you!

For more information about BPB, please visit **www.bpbonline.com**.

Join our book's Discord space

Join the book's Discord Workspace for Latest updates, Offers, Tech happenings around the world, New Release and Sessions with the Authors:

https://discord.bpbonline.com

Table of Contents

CHAPTER 1
Getting Familiar with .NET 7 Application Structure

Introduction

From November 2022, .NET 7 is the latest version of a cross-platform software development framework called .NET, which is being developed and maintained by Microsoft. Although the framework supports a number of programming languages, the most popular .NET language is C#, and the new version of this language, C# 11, is an integral part of .NET 7.

The main benefit of using .NET 7 over some other software development platforms is that it can run on any of the major operating systems on PCs, which include Windows, MacOS, and Linux. In this version, that is, .NET 7, in particular, you will be able to build applications that run on both PCs and mobile devices. Later in this book, you will find out how.

This book will teach you how to use the latest features of both .NET 7 and C# 11. Whether you are an experienced .NET developer or you have only started using C# and .NET recently, this book will provide you with enough knowledge of these subjects so that you will be able to write your own .NET applications.

If you have used .NET and C# before, this book will give you a good introduction to the latest features of both the platform and the language. If you are a beginner to C#, you will be able to follow this book, but you should familiarize yourself with the basic C# syntax first. The primary focus of this book is to showcase the latest features of C# 11 and .NET 7. However, we will still briefly recap all the fundamentals. Also, carefully selected links to the official language documentation will be provided at the end of this chapter. So, whether you are only starting to learn .NET or are already an experienced software engineer that specializes in .NET, you will find this book valuable.

Structure

In this chapter, we will discuss the following topics:

- Setting up your development environment

- Creating a .NET 7 application

- .NET 7 project structure overview

- C# 11 basics and inbuilt data type

Objectives

In this chapter, we will focus on setting up your development environment and creating a basic application by using .NET 7 templates. Then, once we have created our initial project, we will recap some basics of C#.

The following chapters will focus on the new and shiny features of .NET 7 and C# 11. But before we get there, we need to have our fundamental dependencies set up. So, let us begin.

Setting up your development environment

To start working with .NET 7 and C# 11, you will need the following:

- A suitable machine is running either Windows, MacOS, or Linux operating system.

- .NET 7 SDK

- A suitable IDE or a code editor

If you do not have any of these prerequisites installed already, let us go through the steps you need to take to install them.

A suitable development machines

Since .NET is a cross-platform software development framework, it will work on either Windows, Linux, or MacOS. Therefore, a machine running either of these operating systems will be suitable. .NET is also compatible with a variety of CPU architectures. It will work with either Intel/AMD or ARM.

Regarding the processing power, disk space, and memory size, any average consumer-grade laptop or desktop would do. You do not need an extra-powerful machine to run your .NET code on. However, I would recommend a machine with at least 8 GB of RAM.

.NET 7 SDK

.NET software development kit (SDK) contains everything that you need as a .NET developer, including the platform, the compiler, and all supporting tools. The latest .NET 7 SDK can be installed via the following steps:

1. To obtain .NET 7 SDK, you will need to visit the following page:

    https://dotnet.microsoft.com/

2. Once on the page, you will need to click on the **Download** tab, as per *figure 1.1*:

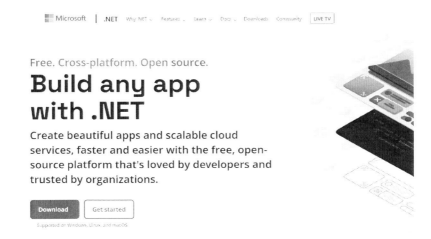

Figure 1.1: *Download tab on Microsoft .NET page*

3. You will then be taken to the download page, where you will need to choose the latest .NET 7 SDK to download and make sure that the option that you choose is SDK rather than Runtime. The .NET 7 runtime will allow you to run .NET 7 applications on your machine, but you will not be able to build them. SDK, on the other hand, contains both the runtime and all the development tools that you will need, including command line interface (CLI) tools that we will cover in detail in *Chapter 3: What is new in .NET 7*.

4. Next, we will set up a suitable IDE or a code editor if you have not done so already.

Setting up a code editor or an IDE

It does not matter whether you will choose a code editor or an IDE for your application development. You will be able to use either. And you will be able to perform all exercises in this book regardless of this choice. However, it would be useful to know the difference between the two, so you can decide which tool would be more suitable for you.

A code editor allows you to write the code and navigate through it. It comes with a variety of code formatters and highlighters, so your code will be easy to read. But this is pretty much what the capabilities of a code editor are limited to. Typically, you will have to use some external tools or install additional plugins to be able to build your application from the source code. However, because code editors are limited in their capabilities, they tend to be substantially lightweight and faster to load than IDEs.

Integrated Development Environment (IDE) can do absolutely everything a code editor can do and much more. Things like creating new projects from various templates, running and debugging your applications, and building your source code into a deployable application are available out of the box. And all of these things can be managed via **Graphical User Interface (GUI)**. But all of this comes at the expense of performance. Typically, an IDE would be slow to install, occupy a reasonably large chunk of disk space, and noticeably slower to load than a code editor, especially if you are running it on a slower machine.

So, which one should you choose for application development with .NET 7? Well, you can choose either of these, depending on your preferences. If you do not mind building and testing your application via a CLI, which comes with .NET 7 SDK, a code editor would probably be sufficient. However, if you prefer the comfort of using a GUI for everything and you do not mind longer loading times and occasional dips in performance, then you should probably use an IDE. Also, I would recommend that you use an IDE if you are a beginner.

Let us now review which code editors and IDEs would work with .NET 7 and C# 11.

Installing a suitable code editor

If you want to use a simple code editor, then the choice would be Visual Studio Code. And it does not matter which OS your development machine runs. There is a version of Visual Studio Code available for all supported operating systems.

Visual Studio Code can be downloaded from the following Web page:

https://code.visualstudio.com/download

You will then need to choose the download option that is relevant for your OS and your CPU architecture, as per *figure 1.2*:

Figure 1.2: Visual Studio Code download page

Once downloaded, you will then just need to follow the installation instructions that are specific to the OS you are using. Once installed, you will need to download a C# plugin for the code editor to make sure that all C# code is highlighted correctly. Either you can do it now, or you will be prompted to do so the first time you use the editor to open any file with the .cs extension. If you choose to do it now, you will need to open Visual Studio Code and click on the Extensions bar on the left-hand side, which is represented by a symbol containing four squares. Then, you will just need to type **C#** in the search panel and install the first plugin that comes up in the results, as per *figure 1.3*:

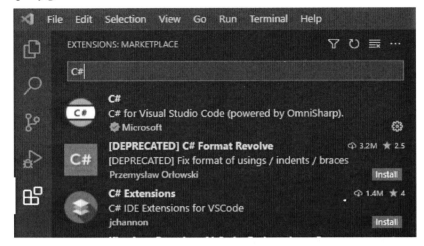

Figure 1.3: C# extension in Visual Studio Code

And this is all you need to start building your apps. However, if you prefer an IDE, then these are the steps you would need to take.

Installing a suitable IDE

Installing an IDE is not as simple as installing a code editor. Visual Studio Code is the only recommended code editor for .NET development, regardless of which OS you are using. But when it comes to an IDE, different operating systems have different options available. The options can be summarized as follows:

Windows

- Microsoft Visual Studio 2022
- JetBrains Rider

MacOS

- Microsoft Visual Studio 2022 for Mac
- JetBrains Rider

Linux

- JetBrains Rider

So, as you can see, the only common IDE is JetBrains Rider. But it has its own caveats too, so it might not be the best option for everyone. In fact, every IDE from this list has its own pros and cons. We will now examine each of the options, so you can decide which IDE to choose.

Microsoft Visual Studio 2022

This is the official .NET IDE from Microsoft. Although it was mainly designed to work with .NET, it supports a range of different platforms, languages, and technologies. Despite its name, it is not related to Visual Studio Code in any way. It looks different and feels different. The only common things between the two is that both are made by Microsoft, and both can be used for writing code.

It comes with all the tools that you need. And you can also get it for free, as it has the so-called *community edition*. There are also premium *professional* and *enterprise* editions that you have to purchase a license for. They come with more tools than the free community edition. However, even the community edition comes with a sufficient amount of tools for developing your .NET applications. You will definitely not need anything more than the community edition to follow the exercises in this book.

The biggest advantage of using Visual Studio 2022 over any other IDE is that it is kept up to date with .NET updates. So, whenever .NET SDK gets updated (even if it is only a preview version of it), an update for Visual Studio will be made available immediately to make it compatible with it. So, you can be certain that your IDE will always be able to handle the latest .NET features.

To download Visual Studio 2022, you can visit its official page via the following link:

https://visualstudio.microsoft.com/downloads/

You will be greeted by the following screen, which is illustrated in *figure 1.4*, where you can choose the version to download. Choose the **Community** option if you are not sure which version you will need. You can always upgrade later if you have to.

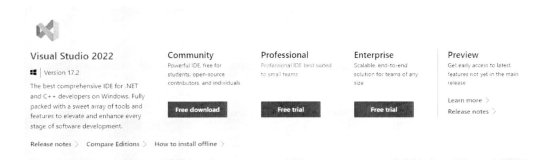

Figure 1.4: Visual Studio 2022 download page

Once the download begins, you will just need to follow the installation instructions. But you will need to be aware that both the downloading and the installation may take a while, as Visual Studio 2022 is a fairly sizeable IDE.

Even though Visual Studio 2022 provides you with all the tools that you need, the main caveat is that it is only available for Windows. There is an IDE called Visual Studio for Mac, but despite its name, it is not a Mac version of the same IDE. It is a completely different piece of software. And this is what we will have a look at next.

Microsoft Visual Studio 2022 for Mac

If you use Mac instead of Windows, Visual Studio 2022 for Mac might be a good IDE option. This IDE comes with sufficient tooling to build your .NET applications, but it is more basic than the Windows version of Visual Studio 2022. It is also that the GUI of the IDE looks completely different, so if you have previously been using Visual Studio on Windows and you have now switched to using Mac, it will take you some time to get used to it.

Another caveat of using Visual Studio for Mac is that its development lags somewhat behind the development of Visual Studio for Windows. And it does not keep up with the evolution of .NET. Sometimes you even have to wait months before you can start using any new .NET features. Sometimes the only way to use any new .NET features in this IDE is to install the preview version of it, which, as a piece of software that has not yet been signed off for an official release, may have some bugs.

You can download Visual Studio for Mac from its official page, which can be accessed via the following link:

https://visualstudio.microsoft.com/vs/mac/

Because there is only one version of this IDE, you will be presented with a single download button, as illustrated in *figure 1.5*:

Figure 1.5: *Visual Studio 2022 for Mac download page*

Then you just need to follow the download and the installation instructions, which should be self-explanatory. There is also a third IDE option. There is an IDE made by JetBrains called Rider. And it is worth examining regardless of the OS you are using.

JetBrains Rider

The main advantage of Rider over any other IDEs is that it comes with a lot of inbuilt tooling by default. It will automatically find potentially problematic code, and it will provide refactoring suggestions. It will be able to decompile third-party libraries, so you will be able to see the original code they were written in. And the list goes on.

If you are a Windows user, then you will get a much richer IDE than Visual Studio at a relatively low price. It will be even more noticeable if you are a Mac user. And if you happen to be a Linux user, this will be your only option. The IDE will look the same and have the same functionality regardless of the OS you run it on.

However, it comes with its own caveats. But there are only two I can think of. There is no free version of it. After the initial 30-day trial, you must purchase the license. However, the price of it tends to be cheaper than either the *professional* or the *enterprise* edition of Visual Studio. The second caveat is that, since it is made by a third party rather than Microsoft, it sometimes lags slightly behind when new .NET SDK updates get released. However, the Rider development team tends to work fast, so these delays do not tend to be big. It tends to get updated quicker than Visual Studio for Mac.

Rider can be obtained from its official **Download** page, which can be found via the following link:

https://www.jetbrains.com/rider/

The Web page should automatically detect which OS you are on, so you will be presented with the download link that is specific to your OS:

Fast & powerful cross-platform .NET IDE

Download   free 30-day trial

Figure 1.6: Rider downloads page

Then all you have to do is just follow the instructions.

By now, you have chosen and installed either an IDE or a code editor that is right for you. Now, we are ready to start creating our first .NET 7 applications and examining their structure.

Creating a .NET 7 application

When you write a .NET application, you work with projects and solutions. A project is a collection of code files that will later be built into a single executable file or a single reference library. These files form an application. An application can consist of a single executable file or have the main executable file alongside some other files that provide additional functionality. The latter types of files are known as libraries, and they can be shared between different applications. The libraries are also represented in the source code by projects.

A solution is something that holds multiple projects together. It is represented by a file with a `.sln` extension that gets placed alongside the project folders in the source code. Although you do not strictly require a solution, having one is helpful if you are using an IDE, as it would make it easier to manage and organize related projects.

Both projects and solutions can be created either via the CLI or via IDE GUI. And in this section, we will go through both of these methods. Later in the book, we will be primarily using the CLI commands, as they will be the same on all operating systems. Plus, .NET CLI comes with the .NET SDK, so if you have the SDK installed, you have the CLI too.

Creating an application via CLI

The most basic type of a .NET application is known as a console application. It does not have any GUI. The only way it can interact with the outside world is via a textual interface, such as the one provided by CMD, PowerShell, Terminal, Shell, and so on. And because it is so basic, it is a perfect application type to use for our demo.

And now, we will go ahead and create our solution. To do so, you can open any command line terminal of your choice, create a folder in which you want to place your solution, navigate to this folder, and execute the following command:

```
dotnet new sln
```

This will create a file inside this folder with the same name as the name of the folder and the `.sln` extension. So, assuming that your folder is called **BasicApp**, the solution file will be called **BasicApp.sln**.

Now, we will create a project. For demonstration purposes, we will call it **BasicConsoleApp**. We will do so by executing the following command:

```
dotnet new console -o BasicConsoleApp
```

The console argument is there to indicate that we are using the Console Application template. The **-o** parameter stands for *output*. This is where we put the name of our project.

After executing this command, you should have ended up with a folder inside the **solution** folder called **BasicConsoleApp**. Inside it, you will see two files: **BasicConsoleApp.csproj** and **Program.cs**. The file with the **.csproj** extension is the project file, which provides information about the project to the compiler. It contains various XML properties, including the .NET version. And, as long as you have version 7 of the SDK installed, it should be picked up automatically. Your project file should look like the following:

```
<Project Sdk="Microsoft.NET.Sdk">

  <PropertyGroup>
    <OutputType>Exe</OutputType>
    <TargetFramework>net7.0</TargetFramework>
    <ImplicitUsings>enable</ImplicitUsings>
    <Nullable>enable</Nullable>
  </PropertyGroup>

</Project>
```

The **Program.cs** file is the entry point into your application. It contains the C# code that will be executed first when the application is launched. By default, it will be just outputting **Hello World!** message into the console, as its content would be as follows:

```
// See https://aka.ms/new-console-template for more information
Console.WriteLine("Hello, World!");
```

You can now add this project to the solution. To do so, you need to navigate to your **solution** folder and execute the following command:

```
dotnet sln add BasicConsoleApp/BasicConsoleApp.csproj
```

Now, we will go through exactly the same process but by using an IDE GUI.

Creating an application via an IDE GUI

In our example, we will use Visual Studio 2022 on Windows. But the process will be very similar regardless of which IDE you will use. The GUI will look different. Some of the labels will be different. But the principles will be the same.

First, you will need to open an IDE and choose the option from the menu that will allow you to create a new project, as it is demonstrated in *figure 1.7*:

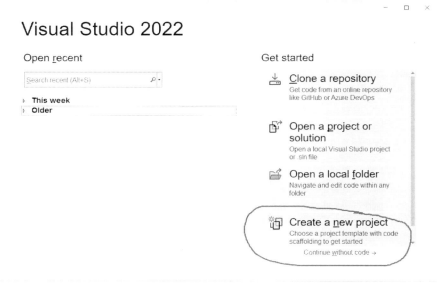

Figure 1.7: *Creating a new project from Visual Studio 2022*

Then you will need to select **Console App** as your project template, as per *figure 1.8*. But make sure you select the **C#** version of it, as this project template is also available in other languages.

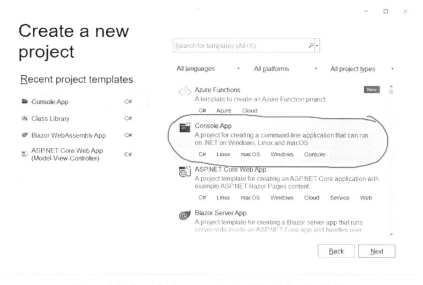

Figure 1.8: *Console App template in Visual Studio 2022*

Then you will be taken through various screens where you will be asked to provide names for your project and solution and select the framework version (which should be .NET 7). The details of how different IDEs do it vary slightly. For example, this is what the naming screen looks like in Visual Studio 2022:

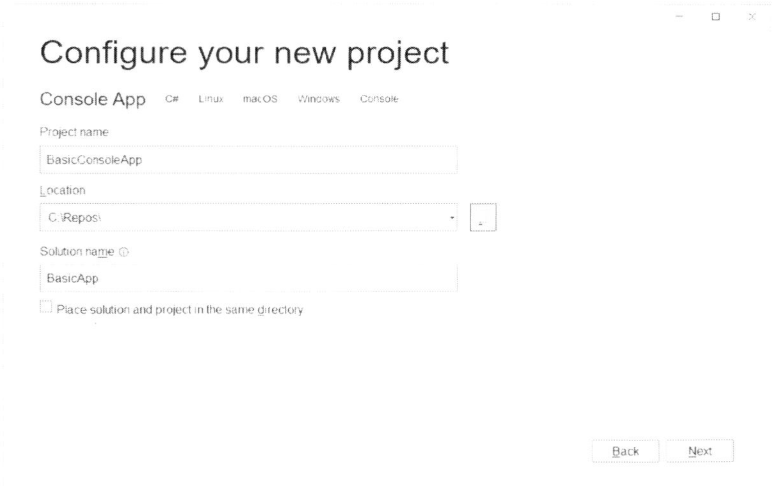

Figure 1.9: Naming your solution and your project

Then, if you just keep the default values in all remaining settings and follow the process till the end, both the solution and the project will be created for you, and the IDE will automatically open the solution. It should look similar to *figure 1.10*:

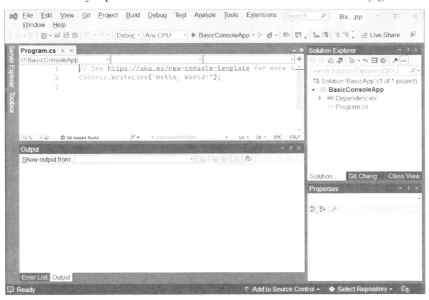

Figure 1.10: Solution opened in Visual Studio 2022

Now, since our solution is ready, we can start adding some useful functionality to it.

.NET 7 project structure overview

To demonstrate .NET 7 project structure, we will add some meaningful capabilities to our application. The complete example can be found via the following URL:

https://github.com/fiodarsazanavets/a-complete-guide-to-implementing-csharp11-and-dotnet7/tree/main/Chapter-01

Adding a struct object

First, we will create a **Customer.cs** file inside our **BasicConsoleApp** project folder. The content of the file will be as follows:

```
namespace BasicConsoleApp;

public struct Customer
{
    public Customer(string name)
    {
        Name = name;
    }

    public string Name { get; set; }
    public short Age { get; set; }
    public int Id => randomId;

    private int randomId = (new Random()).Next();
}
```

Let us use this example to recap a basic C# syntax. We start our file with a namespace declaration statement. Namespaces in C# are used for modularization. If your object is said to work together, you assign them to the same namespace, and then you will be able to reference this namespace to be able to use the custom data types assigned to it.

In our example, the **Customer** data type that we have created is a struct. C# supports other object types, such as class and record. We will recap the differences between them shortly. But for now, we have chosen to use our object as a struct to demonstrate one of the latest C# 11 struct-specific features.

Our **Customer** object has a constructor that accepts the name parameter of a type string. This allows the **Name** property to be given a value as soon as an instance of Customer is created. It also has two other properties: **Age** and **Id**. **Age** property is a short integer. By default, the value of it will be 0. And this demonstrates a new feature that has been added to C# 11. If any properties are not set in the constructor, then they will be automatically set to their default value, which, for the data type short, is 0. However, this only works for struct object types. Prior to C# 11, this would have thrown a compilation error, as all properties had to be given values before the code block inside the constructor executes.

The other property, Id, is a read-only property that cannot be changed after an instance of the object is created. It takes its value from the **randomId** field, which gets a random value assigned to it. And, as the field is private, it is not visible to anything outside this object. The other members of the object are all marked as public. This keyword at the beginning at an object member definition is known as an access modifier.

Adding an interface and a class

Next, we will add **CustomerRepository.cs** file to our project folder, and the first thing we will insert into this file is the following interface definition:

```
namespace BasicConsoleApp;


public interface ICustomerRepository
{
    int Count { get; }

    void AddNewCustomer(Customer customer);
    Customer GetCustomer(int id);
    Customer GetCustomer(string name);
    IEnumerable<Customer> GetCustomers();
    IEnumerable<Customer> GetCustomers(string nameMatch);
}
```

As before, we have added a namespace definition right at the top. Because we are using the same namespace as we used in our **Customer** struct, we do not need to import any additional namespace into our file. We have implicit access to any other object that uses the same namespace.

Interfaces are not functional objects, so you cannot use them directly. They act like contracts for object definitions. An interface provides signatures for all public members that an object that implements the interface must have. Otherwise, the code will not compile. This is why there is neither a body nor an access modifier in the interface members.

However, you can assign an interface as a return data type for fields, properties, methods, and variables. If you do so, then absolutely any object that implements this interface can be assigned to it. And we do have an example of this here. Both versions of our **GetCustomers** method have **IEnumerable** as their data type. **IEnumerable** is an in-built interface that is meant to be implemented by collections. And in our case, we will be able to return absolutely any concrete collection type as long as it implements this interface.

Next, we will add the following class definition to our file:

```csharp
internal class CustomerRepository : ICustomerRepository
{
    private readonly List<Customer> customers;

    public CustomerRepository()
    {
        customers = new List<Customer>();
    }

    public int Count => customers.Count;

    public void AddNewCustomer(Customer customer)
    {
        customers.Add(customer);
    }

    public Customer GetCustomer(int id)
    {
        return customers.SingleOrDefault(c => c.Id == id);
    }

    public Customer GetCustomer(string name)
    {
        return customers.SingleOrDefault(c => c.Name == name);
    }
```

```
public IEnumerable<Customer> GetCustomers()
{
    return customers;
}


public IEnumerable<Customer> GetCustomers(string nameMatch)
{
    return customers.Where(c => c.Name.Contains(nameMatch));
}
}
```

This class implements the interface we have defined earlier, as there is a semicolon followed by the interface name after the class name. In C#, the semicolon is used in this context as an implementation or inheritance operator.

You may have also noticed that the class has internal as its access modifier rather than public. There is a difference between the two. While the public access modifier makes an object visible to every other object, both inside your project and in any project that references your project, the internal modifier restricts visibility to only those objects that exist inside the same project. While implementing interfaces, you can go from a lower restriction level to the higher one, but not the other way around. And this is demonstrated in our example by having a public interface getting implemented by an internal class.

Next, we have a private read-only list of **Customer** objects. When we use a read-only modifier, the value of the field can only be instantiated as the field gets declared or inside the object's constructor. We cannot assign a new value to this field later.

After this, we just provide complementation for all of the members that we have previously defined in the interface. Please note that we have some duplicate method names. But this is OK, as they have different signatures. A method signature is defined by the combination of the name, the return data type, and the input parameters. Being able to define methods with the same name and the same data type but different parameters is known as **polymorphism**.

So, we are implementing the following interface members:

Count: It returns the current count of customers list.

- **AddNewCustomer(Customer customer)**: It accepts a **Customer** object as an input parameter and adds it to the customer list.

- **GetCustomer(int id)**: It retrieves a single **Customer** entry based on the id input parameter.

- **GetCustomer(string name)**: It retrieves a single **Customer** object by name.

- **GetCustomers()**: It returns all entries from the customer's list.

- **GetCustomers(string nameMatch)**: It returns only those entries from the customers list that contain a specific pattern in the name.

The latter two methods demonstrate how we can return a concrete implementation where the return type was defined as an interface. The return type for both of these methods is **IEnumerable**. But we are returning **List**. We can do it because the **List** data type happens to implement **IEnumerable**.

Modifying the entry point of the app

Next, we will replace the content of our **Program.cs** file. We will start by deleting the existing content from it. And then, we will add the following code:

```
using BasicConsoleApp;

// Creating a repository
var customerRepository = new CustomerRepository();


// Creating Customer objects
var customer1 = new Customer("John Smith");
var customer2 = new Customer("David Smith");
var customer3 = new Customer("Gary Rogers");
```

So, since **Program.cs** class does not have any namespace definition, and we need to import the namespace of the objects that we have just created. To do so, we are applying using a statement followed by the namespace name.

Then we create an instance of **CustomerRepository** object and store it in **customerRepository** variable. After this, we create three instances of **Customer** object and store them in named variable. A variable is a temporary data storage in memory. It is normally defined by the **var** keyword. However, you can also provide an explicit data type instead of using this keyword. However, using var is recommended for most situations.

We will then add the following code, where we modify the data in some **Customer** objects and then insert them all into the **customerRepository**:

```
// Applying additional data
customer1.Age = 30;
customer2.Age = 21;
```

```
// Adding customers to the repository
customerRepository.AddNewCustomer(customer1);
customerRepository.AddNewCustomer(customer2);
customerRepository.AddNewCustomer(customer3);
```

Finally, we will add the following code to our file, where we will be trying out different methods of extracting **Customer** object instances from the **CustomerRepository**:

```
// Extracting data from the repository
Console.WriteLine("The following data has been obtained while iterating
through all customers:");

foreach (var customer in customerRepository.GetCustomers())
{
    Console.WriteLine($"""
    Customer id: {customer.Id},
    Customer Name: {customer.Name},
    Customer Age: {customer.Age}

    """);
}


// Extracting filtered data
Console.WriteLine("The following data has been obtained while iterating
through customers while filtering by 'Smith' in name:");

foreach (var customer in customerRepository.GetCustomers("Smith"))
{
    Console.WriteLine($"""
    Customer id: {customer.Id},
    Customer Name: {customer.Name},
    Customer Age: {customer.Age}

    """);
}


// Extracting a single customer by name
```

```
Console.WriteLine("The following data was returned for David Smith:");
var specificCustomer = customerRepository.GetCustomer("David Smith");

Console.WriteLine($"""
    Customer id: {specificCustomer.Id},
    Customer Name: {specificCustomer.Name},
    Customer Age: {specificCustomer.Age}

""");
```

And this example showcases another new language feature that has been added to C# 11, which is multi-line string literals. If you wrap your string value up in triple double-quote symbols, then anything you write inside of it will be treated as a literal character rather than a special C# character. But you can still combine it with interpolated string feature if you place a dollar sign at the beginning of it. This will allow you to insert data from your code into the string. To do so, you need to wrap your code in curly braces inside the string.

We can now launch our application, which we can do either by right-clicking on the IDE and selecting **Run** option or by executing the following command inside the project folder:

dotnet run

We should be expecting to see the following result:

```
The following data has been obtained while iterating through all customers:
Customer id: 452867481,
Customer Name: John Smith,
Customer Age: 30

Customer id: 31176956,
Customer Name: David Smith,
Customer Age: 21

Customer id: 2062322027,
Customer Name: Gary Rogers,
Customer Age: 0

The following data has been obtained while iterating through customers while filtering by 'Smith' in name:
Customer id: 452867481,
Customer Name: John Smith,
Customer Age: 30

Customer id: 31176956,
Customer Name: David Smith,
Customer Age: 21

The following data was returned for David Smith:
Customer id: 31176956,
Customer Name: David Smith,
Customer Age: 21
```

Figure 1.11: The output of our application

As we can see here, the age of Gary Rogers is 0. This is because we have not explicitly set this age for this specific customer. It was just initialized to the default value of its data type, which happens to be 0. And this has proven that the mechanism of auto-initializing struct properties to their default values has worked.

Next, we will briefly recap the fundamentals of C# and its inbuilt data types. If you are just starting your journey to become a C# programmer, links to various online documentation sources will also be provided, so you can study the fundamentals of the C# syntax in more detail.

C# 11 basics and inbuilt data types

Many C# language features have existed since the initial version of the language and many of these are still relevant. However, over time, C# has evolved, and some of the old functionality became obsolete because better ways of doing things were invented. There are also some parts of the language that have changed their paradigm. For example, the string data type used to be a value type, which means that if you use it as a parameter, it is only the value of it that gets passed. So, if the parameter gets modified inside the method that it was passed into, the original string variable would not get modified. But since C# 10, the string is now a reference type. This means that when it gets passed as a parameter, modifications made to the parameter inside the method that it is been passed into will cause these modifications to be applied to the original variable.

There are still various ways of applying old behavior to the parts of the language where the behavior has been changed. Also, the old ways of doing things are still available in the language to make it backward-compatible with the older versions. But in our examples, we will focus purely on how things work in C# 11. We will start by listing all inbuilt data types.

Inbuilt data types

Inbuilt data types are the types of data that are supported by the language out of the box. These are available in the language even without any additional libraries.

Each of the data types has a default value. So, if you are using a variable, field, or property of a particular type and you do not explicitly set a value to it, the default value will be used.

The data types in C# can also be categorized as either value or reference types. When you use a value type and pass a variable of this type into a method, then it will only be the value of this variable that will be passed to the method and not the variable itself (unless you explicitly choose to pass the variable by reference by using ref keyword). When you use a reference type and pass it to the method, it is the reference to the whole variable that gets passed and not just its value. Therefore, if the variable gets modified inside the method, your original variable will be modified too.

The following table shows all built-in data types that are available in C#:

Name	Description	Reference or value type	Default value
bool	A representation of Boolean value that can either be true or false.	Value type	false
byte	A representation of a single byte consisting of 8 bits. Can accept values in the range of 0 to 255 if converted to decimal.	Value type	0
sbyte	A representation of a single byte consisting of 8 bits. Differs from byte by the range of the values it accepts, which is between –128 and 127 if converted to decimal.	Value type	0
char	A single character.	Value type	"\0"
decimal	A numeric data type that supports high-precision decimal fractions.	Value type	0.0M
float	A numeric data type that supports decimal fractions. It is smaller than double but has much lower precision.	Value type	0.0F
double	A numeric data type that is similar to float but comes with double the precision and double the size.	Value type	0.0D
int	A numeric value that does not support decimal point and has a size of 16 bits.	Value type	0
uint	A numeric value that does not support decimal point and negative values. Has a size of 16 bits.	Value type	0
nint	A pointer to a memory location containing an integer value.	Value type	0
nuint	A pointer to a memory location containing an unsigned integer value.	Value type	0
long	A numeric value that does not support decimal point and has the size of 64 bits.	Value type	0
ulong	A numeric value that does not support decimal point and negative values. Has the size of 64 bits.	Value type	0
short	A numeric value that does not support decimal point and has the size of 32 bits.	Value type	0

Name	Description	Reference or value type	Default value
ushort	A numeric value that does not support decimal point and negative values. Has the size of 32 bits.	Value type	0
string	Representation of any arbitrary text.	Reference type as of .NET 6. Used to be a value type prior to this.	""
object	The base type for all other data types in C#.	Reference type	null
dynamic	A data type that accepts any other data type and allows it to be changed dynamically. Not recommended for most situations.	Reference type	null

Table 1.1: *Inbuilt data types that are found in C#*

More detailed information on inbuilt C# data type can be found in the official Microsoft documentation via the following link:

https://docs.microsoft.com/en-us/dotnet/csharp/language-reference/builtin-types/built-in-types

Next, we will have a look at different types of control from the C# 11 supports. These allow you to execute code conditionally, create branches in the executional flow and perform repeated actions.

Control flow

Control flow is what allows your code to make decisions. Some control flow elements allow you to repeatedly execute a given action, whereas others allow you to execute an action only if a specific condition is met.

The following table lists the main control flow elements that are available in C#:

Statement type	Description
if .. else if .. else	Indicates what condition needs to be applied to a block of code for it to get executed.
switch .. case	Another type of conditional logic is where a single distinct scenario is selected from multiple options.
for	A looped execution of a statement that will continue executing until an arbitrarily defined counter reaches a specific value.

Statement type	Description
foreach	A piece of logic is executed for each item of a collection.
while	A block of code keeps executing while a condition remains true.
do .. while	Same as while, but the block of code executes at least ones.

Table 1.2: Control flow elements of C#

To find out about control flow in C# in more detail, you can visit the appropriate section from the official language documentation via the link as follows:

https://docs.microsoft.com/en-us/dotnet/csharp/tour-of-csharp/tutorials/branches-and-loops-local

Next, will have a look at different ways of how we can create our own custom types in C#.

C# custom types

As well as using inbuilt data types, it is very important in programming to be able to build custom objects. And C# supports a number of structures that allow software developers to do it. These structures are listed in *table 1.3*:

Structure type	Description
interface	Provides only the signatures of public members (methods, fields, and properties) that implementing object must have defined.
class	A reference type structure that enables the creation of custom data types with bespoke fields, properties, and methods.
struct	A value type structure that enables the creation of custom data types with bespoke fields, properties, and methods.
record	A class or a struct that is specifically designed to represent database objects and store data. So it typically consists only of properties.

Table 1.3: C# structures that enable the creation of custom data types

To learn more about the C# type system, you can visit the official documentation via the link as follows:

https://docs.microsoft.com/en-us/dotnet/csharp/fundamentals/types/

Next, we will have a recap of the access modifiers available in C#.

Access modifiers

Access modifiers are keywords that control the visibility of the objects and object elements, such as fields, properties, and methods. For example, you can make certain elements of an object completely inaccessible to other objects. You can make a certain object visible to other objects inside the same library but completely inaccessible to any code outside the library.

Table 1.4 provides the full list of access modifiers that are available in C#:

Access modifier	Description
public	Visible to all objects inside the executable and to all objects in any other executable that references it.
private	Visible only to the members of the same object.
protected	Visible only to the members of the same object and the members of any derived object.
internal	Visible to all objects inside the executable.
protected internal	Visible to all objects inside the executable or a derived object created in another executable.
private protected	Visible only to the members of the same object and the members of a derived object, as long as the derived object belongs to the same project.

***Table 1.4**: C# access modifiers*

A more detailed information on the C# access modifier can be found here:

https://docs.microsoft.com/en-us/dotnet/csharp/programming-guide/classes-and-structs/access-modifiers

Of course, there is much more in C# than we have managed to cover in this chapter. But these summaries cover the bulk of language fundamentals.

And this concludes our introduction to C# 11 and .NET 7. Let us summarize what we have learned.

Conclusion

C# 11 and .NET 7 come with some new features. But the old features will still work.

If you are familiar with the previous iteration of the platform and the language, then you may have noticed that hardly anything has changed in terms of the project structure. Once you create a new project, it looks almost identical to what your .NET 6 project would have looked like.

And there is a good reason for it. Microsoft keeps up with its tradition of making as few breaking changes as possible. One of the benefits of this is that migrating your older applications to the new platform is easy. Typically, all you have to do is just change the framework version in the project file.

But there is also a disadvantage to it. Because old features do not get marked as deprecated as the language evolves, the complexity of the language keeps increasing. Therefore, there is a lot more to learn in C# 11 than there was in C# 1.

But there is an approach that you can use to work around it. While studying the language, focus only on the latest of its features. And ignore everything else. If you then happen to come across some old code feature while looking at somebody else's code, you will always be able to look it up easily, as long as you know the language fundamentals, which we have briefly recapped in this chapter.

In the upcoming chapter, you will learn about the new features that have been added to version 11 of the C# language.

Points to remember

- To work with C# 11 and .NET 7, you will need to download the .NET 7 SDK.

- You can either use a code editor or an IDE to work with your code.

- The suitable code editor is Visual Studio Code.

- Depending on your OS, the suitable IDEs are Visual Studio 2022, Visual Studio 2022 for Mac, or Rider.

- One of the new C# features is the auto-initialization of struct properties to the default values of their data type.

- Another new C# feature is a new type of string literal, where you do not have to escape any special characters.

Multiple choice questions

1. **What is the minimum set of tools you need to start working with C# 11 and .NET 7?**

    a. .NET 7 SDK

    b. Code Editor

    c. IDE

    d. All of these

2. **Which data types of support auto-initialization of their properties to their default values?**

    a. class

    b. struct

    c. record

    d. All of these

    e. None of these

3. **Which statement best describes the new string literals from C# 11?**

    a. You cannot combine it with interpolated strings because curly brackets will be treated as literal characters

    b. You cannot combine it with interpolated strings because this string type does not support the dollar sign at the beginning of its value definition

    c. You can combine it with interpolated strings as long as you place the dollar sign at the beginning of its value definition

    d. None of these are true

Answers

1. a

2. b

3. c

Key terms

*   **IDE**: Integrated development environment that provides all tools that you need to manage your code

*   **Code editor**: This allows you to write code, but you will typically need external tools to run it.

*   **SDK**: Software development kit that allows you to use specific languages, platforms, frameworks, and collections of libraries to build your code with.

*   **CLI**: Command line interface that allows you to execute commands inside a text-based terminal.

*   **Access modifier**: A keyword that controls the visibility of your objects or the members of these objects.

Join our book's Discord space

Join the book's Discord Workspace for Latest updates, Offers, Tech happenings around the world, New Release and Sessions with the Authors:

https://discord.bpbonline.com

CHAPTER 2
Overview of C# 11 Features

Introduction

This chapter will cover all the latest features that have been added in C# 11. Some of these language features have already been made available in older versions of the language, but we had to install some external dependencies to enable them. At the same time, some other features are completely brand new. Some of these features are improvements of other new features that have been added to the language in the most recent versions of it, whereas other features are completely stand-alone.

Whatever the new features are, this chapter covers them all. For each of these features, the chapter also provides implementation examples and showcases its benefits.

Structure

In this chapter, we will discuss the following topics:

- Struct auto-defaults
- Generic attributes
- Sequence pattern matching
- New string operations

Objectives

By the end of this chapter, you will have learned how to use each of the C# features that were added to the language with the version 11 update. This will be achieved by demonstrating implementation examples that you can try out in your own code. This will help you to understand the importance and benefits of each of the new features.

Prerequisites

To follow this chapter, you will need the following:

- A machine running either Windows, MacOS, or Linux operating system

- .NET 7 SDK

- A suitable IDE or a code editor

- Being familiar with C# fundamentals

If you do not have any of the preceding listed dependencies installed already, let us know the setup instruction provided in *Chapter 1: Getting Familiar with .NET 7 Application Structure*, which also provides a recap of C# fundamentals.

Struct auto-defaults

We will start by examining auto-default property initialization in struct data types. We have already touched upon it in *Chapter 1: Getting Familiar with .NET 7 Application Structure*. But as we want to keep listing all new C# 11 features in one place, we will examine it in more detail here.

Before we can make start looking at the new C# language features, we will need to create a new .NET console application. In my example, I will call the application project **NewFeatures**.

If you are using an IDE, you can create a new application project via the GUI by selecting a Console Application template. But you can also use the command line interface, which will be available on any system that has .NET SDK installed. And to do it via the CLI, you can execute the following command in a folder of your choice:

```
dotnet new console -o NewFeatures
```

This will create a folder called **NewFeature** with a console application project inside it. And now, we will add a struct, which will allow us to demonstrate the auto-default feature. To do so, create a folder called **AutoDefaults** inside the **NewFeature** project folder. Then create a **StructExample.cs** file inside this folder and populate it with the following content:

```
namespace NewFeatures.AutoDefaults;

public struct StructExample
{
    public int Id { get; set; } // Auto-initialized to 0

    public string Name { get; set; } // Auto-initialized to ""

    public bool Active { get; set; } // Auto-initialized to false
}
```

We have already added some comments to the properties of this **struct** to indicate what each of these properties will auto-initialize to. So, basically, when we create a new instance of the **StructExample** struct, we will be able to read the properties right away. An attempt to read them will not result in a **NullReferenceException** being thrown. And this is despite the fact that we have not explicitly assigned any values to these properties.

To test this behavior, we can replace the content of the **Program.cs** file with the following code:

```
using NewFeatures.AutoDefaults;

Console.WriteLine("Testing auto-defaults.");

var testStruct = new StructExample();

Console.WriteLine($"""

Struct data is as follows:

Id: {testStruct.Id},
Name: {testStruct.Name},
Active: {testStruct.Active}

""");
```

This is something that would have thrown a **NullReferenceException** in the previous versions of C# as soon as we attempted to read any of the properties of the **testStruct** variable. But if we run our application on the latest version of .NET, it will produce the following output, which confirms that all of our properties have been auto-initialized to their default values, as shown in the following figure:

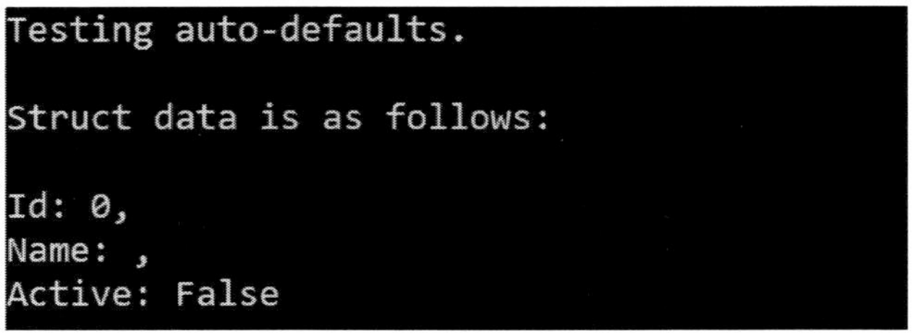

```
Testing auto-defaults.

Struct data is as follows:

Id: 0,
Name: ,
Active: False
```

Figure 2.1: Auto-initialized struct properties

The next C# 11 feature that we will have a look at is generic attribute classes.

Generic attributes

In C#, attribute classes are used for extending the functionality of classes and class members and adding metadata to them. For example, placing the **Authorize** attribute above a method in a Web API controller will ensure that the endpoint that this method represents will only be accessible by authenticated users. And passing some additional parameters into this attribute will apply even stricter authorization requirements to the endpoint.

All attribute classes inherit from **System.Attribute** class. By convention, the name of an attribute class should end with **Attribute** suffix, which can be stripped out when the attribute is applied in the code. For example, the previously-mentioned Authorize attribute is actually defined as **AuthorizeAttribute** at its source.

An attribute is placed above a class or a class member in square brackets. And the syntax for applying attributes to classes and class members is as follows:

[<attribute class name without Attribute suffix><optional: attribute properties in brackets>]

Just like any other class, attributes have methods, fields, and properties. But prior to C# version 11, they did not support generics. So, if you need to be able to pass any arbitrary type into an attribute class, the only way to do it is to pass it into the attribute constructor and store it in some field or property. But now, generic attributes have been added. And this has made things a lot simpler.

But why would you even want to pass an arbitrary type definition into an attribute class? Well, there are many scenarios where such an ability may be useful. For example, you may want to add some behavior to the attribute that is specific to the return data type of the class member that the attribute is placed on. And to make sure that the attribute can be applied anywhere, the type should be injectable at runtime.

Generic attribute example

To demonstrate how generic attributes work, we will compare them against the old way of passing arbitrary type definitions into attribute classes. This way, the benefit of using a generic attribute will be demonstrated more clearly.

To make a start, we will add a **GenericAttributes** folder to our project and will place **OldTypeAttribute.cs** file into it with the following content:

```
namespace NewFeatures.GenericAttributes;


public class OldTypeAttribute : Attribute
{
    public OldTypeAttribute(Type attributeType) => AttributeType =
attributeType;

    public Type AttributeType { get; }
}
```

As you can see, we have a read-only property in this class that holds a type. It is set during the class initialization via the class constructor. And to find out what type the attribute holds, you actually need to have a look at this property once the attribute has been initialized.

And we will now add a new generic attribute. To do so, we will create **NewTypeAttribute.cs** file inside the same folder and will populate it with the following content:

```
namespace NewFeatures.GenericAttributes;


public class NewTypeAttribute<T> : Attribute { }
```

As you can see, there is no longer any need for an additional class member to store the attribute in. This also makes it easier to obtain the type at runtime. Also, it makes for a cleaner syntax when applying the attribute.

To demonstrate how both of these attributes are applied, we will add **ParametrizedClass.cs** file to the same folder. It will contain the following code:

```
namespace NewFeatures.GenericAttributes;


public class ParametrizedClass
{
```

```
[OldType(typeof(int))]
public int DoOldStyleJob() => default;


[NewType<int>]
public int DoNewStyleJob() => default;


}
```

As you can see, the generic attribute syntax is cleaner. There is one less keyword we have to use. But what is even better is that the type that the attribute stores can be instantly obtained by reflections without having to look at its members. To demonstrate this, we will add some code to our **Program.cs** file. First, we will add the following using statement at the beginning of the code in the file:

```
using NewFeatures.GenericAttributes;
```

Then, we will add the following code at the end of the file:

```
Console.WriteLine("Testing Generic Attributes.");


var methods = typeof(ParametrizedClass).GetMethods();


foreach (var method in methods)
{
    var attribute = method?
        .GetCustomAttributes(false)
        .FirstOrDefault();

    if (attribute != null)
        Console.WriteLine($"""

        Method name: {method?.Name},
        Method attribute: {attribute.GetType()}
        """);
}
```

And the output of this code will look like the following:

```
Testing Generic Attributes.

Method name: DoOldStyleJob,
Method attribute: NewFeatures.GenericAttributes.OldTypeAttribute

Method name: DoNewStyleJob,
Method attribute: NewFeatures.GenericAttributes.NewTypeAttribute`1[System.Int32]

Method name: GetType,
Method attribute: System.Runtime.CompilerServices.NullableContextAttribute
```

Figure 2.2: Generic versus non-generic attribute class

As you can see, with a generic attribute, we can see what data type it represents right away. The old style attribute, however, does not show this information when we use reflections to obtain the definition of its instance. So, not only a generic attribute is easier to set up, but it is also easier to read.

Next, we will have a look at some improvements to a C# feature that has been added to the language in its fairly recent versions: sequence pattern matching.

Sequence pattern matching

Pattern matching feature in C# allows you to identify whether a specific value adheres to a specific pattern. And in C# 11, this feature has been applied to collections.

There are various patterns that you can match a collection against. There is an exact match, where the sequence that you are testing the collection against must be identical to the sequence inside the collection. But you can also do a loose match, where certain places in the sequence can match against any value or a range thereof.

Sequence pattern matching completely disregards collection types. It only cares about the sequences in the collections. It does not matter if you are working with arrays, lists, or anything else. As long as your collection contains a specific sequence of values, it will match if this is the sequence that has been specified.

The syntax for sequence pattern matching is as follows:

```
<collection variable> is [<sequence>]
```

To check whether the collection that you are comparing the sequence against contains exactly the same sequence as specified, you just put the full list of the exact comma-separated values inside the square brackets in the same order as you expect them to appear inside the collection. To see if the collection contains specific values in specific positions, while you do not care about any other values, you can just use the discard (underscore; _) character in the positions of the values you do not care about. If you are looking for a specific sequence of values, while you do not care where exactly in the collection this sequence resides, you can use a double-dot character to represent a range of any values. And, of course, you can combine all of these to perform more sophisticated pattern matching.

Sequence pattern matching demonstrated

To demonstrate how sequence pattern matching works, we will create a **PatternMatching** folder inside our project. Then, we will add a **Collection Operations.cs** file to it and populate it with the following content:

```
namespace NewFeatures.PatternMatching;

public class CollectionOperations
{
    private List<int> items = new List<int>
    {
        2, 3, 6, 7, 8
    };

    public bool MatchExactSequence => items is [2, 3, 6, 7, 8];

    public bool MatchWithDiscard => items is [2, _, 6, _, 8];

    public bool MatchWithRange => items is [2, ..];
}
```

In this class, we have the following three fields:

1. **MatchExactSequence** performs an exact match. This means that the collection the sequence is being compared against must be comprised of exactly the same sequence as the one specified.

2. **MatchWithDiscard** method only cares that the collection has a specific number of items and that items at the index of 0, 2, and 4 have specific values. It does not care what values the items at the indexes of 1 and 3 have.

3. **MatchWithRange** method only cares that the first item of the collection is 2. It does not care how many more items there are in the collection and what they are.

But the good news is that this new pattern matching feature does not only work with classic collection types but also with fairly recently added char span types. And this is what we will have a look at next.

Sequence pattern matching with char span

Span is a data type that has been added to version 8 of C# language. It is a collection type that is meant to represent a specific span of another collection. For example, if you are using an array and you only ever want to modify a specific set of items inside of it, you can assign this set of items to a Span object. This way, you will be protected from accidentally modifying the members of the original collection that you did not want to modify.

In C# 11, you can use sequence pattern matching against a span. To demonstrate how this works, we will add a **CharSpanOperations.cs** file to our **PatternMatching** folder. In this class, we will first create the following class definition:

```
namespace NewFeatures.PatternMatching;

public class CharSpanOperations
{
    private char[] charArray = new char[3]
    {
        'a',
        'b',
        'c'
    };

    private Span<char> GetSpan()
    {
        Span<char> span = charArray;
        return span;
    }

    private ReadOnlySpan<char> GetReadonlySpan()
    {
        ReadOnlySpan<char> span = charArray;
        return span;
    }
}
```

And then, we will add the following public properties to it:

```
public bool MatchWholeSpan => GetSpan() is ['a', 'b', 'c'];

public bool MatchWholeReadOnlySpan => GetReadonlySpan() is ['a', 'b',
'c'];
```

```
public bool MatchWholeSpanWithDiscard => GetSpan() is ['a', _, 'c'];

public bool MatchWholeReadOnlySpanWithDiscard => GetReadonlySpan() is
['a', _, 'c'];

public bool MatchWholeSpanByRange => GetSpan() is ['a', ..];

public bool MatchWholeReadOnlySpanBtRange => GetReadonlySpan() is ['a',
..];
```

Now, we can test whether all our examples of sequence pattern matching work. To do so, we will add the following using statement to our **Program.cs** file:

```
using NewFeatures.PatternMatching;
```

And then, we will add the following code to the file:

```
Console.WriteLine("Testing Pattern Matching.");


var collectionOperations = new CollectionOperations();


Console.WriteLine($"""


MatchExactSequence returns {collectionOperations.MatchExactSequence},

MatchWithDiscard returns {collectionOperations.MatchWithDiscard},

MatchWithRange returns {collectionOperations.MatchWithRange}


""");


var charSpanOperations = new CharSpanOperations();


Console.WriteLine($"""

MatchWholeSpan returns {charSpanOperations.MatchWholeSpan},

MatchWholeReadOnlySpan returns {charSpanOperations.
MatchWholeReadOnlySpan},

MatchWholeSpanWithDiscard returns {charSpanOperations.
```

```
MatchWholeSpanWithDiscard},

MatchWholeReadOnlySpanWithDiscard returns {charSpanOperations.
MatchWholeReadOnlySpanWithDiscard},

MatchWholeSpanByRange returns {charSpanOperations.
MatchWholeSpanByRange},

MatchWholeReadOnlySpanBtRange returns {charSpanOperations.
MatchWholeReadOnlySpanBtRange}


""");
```

If the sequence pattern matching works the way we expect it to, we expect every **public** property in the newly created classes to return true. And, as the following console output in *figure 2.3* indicates, this is indeed what happens:

```
Testing Pattern Matching.

MatchExactSequence returns True,
MatchWithDiscard returns True,
MatchWithRange returns True

MatchWholeSpan returns True,
MatchWholeReadOnlySpan returns True,
MatchWholeSpanWithDiscard returns True,
MatchWholeReadOnlySpanWithDiscard returns True,
MatchWholeSpanByRange returns True,
MatchWholeReadOnlySpanBtRange returns True
```

Figure 2.3: *Sequence pattern matching demonstrated*

So, as you can see, C# 11 has substantially expanded the pattern-matching capabilities of the language. But it has also improved the way programmers can work with strings. And this is what we will have a look at next.

New string operations

C# 11 has included some new things you can do with strings. These new operations make your code less verbose and easier to read. One of the new improvements is being able to use multiple lines in interpolated string. This feature is especially helpful when you want to insert the results of some complex expression into a string. Another newly added feature is the new raw string literal, which we briefly touched upon in *Chapter 1: Getting Familiar with .NET 7 Application Structure*.

We will start by applying multi-line string interpolation. We will use a multi-step LINQ expression as the code we will insert into the string. And to showcase the benefits of this feature, we will apply it twice. On the first occasion, we will use the old-style single-line string interpolation. And then, we will apply the new-style multi-line string interpolation.

We will create a **StringOperations** folder inside our project folder and add an **InterpolatedStrings.cs** file to it. The content of the file will be as follows:

```csharp
namespace NewFeatures.StringOperations;


public class InterpolatedStrings
{
    private List<(string, int)> names = new List<(string, int)>
    {
        ("John", 25),
        ("Mike", 34),
        ("Laurence", 42)
    };


    public string OldStyleInterpolation => $"The age of Laurence
is: {names.Where(n => n.Item1 == "Laurence").Select(n => n.Item2).
FirstOrDefault()}.";


    public string NewStyleInterpolation => $"The age of Laurence is: {
        names
            .Where(n => n.Item1 == "Laurence")
            .Select(n => n.Item2)
            .FirstOrDefault()
        }.";
}
```

So, we have two string properties: OldStyleInterpolation and NewStyleInterpolation. Both of these are read-only properties that return identical values. The only difference between them is how the code is formatted.

By looking at this code, you can immediately see what makes multi-line string interpolation so useful. When we have a look at the OldStyleInterpolation property, a long LINQ expression has been placed on a single line, which makes it difficult to read. In fact, the expression is so long that it does not fit the width of the page.

NewStyleInterpolation, on the other hand, has the same LINQ expression split across multiple lines. This makes the code much easier to read. And each line of the expression neatly fits within the width of the page.

Next, we will examine a raw string literal. To do so, we will create another file inside the StringOperations sub-folder and call it StringLiterals.cs. The content of this file will be as follows:

```
namespace NewFeatures.StringOperations;

public class StringLiterals
{

    public string RawStringLiteral => """
    This text may contain any symbols, including
    newlines, "quoted text",
        indentations, and so on.

    There is no need to escape any characters.
    """;


    public string NewStyleInterpolation => $"""
    This is a combination of a new string
        literal and interpolated string.

    This is a value from inserted code: {5 + 8}.

    """;
}
```

So, we have the new raw string literal applied in two varieties: on its own and combined with string interpolation. The syntax for this new string literal is to surround the text value in triple double-quote characters on both ends. And both the start and the end sequence of three double quotes must be placed on their own line.

Anything in between will be interpreted as text, even if a character that you use happens to have a special meaning in C#. You will not have to perform the escape of any special characters. In fact, the backslash (\) symbol that you would normally have used to escape special characters will also be interpreted just as a normal character in the text. And so will be double quotes until we reach a new line where double quotes are presented in a sequence of three. This is how we know we have reached the end of the text.

If you place a dollar sign in front of the opening double-quote sequence, you will be able to insert the code into the string by using curly braces, as you would do with any other type of string interpolation. And this is the only scenario where you will need to escape curly braces if you want to include them as part of your text instead of using them for string interpolation.

And now, we can test all of the string features that we have added. So, we will place some code into **Program.cs** file. And the first thing we will do is add the following statement at the beginning of the file:

```
using NewFeatures.StringOperations;
```

Then, we will test our multi-line string interpolation feature and see if it produces the same result as a single-line version of it. To do this, we will add the following block of code to the file:

```
Console.WriteLine("Testing String Operations.");

var interpolatedStrings = new InterpolatedStrings();

Console.WriteLine($"""

Old style interpolation:

{interpolatedStrings.OldStyleInterpolation}

New style interpolation:

{interpolatedStrings.NewStyleInterpolation}

""");
```

Figure 2.4 shows the result it produces, which indeed confirms that multi-line string interpolation works as expected:

```
Testing String Operations.

Old style interpolation:

The age of Laurence is: 42.

New style interpolation:

The age of Laurence is: 42.
```

Figure 2.4: *Testing multi-line string interpolation*

Next, we will test our string literals to confirm that they produce the results we expect. To do so, we will add the following code to the **Program.cs** file:

```
var stringLiterals = new StringLiterals();


Console.WriteLine($"""


Raw string literal:


{stringLiterals.RawStringLiteral}


String literal with interpolation:


{stringLiterals.NewStyleInterpolation}


""");
```

This code produces the results as shown in *figure 2.5*, which confirms that the new string literals work properly both with and without interpolation:

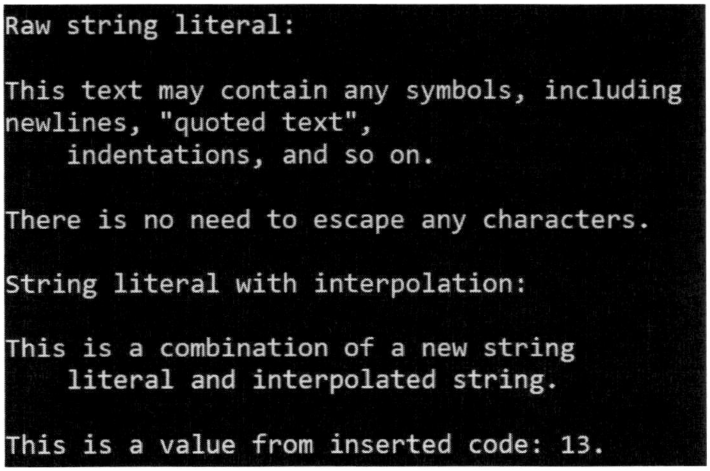

Figure 2.5: Testing string literals

Also, we see the obvious benefits of these new-style string literals when we use them inside the Console logger. We no longer have to make multiple calls to **Console. WriteLine**. We can now make a single call and add multiple lines to the text itself.

This completes the overview of the newly introduced C# 11 features. Let us summarize what we have learned.

Conclusion

C# 11 has added an array of useful features which make the code easier to read, write, and execute. One of such feature is auto-default properties on non-nullable fields in a struct, which allows us to have less verbosity in our code and to prevent our code from accidentally throwing errors if we have not explicitly set any of the properties of a struct object.

Another useful feature is generic attribute classes. This feature allows us to easily determine what exact type is associated with an attribute. We no longer have to store a type in one of the members of the attribute class. This makes our code less verbose and easier to use.

As well as this, we have new sequence pattern matching available in C# 11. This is a powerful feature that provides multiple ways of how various collection types can be used inside conditional logic. The feature works with any collection type, including Span and `ReadOnlySpan`.

C# 11 has also substantially improved how strings are used. First, there is now an ability to use multiple lines in interpolated strings. This allows us to format the code in such a way that it becomes much easier to read. Second, there is a new type of string literal, which does not require programmers to use escape characters. And this new string literal can work with and without string interpolation.

In the upcoming chapter, we will cover the features that have been newly added to .NET 7, including its base SDK, its command line interface, and its core libraries.

Points to remember

- Auto-default properties ensure that non-nullable properties inside a struct data type are always set.

- Generic attribute classes enable the insertion of any arbitrary type into an attribute.

- Sequence pattern matching enables pattern matching on collections.

- Multi-line interpolated strings enable the programmers to use multi-line expressions inside interpolated strings.

- New string literal allows for the construction of string literal that do not require escaping special characters.

Multiple choice questions

1. **What makes auto-default properties useful?**

    a. Less verbosity in the code

    b. Prevents errors from being accidentally thrown

    c. No need to use a constructor

    d. All of these

2. **What makes generic attributes useful?**

    a. Easier to determine a type associated with it

    b. No need to store the type in a dedicated class member

    c. Both of these

    d. None of these

3. **What characters do you need to escape while using raw string literals without interpolation?**

    a. Curly braces

    b. Newlines

    c. Double quotes

    d. None of these

4. **What characters do you need to escape while using raw string literals with interpolation?**

    a. Curly braces

    b. Newlines

    c. Double quotes

    d. None of these

Answers

1. d

2. c

3. d

4. a

Key terms

- **Auto-default properties**: The non-nullable properties that are set to the default value of their data type if not set explicitly.

- **Generic attribute class**: An attribute class that can use generic syntax and be associated with any arbitrary type.

- **Raw string literal**: A string literal that is surrounded by sequences of three double-quote characters. None of the characters inside such a string literally requires escaping.

Join our book's Discord space

Join the book's Discord Workspace for Latest updates, Offers, Tech happenings around the world, New Release and Sessions with the Authors:

https://discord.bpbonline.com

CHAPTER 3
What is New in .NET 7?

Introduction

We have already covered core changes to the C# 11 language. However, .NET 7 platform is more than C#. Some exciting changes were added to the platform itself.

Broadly speaking, .NET consists of a wide range of components. These include build tools, code generation tools, code analysis tools, compilers, and so on. But it also includes **command line interface (CLI)** and various core libraries that can be used by any .NET-compatible programming language.

As you can see, the .NET platform is a fairly broad topic. And this chapter aims to cover the main improvements that have been introduced to all parts of it.

Structure

In this chapter, we will discuss the new features of .NET 7, which will include the following topics:

- SDK and build tool improvements
- System and Microsoft library updates
- Observability improvements
- Breaking changes of .NET 7

Objectives

By the end of this chapter, you will be familiar with the new features that have been added to version 7 of the .NET platform. You will also learn which of the older features have been either marked as deprecated, removed, or had their behavior changed. This way, you will be able to migrate your code base to .NET 7 without breaking any of your existing code.

Prerequisites

To follow this chapter, you will need the following:

- A machine running either Windows, MacOS, or Linux operating system

- .NET 7 SDK

- A suitable IDE or a code editor

- Being familiar with C# fundamentals

If you do not have any of the preceding listed dependencies installed already, let us know the setup instruction provided in *Chapter 1: Getting Familiar with .NET 7 Application Structure*, which also provides a recap of C# fundamentals.

SDK and build tool improvements

We will start by covering the most fundamental components of .NET—it is SDK and the build tools that come with it. That also includes the CLI.

Many improvements have been made to .NET 7 that are purely performance related. But there are also some functional changes that are easy to demonstrate. And this is precisely what we will do now, starting with the CLI improvements.

CLI tools improvements

One of the major improvements to the .NET CLI tools is the output of **dotnet --help** command. It has been made much more detailed than before. The output you will get after executing this command will look similar to the following:

```
Usage: dotnet [runtime-options] [path-to-application] [arguments]

Execute a .NET application.

runtime-options:
  --additionalprobingpath <path>    Path containing probing policy and
```

```
assemblies to probe for.
  --additional-deps <path>        Path to additional deps.json file.
  --depsfile                      Path to <application>.deps.json file.
  --fx-version <version>          Version of the installed Shared
                          Framework to use to run the application.
  --roll-forward <setting>        Roll forward to framework version
(LatestPatch, Minor, LatestMinor, Major, LatestMajor, Disable).
  --runtimeconfig                 Path to <application>.runtimeconfig.
json file.


path-to-application:
  The path to an application .dll file to execute.


Usage: dotnet [sdk-options] [command] [command-options] [arguments]


Execute a .NET SDK command.


sdk-options:
  -d|--diagnostics  Enable diagnostic output.
  -h|--help         Show command line help.
  --info            Display .NET information.
  --list-runtimes   Display the installed runtimes.
  --list-sdks       Display the installed SDKs.
  --version         Display .NET SDK version in use.


SDK commands:
  add           Add a package or reference to a .NET project.
  build         Build a .NET project.
  build-server  Interact with servers started by a build.
  clean         Clean build outputs of a .NET project.
  format        Apply style preferences to a project or solution.
  help          Show command line help.
  list          List project references of a .NET project.
  msbuild       Run Microsoft Build Engine (MSBuild) commands.
  new           Create a new .NET project or file.
  nuget         Provides additional NuGet commands.
  pack          Create a NuGet package.
```

publish	Publish a .NET project for deployment.
remove	Remove a package or reference from a .NET project.
restore	Restore dependencies specified in a .NET project.
run	Build and run a .NET project output.
sdk	Manage .NET SDK installation.
sln	Modify Visual Studio solution files.
store	Store the specified assemblies in the runtime package store.
test	Run unit tests using the test runner specified in a .NET project.
tool	Install or manage tools that extend the .NET experience.
vstest	Run Microsoft Test Engine (VSTest) commands.
workload	Manage optional workloads.

Additional commands from bundled tools:

dev-certs	Create and manage development certificates.
fsi	Start F# Interactive / execute F# scripts.
user-jwts	Manage JSON Web Tokens in development.
user-secrets	Manage development user secrets.
watch	Start a file watcher that runs a command when files change.

Run **dotnet [command] --help** for more information on a command.

But this is not the only improvement to .NET CLI. There is also an inclusion of tab completion. So, pressing the *Tab* key after partially typing a command attribute will complete the attribute for you. This makes the CLI consistent with other CLIs.

NativeAOT and enabling library trimming

Ahead of Time (AOT) is a mechanism used to compile the code into binaries that are specific to a particular platform. There is no longer any intermediate code running between the application and the machine it is running on. The application was already pre-compiled to run on a machine with a specific operating system and CPU architecture. Because there is no intermediate code that needs to be interpreted as it runs, such pre-compiled applications perform significantly faster than their .NET runtime counterparts. And NativeAOT is a .NET 7 feature that enables this type of compilation on .NET.

Because the application has been pre-compiled to run on a specific type of machine, it no longer relies on .NET components. But there are also some .NET components that actually prevent the code to be compliable into a fully native application. To make your .NET application work with NativeAOT if it needs to be trimmed.

Luckily, there is a feature that has been added to the .NET 7 project templates that make the process of trimming the libraries easy. All we need to do is add the following entry to the project file markup:

```
<IsTrimmable>true</IsTrimmable>
```

The complete content of the **.csproj** file may look as follows:

```
<Project Sdk="Microsoft.NET.Sdk">


  <PropertyGroup>
    <OutputType>Exe</OutputType>
    <TargetFramework>net7.0</TargetFramework>
    <ImplicitUsings>enable</ImplicitUsings>
    <LangVersion>preview</LangVersion>
    <Nullable>enable</Nullable>
    <IsTrimmable>true</IsTrimmable>
  </PropertyGroup>


</Project>
```

Central package manager

The central package manager is a new feature that has been added to the NuGet package management system. This is a feature that allows us to easily manage common dependencies for multiple projects in complex solutions.

To enable this feature, you will need to create a **Directory.Packages.props** file inside your solution. This file will contain XML with the **Project** root element. You will need to then have the following markup inside this element to enable the central package manager:

```
<PropertyGroup>
<ManagePackageVersionsCentrally>true</ManagePackageVersionsCentrally>
</PropertyGroup>
```

Then, you can have **ItemGroup** element that will contain references to each individual package you want to use in your projects. This will be represented by **PackageVersion** element, which will be added in the following format:

```
<PackageVersion Include="{ NuGet package name }" Version="{ NuGet
package version }" />
```

This will be the only reference to a specific package you will need in your entire solution. To apply it in your project, you will just need to add the following element to any arbitrary **ItemGroup** element inside your **.CSPROJ** file:

```
<PackageReference Include="{ NuGet package name }" />
```

This concludes our overview of the SDK and builds tool improvements. Now, we will move on to the improvements that have been introduced to the core .NET libraries.

System and Microsoft library updates

We will now have a look at some improvements that have been added to the core libraries used by .NET, which primarily come from **System** and **Microsoft** namespaces. To showcase these new features, we will create a console application project. We will call our project **CoreLibraryImprovements**. You can either create it via a GUI of an IDE of your choice, or you can execute the following command inside any folder on your computer:

```
dotnet new console -o CoreLibraryImprovements
```

This will create a **CoreLibraryImprovements** folder with the project structure inside it. Thereafter, we will start adding classes to the project to showcase the new core library features. The first feature we will have a look at is the improvement to the time-related data types in the System library.

Microseconds and nanoseconds support

Prior to .NET 7, millisecond was the smallest unit of time that .NET has supported. But now, you can work with microseconds and nanoseconds. Both of these units of measure have been added to **DateTime**, **DateTimeOffset**, **TimeOnly**, and **TimeSpan** objects.

To demonstrate how these units can be applied, follow the following steps:

1. We will add **TimeDatatypeImprovements.cs** file to our **CoreLibrary Improvements** project folder. The initial content of this file will be as follows:

```
namespace CoreLibraryImprovements;

public class TimeDatatypeImprovements
{
    public static void DemoNewTimeFeatures()
    {
```

```
        }
}
```

2. Inside the **DemoNewTimeFeatures** method, we will place some code for every data type that had microseconds and nanoseconds added. First, we will insert the following code into the method to demonstrate the new **DateTime** API:

```
var dateTime = new DateTime(2022, 3, 2, 15, 00, 30, 30, 30);


Console.WriteLine($"""
    DateTime object is {dateTime} with {dateTime.Microsecond
    } microseconds and {dateTime.Nanosecond} nanoseconds.

    """);
```

3. In this code, we are setting microsecond and nanosecond values while creating a new instance of a **DateTime** object.

4. Then, we are printing those values in the console.

5. Apply a similar action to the **DateTimeOffset** object by inserting the following code into the method:

```
var dateTimeOffset = new DateTimeOffset(2022,
    3, 2, 15, 00, 30, 30, 30,
    TimeSpan.FromMicroseconds(60 * 1000 * 1000));


Console.WriteLine($"""
    DateTimeOffset object is {dateTimeOffset } with
{dateTimeOffset.Microsecond
    } microseconds and {dateTimeOffset.Nanosecond} nanoseconds.

    """);
```

6. Next, we will insert the following code that demonstrates the new API on the **TimeOnly** object type:

```
var timeOnly = new TimeOnly(15, 00, 30, 30, 30);


Console.WriteLine($"""
```

```
TimeOnly object is {timeOnly} with {timeOnly.Microsecond
} microseconds and {timeOnly.Nanosecond} nanoseconds.

""");
```

7. As you may have noticed, the **TimeOnly** object is very similar to **DateTime**, but it does not have the date part in it.

8. And finally, we will add the following code to demonstrate the new API of the **TimeOffset** data type:

```
var timeSpan = new TimeSpan(19, 3, 40, 20, 30, 30);

Console.WriteLine($"""
    TimeSpan object is {timeSpan} with {timeSpan.Microseconds
    } microseconds and {timeSpan.Nanoseconds} nanoseconds.
    Ticks per microsecond: {TimeSpan.TicksPerMicrosecond}.
    Nanoseconds per tick: {TimeSpan.NanosecondsPerTick}.

    """);
```

As you may have noticed, this data type has some additional constant static fields, namely, **TicksPerMicrosecond** and **NanosecondsPerTick**.

9. And now, to see our code in action, we can replace the content of the **Program. cs** file inside the project folder with the following:

```
using CoreLibraryImprovements;

Console.WriteLine("Demonstrating time-related data type improvements.");

TimeDatatypeImprovements.DemoNewTimeFeatures();
```

And if we now run the application, the output of it is expected to look similar to what is displayed in *figure 3.1*:

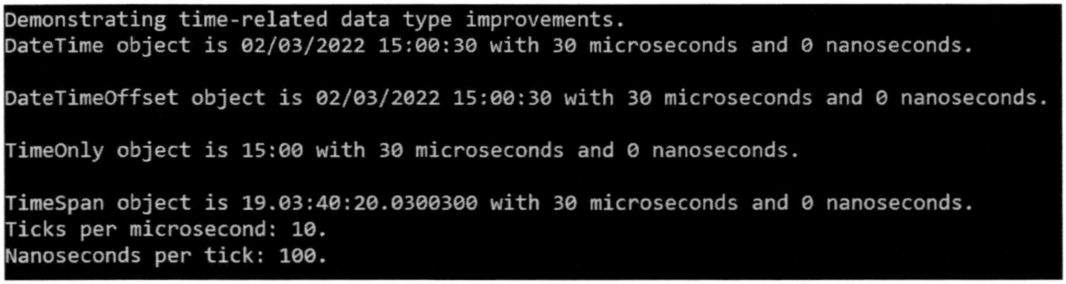

Figure 3.1: *Demonstration of new time-related APIs*

This concludes the overview of the new time-related .NET functionality. Next, we will examine the new features related to JSON processing.

New JSON features

The improvements to JSON that have been added to .NET 7 include the following:

- **MaxDepth** property has been added to **JsonWriterOptions** class from **System.Text.Json** library.
- The default **JsonSerializerOptions** is being made accessible externally, so developers can see what the options are.
- An implementation of HTTP PATCH calls specific to JSON
- JSON object polymorphism features have been added.

To demonstrate these JSON features, we will add **NewJsonFeatures.cs** file to our project folder, and we will initially populate it with the following content:

```
using System.Net.Http.Json;
using System.Text.Json;
using System.Text.Json.Serialization;


namespace CoreLibraryImprovements;


public static class NewJsonFeatures
{
}
```

Next, we will add a method to this class that will demonstrate how to use the **MaxDepth** of the **JsonWriterOptions** class.

MaxDepth property of JsonWriterOptions class

MaxDepth property enforces the maximum depth of inner objects inside the JSON output. If this number is exceeded and the structure of an object is deeper, an exception will be thrown. The method that we will add to demonstrate this will look as follows:

```
public static void DemoJsonWriterOptions()
{
    var options = new JsonWriterOptions
    {
```

```
        Indented = true,
        MaxDepth = 5
    };

    using var fileStream = File.Create("output.json");
    using var writer = new Utf8JsonWriter(fileStream, options: options);
    using JsonDocument document = JsonDocument.Parse("""
    {
        "level1": {
            "level2": {
                "level3": {
                    "key": "value"
                }
            }
        }
    }
    """);

    var root = document.RootElement;

    if (root.ValueKind == JsonValueKind.Object)
    {
        writer.WriteStartObject();
    }
    else
    {
        return;
    }

    foreach (JsonProperty property in root.EnumerateObject())
    {
        property.WriteTo(writer);
    }

    writer.WriteEndObject();
    writer.Flush();
}
```

In this method, we are setting JSON writer that writes indented JSON and is only capable of dealing with up to five levels of depth. Then, we use this writer to write a JSON document into a file.

In the JSON that we are using in our example, we only have three levels of depth, so it fits within our maximum value of 5. However, if we had more than five levels, this code would throw an exception.

Default JsonSerializerOptions configuration

Next, we will add the following method that demonstrates the accessibility of the default values in the **JsonSerializerOptions** object. The method will look like the following:

```
public static void ShowDefaultJsonSerializerOptions()
{
    var options = new JsonSerializerOptions
    {
        WriteIndented = true
    };

    Console.WriteLine("Showing default JsonSerializerOptions.");
    Console.WriteLine(JsonSerializer.Serialize(JsonSerializerOptions.
Default, options));
}
```

In this method, we are serializing the Default static property of the **JsonSerializerOptions** object to see what the default settings are if you do not set any explicit values in any of the fields.

JSON-specific HTTP PATCH

Next, we will add the following method to demonstrate how a JSON-specific **HTTP PATCH** request can be made from an instance of the **HttpClient** class. The method will have the following structure:

```
public static async Task DemoPatchAsJsonAsync()
{
    var client = new HttpClient();
    client.DefaultRequestHeaders.Add("Accept", "application/json");
    var jsonBody = new { Key = "value" };
var response =
```

```
await client.PatchAsJsonAsync("https://localhost", jsonBody);
}
```

To see how this method works, we will need to host a server application with an appropriate endpoint that accepts the **PATCH** verb and **JSON** payload. In this example, the application is expected to be hosted at the **https://localhost** address. However, if you want to see how this method works, you may want to host an appropriate application at any address that suits you.

Finally, we will have a look at the new JSON polymorphism feature.

JSON polymorphism

To demonstrate JSON polymorphism, we will need to add some classes that will represent JSON objects. We can add them in the same file immediately below the **NewJsonFeatures** class definition. And the first pair of classes will look as follows:

```
[JsonDerivedType(typeof(BasicBaseObject))]
[JsonDerivedType(typeof(BasicDerivedObject))]
public class BasicBaseObject
{
    public int BaseData { get; set; } = 1;
}

public class BasicDerivedObject : BasicBaseObject
{
    public int ExtraData { get; set; } = 2;
}
```

Here, we have two classes. As indicated by the **JsonDerivedType** attributes, both of these types are meant to represent a JSON object. Both of these can inherit and be inherited from. This is why, when we derive **BasicDerivedObject** class from **BasicBaseObject**, this will be known by JSON serializer and deserializer.

This is the most basic setup of JSON polymorphism. Now we will add two more classes that will demonstrate more advanced usage. These classes will look as follows:

```
[JsonDerivedType(typeof(BaseStringDiscriminator), typeDiscriminator:
"baseObject")]

[JsonDerivedType(typeof(DerivedStringDiscriminator), typeDiscriminator:
"derivedObject")]

public class BaseStringDiscriminator
```

```
{
    public int BaseData { get; set; } = 1;
}


public class DerivedStringDiscriminator : BaseStringDiscriminator
{
    public int ExtraData { get; set; } = 2;
}
```

These classes have **typeDiscriminator** parameters set inside the **JsonDerivedType** attribute. This parameter allows you to derive a JSON string into the correct type during the deserialization. In C#, when you derive one class from another, the derived class implicitly matches its type with its base type. So, if your method expects a parameter of the **BaseStringDiscriminator** type, you can pass a variable of **DerivedStringDiscriminator** into it.

The **typeDescriminator** parameter allows you to use this feature of the language while deserializing a JSON string into a class. The value specified in this parameter corresponds to the value of the $type field inside the JSON string. When you specify **BaseStringDiscriminator** type as the target of your deserialization, the JSON string will be deserialized into this type if you specify **baseObject** as the value of the $type field. But it will be deserialized into **DerivedStringDiscriminator** type if the value that you have specified is **derivedObject**.

You can also use a numeric type discriminator. And the following pair of classes demonstrates how you can use it:

```
[JsonDerivedType(typeof(BaseIntDiscriminator), 0)]
[JsonDerivedType(typeof(DerivedIntDiscriminator), 1)]
public class BaseIntDiscriminator
{
    public int BaseData { get; set; } = 1;
}


public class DerivedIntDiscriminator : BaseIntDiscriminator
{
    public int ExtraData { get; set; } = 2;
}
```

In this case, the same principle applies as with the string type discriminator. But this time, it will be an integer number inside the **$type** field.

Now, we will add some code that will help us to see these features in action. We will do it by adding the following method to our **NewJsonFeatures** class:

```
public static void DemoJsonPolymorphism()
{
    Console.WriteLine("Demonstrating basic JSON polymorphism:");
    Console.WriteLine(JsonSerializer.Serialize(new
BasicDerivedObject()));


    Console.WriteLine(
"Demonstrating JSON polymorphism with string type discriminator:");
    var jsonStringDiscrimnator = JsonSerializer.
Deserialize<BaseStringDiscriminator>("""
    {
        "$type": "derivedObject",
        "ExtraData":2,
        "BaseData":1
    }
""");

    Console.WriteLine($"JSON is of derived type: {jsonStringDiscrimnator
is DerivedStringDiscriminator}.");

Console.WriteLine(
"Demonstrating JSON polymorphism with integer type discriminator:");

    var jsonIntDiscrimnator = JsonSerializer.
Deserialize<BaseIntDiscriminator>("""
    {
        "$type": 1,
        "ExtraData":2,
        "BaseData":1
    }
    """);
Console.WriteLine($"JSON is of derived type: {jsonIntDiscrimnator is
DerivedIntDiscriminator}.");
}
```

So, we are serializing an object with basic JSON polymorphism into a JSON string. Then, we are testing the type discriminator features while deserializing a JSON string into a class. We test both the numeric and the textual type discriminators.

Now, we will add some logic to execute the code that we have added.

Testing JSON features

We will add the following code to our Program.cs file:

```
Console.WriteLine("Demonstrating JSON improvements.");

NewJsonFeatures.DemoJsonWriterOptions();

NewJsonFeatures.ShowDefaultJsonSerializerOptions();

NewJsonFeatures.DemoJsonPolymorphism();
```

And this should produce results similar to what is displayed in *figure 3.2*:

```
Demonstrating JSON improvements.
Showing default JsonSerializerOptions.
{
  "Converters": [],
  "PolymorphicTypeConfigurations": [],
  "AllowTrailingCommas": false,
  "DefaultBufferSize": 16384,
  "Encoder": null,
  "DictionaryKeyPolicy": null,
  "IgnoreNullValues": false,
  "DefaultIgnoreCondition": 0,
  "NumberHandling": 0,
  "IgnoreReadOnlyProperties": false,
  "IgnoreReadOnlyFields": false,
  "IncludeFields": false,
  "MaxDepth": 0,
  "PropertyNamingPolicy": null,
  "PropertyNameCaseInsensitive": false,
  "ReadCommentHandling": 0,
  "UnknownTypeHandling": 0,
  "WriteIndented": false,
  "ReferenceHandler": null
}
Demonstrating basic JSON polymorphism:
{"ExtraData":2,"BaseData":1}
Demonstrating JSON polymorphism with string type discriminator:
JSON is of derived type: True.
Demonstrating JSON polymorphism with integer type discriminator:
JSON is of derived type: True.
```

Figure 3.2: The output of our JSON-related methods

This concludes the demonstration of the new JSON-related features in .NET 7. Next, we will have a look at the new Stream features.

New stream features

The main improvement to the **Stream** class in the core **System** library of .NET is that it had two methods added to it: ReadExactly and ReadAtLeast. These methods allow for greater flexibility while reading data from the stream into the byte array buffer.

ReadExactly method will read the exact number of bytes that the buffer contains. If there is insufficient data to fill the buffer, an exception will be thrown.

ReadAtLeast method will read at least as many bytes as specified in a specific parameter. It does not have to fill the entire buffer. It will throw an exception if there are fewer bytes to read than are specified in the parameter.

To demonstrate both of these methods in action, we will add NewStreamFeatures. cs file to our CoreLibraryImprovements project and populate it with the following content:

```csharp
namespace CoreLibraryImprovements;

public static class NewStreamFeatures
{
    public static void DemoReadExactly()
    {
        using var fileStream = File.Open("output.json", FileMode.Open);

        var buffer = new byte[10];
        fileStream.ReadExactly(buffer);

        Console.WriteLine($"""
        Bytes read with ReadExactly:
        {BitConverter.ToString(buffer)}
        """);
    }

    public static void DemoReadAtLeast()
    {
        using var fileStream = File.Open("output.json", FileMode.Open);

        var buffer = new byte[10];
        fileStream.ReadAtLeast(buffer, 10);
```

```
        Console.WriteLine($"""
        Bytes read with ReadAtLeast:
        {BitConverter.ToString(buffer)}
        """);
    }
}
```

So, we have two methods in here: **DemoReadExactly** and **DemoReadAtLeast**. Both methods read data from the file that was created when we were testing some new JSON-related features. **DemoReadExactly** method demonstrates how to use **ReadExactly** method on the **Stream** class, which is accessible to any class that inherits from **Stream**, such as **FileStream** from our example. **DemoReadAtLeast** method demonstrates how to use **ReadAtLeast**. Here, we are setting both the buffer length and the minimum number of bytes to 10, which will make the behavior of this method identical to that of **ReadExactly**.

Now, we will add the following code to the **Program.cs** file to test these newly added methods:

```
Console.WriteLine("Demonstrating Stream improvements.");

NewStreamFeatures.DemoReadExactly();

NewStreamFeatures.DemoReadAtLeast();
```

And if we now run our program, we should expect to see an output similar to that shown in *figure* 3.3:

```
Demonstrating Stream improvements.
Bytes read with ReadExactly:
7B-0D-0A-20-20-22-6C-65-76-65
Bytes read with ReadAtLeast:
7B-0D-0A-20-20-22-6C-65-76-65
```

Figure 3.3: The data read by ReadExactly and ReadAtleast methods

This concludes the overview of the new streaming features from .NET 7. Now, we will look at the improvements to the **RegEx** engine.

RegEx improvements

RegEx is a technology that allows programmers to verify if some arbitrary text matches a specific pattern. It is very powerful because you can construct any pattern with a relatively low number of symbols. But because of its ability to work with virtually limitless patterns, rules, and combinations thereof, it is relatively computationally expensive to use RegEx.

.NET 7, however, has introduced a feature that substantially improves the performance of the RegEx engine. If you want your code path to only work with a specific RegEx expression, you can pre-compile it. So, the pattern comparison will be very quick to execute during the runtime. And this is what we will have a look at now.

We will add **NewRegexFeatures.cs** file to our **CoreLibraryImprovements** project. The content of this file will be as follows:

```
using System.Text.RegularExpressions;


namespace CoreLibraryImprovements;


public partial class NewRegexFeatures
{
    [RegexGenerator(@"^[a-z]+$", RegexOptions.IgnoreCase)]
    public static partial Regex LettersRegex();

    public static void DemoPrecompiledRegex(string input)
    {
        Console.WriteLine(
$"'{input}' matches '^[a-z]+$' RegEx: {
LettersRegex().IsMatch(input)}.");
        Console.WriteLine(
$"The number of matches: {LettersRegex().Count(input)}.");

        var matchEnumerator = LettersRegex().EnumerateMatches(input);

        while (matchEnumerator.MoveNext())
            Console.WriteLine($"Match of {matchEnumerator.Current.Length
            } found at index {matchEnumerator.Current.Index}.");
    }
}
```

Here, we first define a method that returns a RegEx object. The **RegexGenerator** attribute above indicates that this object comes with a pre-compiled pattern. To make this work, it needs to have static and partial access modifiers. In our case, the pattern determines whether a specific text consists entirely of letters. No other characters are allowed.

Then, we have the **DemoPrecompiledRegex** method that uses the pre-compiled RegEx pattern. It takes an input text and compares it against the pattern. Then, it creates outputs in the console as a result of this comparison.

This method also showcases another RegEx improvement that is new to .NET 7—the **EnumerateMatches** method. This method allows you to go throw all parts of the input text that match the pattern.

Another useful feature about this new pre-compiled RegEx that is worth mentioning is that the Roslyn analyzer will automatically highlight the places in the code where the existing RegEx logic can be replaced with this. This will allow you to refactor and optimize your old code with just a few clicks if you are using Roslyn-compatible IDE like Visual Studio.

Now, we will test this method. We will do so by adding the following lines of code into the **Program.cs** file of the project:

```
Console.WriteLine("Demonstrating RegEx improvements.");


var lettersOnlyText = "letters";
var mixedText = "fwef340";


NewRegexFeatures.DemoPrecompiledRegex(lettersOnlyText);
NewRegexFeatures.DemoPrecompiledRegex(mixedText);
```

Here, we are running the comparison against two strings. One of them contains only letters, as expected by our RegEx pattern, while the other contains numbers too. Figure 3.4 demonstrates the kind of results you are expected to see if you execute this code:

```
Demonstrating RegEx improvements.
'letters' matches '^[a-z]+$' RegEx: True.
The number of matches: 1.
Match of 7 found at intex 0.
'fwef340' matches '^[a-z]+$' RegEx: False.
The number of matches: 0.
```

Figure 3.4: Demonstration of pre-compiled RegEx

This concludes our demonstration of RegEx improvements. Now, we will have a look at the new cryptography-related features.

Cryptography improvements

.NET always had many ways to work with SSL/TLS encryption certificates. Previously, working with the certificate name attributes was not always easy. The primary way of doing so was to pass a string where different attributes were encoded. But it was not the most convenient thing to work with if any of the names had some special characters in them. Plus, because you were dealing with raw strings, it was easy to make a typo somewhere.

.NET 7 fixed this problem by adding the **X500DistinguishedNameBuilder** class. This class comes with methods that allow you to add the naming attributes that are commonly used in encryption certificates. This way, each name will be short enough to minimize the chance of accidental misspelling. And, as it is treated as a separate unit, using special characters inside of it will not affect the integrity of the entire attribute structure.

To demonstrate the **X500DistinguishedNameBuilder** class, we will add the **CryptographyEnhancements.cs** file to our project and will populate it with the following content:

```
using System.Security.Cryptography.X509Certificates;

namespace CoreLibraryImprovements;

public static class CryptographyEnhancements
{
    public static void DemoCertificateNameBuilder()
    {
        var builder = new X500DistinguishedNameBuilder();
        builder.AddCommonName("CertificateSubject");
        builder.AddOrganizationalUnitName("TestUnit");
        builder.AddOrganizationName("Scientific Programmer Ltd.");

        Console.WriteLine($"The certificate name is: {
            builder.Build().Decode(X500DistinguishedNameFlags.None)}");
    }
}
```

Here, we are adding some arbitrary names to the builder, building the name structure, and then decoding it to see what it consists of. We will now add the following code to the Program.cs class, which will allow us to run this method:

```
Console.WriteLine("Demonstrating cryptography improvements.");
CryptographyEnhancements.DemoCertificateNameBuilder();
```

Now, if we run it, we are expected to see the following output:

```
Demonstrating cryptography improvements.
The certificate name is: O=Scientific Programmer Ltd., OU=TestUnit, CN=CertificateSubject
```

Figure 3.5: *Decoded result of using X500DistinguishedNameBuilder*

We will now move on to another extremely useful feature of .NET 7—the TAR API.

New TAR API

TAR is one of the popular file-archiving algorithms. But despite its popularity, .NET did not have any inbuilt functionality to deal with it. But now it does.

To demonstrate what this new functionality consists of, we will add TarApi.cs file to our project, which will then be populated with the following content:

```
using System.Formats.Tar;
using System.IO.Compression;


namespace CoreLibraryImprovements;


public static class TarApi
{
}
```

Next, we will add the following method to the class. This method demonstrates how you can use the TAR API to take all the files inside a specified folder and save them in a TAR archive at a specified location.

```
public static void CreateTarFile(
    string sourceDirectoryName,
    string destinationFileName)
{
    TarFile.CreateFromDirectory(
        sourceDirectoryName: sourceDirectoryName,
        destinationFileName: destinationFileName,
        includeBaseDirectory: true);
}
```

Next, we will add the following method to demonstrate how to use the API to extract the content of a TAR file into a specified directory:

```
public static void ExtractTarFile(
    string sourceFileName,
    string destinationDirectoryName)
{
    TarFile.ExtractToDirectory(
        sourceFileName: sourceFileName,
        destinationDirectoryName: destinationDirectoryName,
        overwriteFiles: false);
}
```

The API can also work with streams, including the memory stream. This allows you to process some complex logic without storing intermediate files on the drive. For example, this method demonstrates how you can extract a TAR archive into the memory stream and then write another TAR archive from this stream:

```
public static void CreateTarFileFromStream(
    string sourceDirectoryName,
    string destinationDirectoryName)
{
    using var stream = new MemoryStream();
    TarFile.CreateFromDirectory(
        sourceDirectoryName: sourceDirectoryName,
        destination: stream,
        includeBaseDirectory: true);

    TarFile.ExtractToDirectory(
        source: stream,
        destinationDirectoryName: destinationDirectoryName,
        overwriteFiles: false);
}
```

You can also use the API to transfer the full or partial content of one TAR file to another. And the following method demonstrates how this can be done:

```
public static void TransferFilesToDifferentArchive(
    string sourceFileName,
    string destinationFileName)
{
    using var stream = File.OpenRead(sourceFileName);
```

```
using var reader = new TarReader(stream, leaveOpen: false);


TarEntry? entry;
while ((entry = reader.GetNextEntry()) != null)
{
    destinationFileName = Path.Join(destinationFileName, entry.
Name);
    entry.ExtractToFile(destinationFileName, overwrite: true);
}
}
```

Also, you can use GZIP compression algorithm together with TAR. This method is demonstrated as follows:

```
public static void ExtractFromGzipArchive(
    string sourceFileName,
    string destinationDirectoryName)
{
    using var compressedStream = File.OpenRead(sourceFileName);
    using var decompressor = new GZipStream(compressedStream,
CompressionMode.Decompress);
    TarFile.ExtractToDirectory(
        source: decompressor,
        destinationDirectoryName: destinationDirectoryName,
        overwriteFiles: false);
}
```

This concludes the overview of the new TAR API that has been added to version 7 of the .NET platform.

There are also some core library improvements in .NET 7 that deserve a category of their own. Those are related to observability. We will discuss that next.

Observability improvements

.NET 7 added some new ways that can help you monitor your applications. A whole new set of improvements was added to the platform because its developers want it to be in line with the emerging cloud-native **OpenTelemetry** standards.

The new observability features in .NET 7 can be broadly split into the following categories:

- New ways to monitor activities

- **UpDownCounter** metric

And to demonstrate these improvements, we will create a new console application project and call it **ObservabilityImprovements**. It can either be created from a GUI of an IDE or by executing the following command:

```
dotnet new console -o ObservabilityImprovements
```

Now, we will start adding content to it too. First, we will have a look at the new ways we can monitor activities.

New ways to monitor activity

System.Diagnostics.Activity is a class that represents a running process from the context of logging. Its main purpose is to obtain the status and some other supporting information about the running processes and log it.

To have a look at what activity monitoring options are available in .NET 7, we will add the **ActivityMonitoring.cs** file to the **ObservabilityImprovements** project with the following content:

```
using System.Diagnostics;


namespace ObservabilityImprovements;


public static class ActivityMonitoring
{
}
```

Now, we will start adding various methods to it to showcase new activity monitoring features. We will start by adding the logic that monitors a stopped activity.

Monitoring stopped activities

To monitor stopped activities, an **IsStopped** property has been added to the **Activity** class. And to demonstrate its usage, we can add the following method to our newly created class:

```
public static void MonitorStoppedActivity()
{
    var activity = new Activity("test");
    activity.Start();
    activity.Stop();
```

```
        Console.WriteLine($"Is activity stopped? {activity.IsStopped}");
}
```

Here, we start an activity. Then we stop it and check its stopped status.

Next, we will have a look at the ability to trigger an event when the current activity changes.

Current activity changed event

To demonstrate how a change of the current activity can trigger an event, we will add the following method:

```
public static void DemoCurrentChangedEvent()
{
    Activity.CurrentChanged += ChangeEvent;

    var activity = new Activity("test");
    activity.Start();
    activity = new Activity("test2");
    activity.Start();

    void ChangeEvent(object? sender, ActivityChangedEventArgs e)
    {
        Console.WriteLine($"Operation changed from {
            (e.Previous?.OperationName ?? "[No Activity]")} to {
                e.Current?.OperationName}.");
    }
}
```

Here, we are associating an event handler with the static **CurrentChange** event on the **Activity** class. Then, we start a new activity that will create a trigger for this event. The event gets triggered even if the current activity changes from no activity. Then, we create another activity, which will trigger the change even once again.

Now, we will have a look at the newly added ability to enumerate activity properties.

Enumerating activity properties

.NET 7 has added the ability to enumerate tags, links, and events of activity. This ability has been enabled by adding **EnumerateTagObjects**, **EnumerateLinks**, and **EnumerateEvents** methods. To demonstrate how it works, we will add the following method:

```csharp
public static void DemoActivityEnumerators()
{
    var activity = new Activity("test");

    activity.SetTag("tag1", "value1");
    activity.SetTag("tag2", "value2");
    activity.SetTag("tag3", "value2");

    Console.WriteLine("Activity has the following tags:");

    foreach (ref readonly KeyValuePair<string, object?> tag
        in activity.EnumerateTagObjects())
    {
        Console.WriteLine($"Tag name: {tag.Key}, tag value: {tag.Value}");
    }

    activity.AddEvent(new ActivityEvent("event1"));
    activity.AddEvent(new ActivityEvent("event2"));

    Console.WriteLine("Activity has the following events:");

    foreach (var ev in activity.EnumerateEvents())
    {
        Console.WriteLine($"Event name: {ev.Name}");
    }
}
```

In addition to this, these properties themselves have tags that can be enumerated. This can be demonstrated in the following method:

```csharp
public static void DemoInnerTagEnumerators()
{
    var tagCollection = new List<KeyValuePair<string, object?>>()
    {
        new KeyValuePair<string, object?>("tag1", "value1"),
        new KeyValuePair<string, object?>("tag2", "value2"),
```

```
    };

    var activityLink = new ActivityLink(default, new
ActivityTagsCollection(tagCollection));

    Console.WriteLine("ActivityLink has the following tags:");

    foreach (ref readonly KeyValuePair<string, object?> tag
        in activityLink.EnumerateTagObjects())
    {
      Console.WriteLine($"Tag name: {tag.Key}, tag value: {tag.Value}");
    }

    var e = new ActivityEvent("TestEvent", tags: new
ActivityTagsCollection(tagCollection));

    Console.WriteLine("ActivityEvent has the following tags:");

    foreach (ref readonly KeyValuePair<string, object?> tag
        in e.EnumerateTagObjects())
    {
      Console.WriteLine($"Tag name: {tag.Key}, tag value: {tag.Value}");
  }
}
```

Next, we will examine a new metric type that has been added to the .NET 7 platform—the **UpDownCounter**.

UpDownCounter metric

UpDownCounter is a class that has been added to **System.Diagnostics.Metrics** namespace. It is meant to be used alongside the **Meter** class from the same namespace.

This is a type of metric that is frequently referred to as a gauge in other telemetry libraries. A normal counter metric would only go up. However, a gauge (or up-down counter) is meant to go either up or down. The following example demonstrates how this metric can be used.

```
public static Meter MeterObject = new Meter("HTTP.Connections",
"1.0.0");
```

```
public static UpDownCounter<int> ActiveConnections = MeterObject.
CreateUpDownCounter<int>("Active-Connections");
```

Then, to change the values of the metric, we can call the **Add** method on it with either positive or negative integer parameters.

```
ActiveConnections.Add(10);
ActiveConnections.Add(-2);
```

The normal counter metric is intended for monitoring the things that can only have their count increased. For example, it can be used for monitoring the number of requests that the system receives. An up-down counter, on the other hand, is there to monitor the counts that are meant to be changed in real time. For example, you can use it to monitor the real-time number of logged-in users. As a user logs in, the count increases. And as someone logs off, the count decreases.

This concludes the overview of the changes that were introduced into .NET 7. Now, we will cover the breaking changes that may cause your old code to not be fully compatible with .NET 7.

Breaking changes of .NET 7

This is a list of the main changes that may make your old code either behave differently once it has been migrated to .NET 7 or does not work at all. And that is why it is important to know these.

Microsoft.Extensions nullability

.NET 6, the nullability of various types has changed. For example, until .NET 6, objects were nullable, and so were strings. Now, it has been changed. You now have to explicitly mark them as nullable to make them nullable.

On the one hand, you can still configure your applications to use the old behavior. But on the other hand, there are plenty of libraries that just did not keep up with these nullability changes. And those include various libraries that use **Microsoft. Extensions** namespace.

But now this has been fixed, and the libraries fully adhere to the nullability rules of both the new and the old versions of .NET. This, however, may cause potential problems if you have been using the libraries against .NET 6 with the new nullability rules enabled. If you are using any libraries with this namespace and you have migrated your application to .NET 7, make sure those code paths still work as intended.

Obsolete and non-nullable endpoints

There are some other endpoints in various .NET libraries that had their nullability behavior changed. There are also some endpoints that have been either deprecated or removed. The first type of endpoint will give you a warning. The endpoints from the second type will prevent your code from compiling.

The easiest way to identify if your code is affected is to migrate your solution to .NET 7 and then build it. If there are any new deprecation warnings or errors, you will know that you need to make some changes to your code to adhere to the new APIs.

PatternContext constraint

Generic **PatternContext<T>** allowed any type to be used as **T**. However, in .NET 7, you can only use struct for this purpose. If you have been using any other type before, your code will no longer compile.

Multi-level lookup is disabled on Windows

Previously, if you were running the dotnet command, the command was looking for the framework in multiple install locations. And now, it only looks inside a single install location that is specified inside the **DOTNET_ROOT** environment variable. This will probably not be an issue for most developers, but it is still worth knowing about.

MSBuild serialization of custom types

In .NET 7, **MSBuild** no longer supports the serialization of the types derived from **BuildEventArgs** and **ITaskItem** via **BinaryFormatter** serializer. So, you will need to change your code that was previously using these types.

Conclusion

.NET 7 platform had many useful features added to it. They cover both the core SDK and the core libraries, which exist under either **System** or **Microsoft** namespace. Some of these improvements are non-functional, such as performance improvements to the compiler. But there are plenty of functional improvements too, the most notable of which have been covered in this chapter.

The notable SDK improvements that we have covered in this chapter are the new CLI features, the NativeAOT functionality, and the central package manager feature for NuGet. The core library improvements that we had a look at included new time-related APIS, new JSON features, new stream-related features, pre-compiled RegEx, cryptography improvements, and the new TAR API.

A notable category of the new core library features is the collection of observability improvements that were added to bring .NET more in line with **OpenTelemetry** standards. These include new ways to monitor activities and new metric types.

But there are also some breaking changes that have been introduced into .NET 7. But most of these are fairly easy to identify by migrating your code to .NET 7 and building your application. Deprecated features will then produce warnings, whereas the features with completely changed functionality will prevent your code from being built.

In the upcoming chapter, we will talk about MAUI, which is a framework for building native applications that can be ported to either mobile devices or desktop computers.

Points to remember

- .NET 7 CLI is now more intuitive and provides more information on the available commands.

- .NET 7 applications can be compiled into native executables and automatically trimmed.

- NuGet central package manager feature allows developers to easily manage dependencies inside complex solutions.

- Microseconds and nanoseconds have been added to the time-related objects.

- .NET 7 has new JSON functionalities, which include JSON polymorphism, access to default serialization options, and so on.

- New stream options allow you to specify the exact number of bytes to read into the stream.

- Pre-compiled RegEx allows you to execute textual pattern matching much quicker.

- With .NET 7, you can easily construct the name attributes of cryptographic certificates.

- A new API has been added to .NET 7 to deal with TAR files.

- Observability improvements that have been added to .NET 7 include activity monitoring and new metric types.

- Some breaking changes have been introduced into .NET 7 too, so developers need to be aware of those.

Multiple choice questions

1. **What is NativeAOT?**

   a. A framework for building mobile applications

   b. A framework for building desktop applications

   c. A technology that complied code into an application that runs directly on a specific hardware type

   d. None of these

2. **What is JSON polymorphism?**

   a. The ability to inherit from a JSON-specific class and deserialize JSON string into an appropriate type

   b. The ability to replace data types in JSON fields

   c. The ability to add or remove JSON fields at will

   d. The ability to store either a singular JSON object or a collection thereof in the same field

3. **What can .NET TAR API be used for?**

   a. Unpacking and packing TAR files

   b. Transferring the content between TAR archives

   c. Transferring the content between TAR archives and memory

   d. All of the above

4. **Which of the following properties of `System.Diagnostics.Activity` class you can enumerate?**

   a. Tags

   b. Links

   c. Events

   d. All of the above

Answers

1. c

2. a

3. d

4. d

Key terms

- **NativeAOT**: A technology that allows developers to compile their application into a format that would run close to the hardware on a particular type of a machine

- **Library trimming**: The process of removing .NET-specific components from the libraries to make them compatible with NativeAOT

- **NuGet Central Package Manager**: The feature that allows NuGet dependencies to be managed in a single place for the whole solution

- **JSON**: JavaScript Object Notation—a format for transferring data

- **JSON serialization**: The process of converting an object from the code into a JSON string

- **JSON deserialization**: The process of converting a JSON string into a specified class

- **JSON polymorphism**: The ability for the JSON-specific classes to inherit from one another and get a JSON string to deserialize into an appropriate derived class when the base class is specified as the target of deserialization

- **RegEx**: Regular expression, which is a technology for string pattern matching

- **TAR**: File archiving format

- **GZIP**: Data compression algorithm that works alongside TAR

- **OpenTelemetry**: A framework for applying observability features to cloud-native applications

Join our book's Discord space

Join the book's Discord Workspace for Latest updates, Offers, Tech happenings around the world, New Release and Sessions with the Authors:

https://discord.bpbonline.com

CHAPTER 4

MAUI and Cross-platform Native Applications

Introduction

Multi-platform UI (MAUI) is a framework for developing native applications for mobile devices and desktop computers using the same codebase. MAUI framework was initially introduced into .NET 6, but it reached its maturity several months after the initial .NET 6 releases. Therefore, it is still appropriate to consider this technology new at the time of the .NET 7 release.

Prior to MAUI, there was a mixture of native application development options on .NET. WinForms and Windows Presentation Framework enabled us to build desktop applications for Windows. Xamarin.Forms allowed us to develop cross-platform mobile applications. It had some limited capacity to build Windows applications via the Unified Windows Platform. But there was no inbuilt framework in .NET for developing desktop applications for non-Windows operating systems. And there was not a unified framework that enabled the development of applications for both desktop computers and mobile devices equally well.

And now, MAUI has changed all of this. It is one true unified platform for developing any type of native application from the same codebase. In this chapter, you will learn how to use it.

Structure

In this chapter, we will discuss the new features of .NET 7, which will include the following topics:

- Introducing MAUI
- Using MAUI to build desktop applications
- Using MAUI to build mobile apps
- Limitations of developing for Mac OS and iOS

Objectives

By the end of this chapter, you will be able to create your own MAUI application. You will have learned the main designed patterns used by MAUI. You will also learn how to compile your codebase into a platform-specific application for any operating system supported by MAUI.

Prerequisites

To follow this chapter, you will need the following:

- A machine running either Windows, MacOS, or Linux operating system
- .NET 7 SDK
- A suitable IDE or a code editor
- Being familiar with C# fundamentals

If you do not have any of the preceding listed dependencies installed already, let us setup using the instruction provided in *Chapter 1: Getting Familiar with .NET 7 Application Structure*, which also provides a recap of C# fundamentals.

Introducing MAUI

For those who have previously used Xamarin.Forms to build mobile applications would find MAUI relatively easy to learn. There is a good reason for it because MAUI is an evolution of Xamarin.Forms.

But it is not just a new version of Xamarin.Forms that happen to have additional desktop deployment capabilities. It is different from its predecessor in many fundamental ways. For example, it uses a much simpler project structure, where all supported deployment platforms, both desktop and mobile, share the same project. Of course, you can still use additional projects in your application. There is even a new type of class library project template that is specific to MAUI. But we no longer need a separate project for every target operating system.

There are also some differences in the markup syntax for building user interfaces between Xamarin.Forms and MAUI. Even though both technologies can use XAML as their main markup language, they use different libraries of elements. Therefore, some elements in the application layouts will have different names and attributes.

But perhaps, the most fundamental difference between Xamarin.Forms and MAUI is that the former was a separate framework, whereas the latter has been fully integrated in .NET since version 6. Therefore, MAUI has access to all the latest language features and all other framework features. For example, you can use .NET CLI commands with MAUI applications. And this is what we will do next.

Enabling MAUI development environment

Before you can start writing MAUI applications, you need to enable MAUI workload on your development machine. You can do it via .NET CLI by executing the following command:

```
dotnet workload install maui
```

Then, you can install a tool that will check if your environment has any missing MAUI dependencies:

```
dotnet tool install -g Redth.Net.Maui.Check
```

To then use this tool, you can execute the following command:

```
maui-check
```

Alternatively, you can set up the MAUI workload via your IDE tools. For example, if you are using Visual Studio on Windows, you can open Visual Studio Installer and click Modify button next to the latest version of the IDE, like it is shown in *figure 4.1*:

Figure 4.1: *Modifying workloads via Visual Studio Installer*

Then, you would need to enable the workloads with the title of .NET Multi-platform App UI development, as demonstrated in *figure 4.2*:

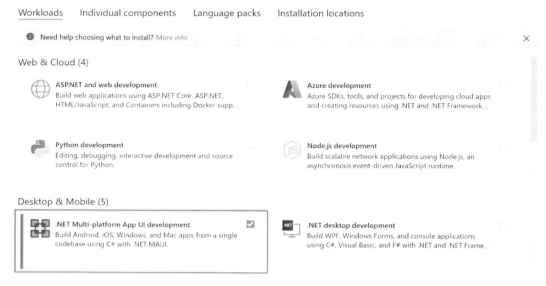

Figure 4.2: *Enabling MAU workload via Visual Studio Installer*

Now, we can start creating MAUI apps to see how they work.

Creating a basic MAUI applications

To create a new MAUI app with the name of **SampleMauiApp**, you can execute the following command:

```
dotnet new maui -o SampleMauiApp
```

And now, we can have a look at the basic structure of the MAUI app project, which can be seen in *figure 4.3*:

Figure 4.3: *The root folder of MAUI project*

By default, we have a couple of files with the code in the root folder. **MauiProgram.cs** is the file that contains the entry point into the application that is shared by all platforms. **App.xaml** is the base file used by the app. It contains links to all shared resources, such as specific fonts and styles. It has a code-behind file with the name of **App.xaml.cs**. This file tells the application which shell layout to load.

AppShell.xaml file represents the main application layout. Its purpose is to provide a common structure to all pages of your application. It is not meant to represent the application UI by itself. For this purpose, we have **MainPage.xaml** file in our example. Just like all other XAML files, it has a code-behind C# file with a CS extension.

MAUI project also has **Platforms** folder, which has platform-specific **entrypoint** code and any other native code that is applicable to platforms. Its structure can be demonstrated as shown in *figure 4.4*:

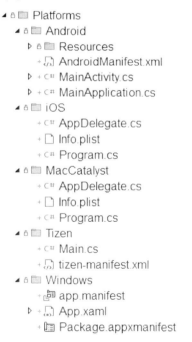

Figure 4.4: *The structure of Platforms folder*

And finally, another noteworthy folder of an MAUI project is **Resources**. It is a folder that contains all images, fonts, locale-specific text, and any other resource that your application might need. The structure of this folder can be seen in *figure 4.5*:

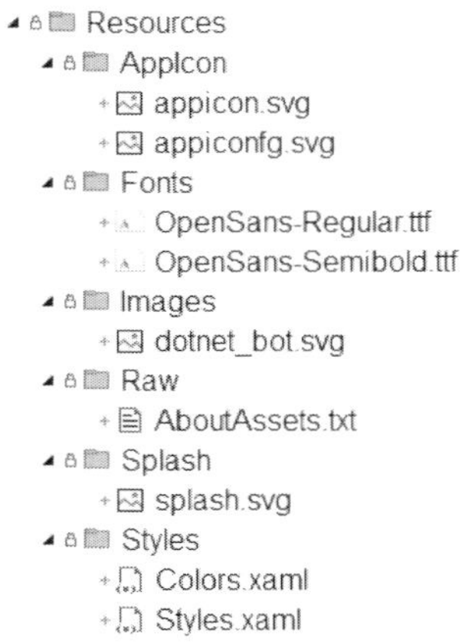

```
▲ 🔒 📁 Resources
    ▲ 🔒 📁 AppIcon
        + 🖼 appicon.svg
        + 🖼 appiconfg.svg
    ▲ 🔒 📁 Fonts
        + ᴀ OpenSans-Regular.ttf
        + ᴀ OpenSans-Semibold.ttf
    ▲ 🔒 📁 Images
        + 🖼 dotnet_bot.svg
    ▲ 🔒 📁 Raw
        + 📄 AboutAssets.txt
    ▲ 🔒 📁 Splash
        + 🖼 splash.svg
    ▲ 🔒 📁 Styles
        + 🗋 Colors.xaml
        + 🗋 Styles.xaml
```

Figure 4.5: The structure of Resources folder

Now we will apply some modifications to our **MainPage.xaml** file to demonstrate how it works. If we open it, we will see various nested elements. The root element is called **ContentPage**. It is a container element that represents the whole page. Immediately inside it, we have **ScrollView**. This is a container element that has an inbuilt ability to scroll if the entire content of the page does not fit on a single screen. Next, we have **Image** and **Label** elements, which represent an image and textual labels, respectively.

We also have a **Button** element, which represents a clickable button. But other than that, we do not have any elements that the user can interact with. So, we will add one. We will insert an **Entry** element just above **the Button**. This element represents a field with editable text. And now, the content of our **MainPage.xaml** file will look like the following:

```xml
<?xml version="1.0" encoding="utf-8" ?>
<ContentPage xmlns="http://schemas.microsoft.com/dotnet/2021/maui"
xmlns:x="http://schemas.microsoft.com/winfx/2009/xaml"
  x:Class="SampleMauiApp.MainPage">

<ScrollView>
    <VerticalStackLayout
      Spacing="25"
      Padding="30,0"
      VerticalOptions="Center">
```

```
        <Image
            Source="dotnet_bot.png"
            SemanticProperties.Description="Cute dot net bot waving hi
to you!"
            HeightRequest="200"
            HorizontalOptions="Center" />

        <Label
          Text="Hello, World!"
          SemanticProperties.HeadingLevel="Level1"
          FontSize="32"
          HorizontalOptions="Center" />

        <Label
          Text="Welcome to .NET Multi-platform App UI"
          SemanticProperties.HeadingLevel="Level2"
          SemanticProperties.Description="Welcome to dot net Multi
platform App U I"
          FontSize="18"
          HorizontalOptions="Center" />

        <Entry
          x:Name="IncrementInput"
          Placeholder="1"
          HorizontalOptions="Center" />

        <Button
          x:Name="CounterBtn"
          Text="Click me"
          SemanticProperties.Hint="Counts the number of times you click"
          Clicked="OnCounterClicked"
          HorizontalOptions="Center" />

    </VerticalStackLayout>
</ScrollView>
</ContentPage>
```

This adds the ability to change the increment by which the counter gets increased when the button gets clicked. To make it work, we will replace the content of the **MainPage.xaml.cs** file with the following:

```
namespace SampleMauiApp;

public partial class MainPage : ContentPage
{
    int count = 0;

    public MainPage()
{
InitializeComponent();
}

private void OnCounterClicked(object sender, EventArgs e)
{
var increment = int.Parse(IncrementInput.Text);

count += increment;

if (count == 1)
CounterBtn.Text = $"Clicked {count} time";
else
CounterBtn.Text = $"Clicked {count} times";

SemanticScreenReader.Announce(CounterBtn.Text);
}
}
```

As we can see, the **IncrementInput** property became accessible in our code behind. This is the same name as we have specified in **x.Name** attribute of the newly added **Entry** element. We parse the content of this element as int. Then, we apply this number as our increment.

We have just briefly touched upon MAUI XAML syntax. Now, let us have a look at the elements available in XAML in more detail.

MAUI XAML references

XAML elements used by MAUI can be broadly separated into pages, layouts, and views, the latter of which are also commonly referred to as controls. We will have a look at all categories, starting with pages, which are listed in the following table:

Page type	Description
ContentPage	The most basic page type that displays a single page.
FlyoutPage	Managed two related pages: flyover that represents items and details page containing details of an individual item.
NavigationPage	A page that represents navigation hierarchy.
TabbedPage	A page that contains a series of pages represented by tabs.

Table 4.1: *MAUI XAML pages*

Next, we will talk about layouts. In the context of MAUI, a layout is a control that is positioned inside of a page control. Its responsibility is to act as a container for the views. *Table 4.2* shows the layouts that MAUI supports:

Layout Type	Description
AbsoluteLayout	Positions each child element at a specific location.
BindableLayout	Can auto-generate its content by binding it to a collection of items.
FlexLayout	Allows children to be stacked or wrapped with different styling options.
Grid	A table-like layout where child controls are placed in rows and columns.
HorizontalStackLayout	Stacks child elements horizontally.
StackLayout	Stacks child elements either horizontally or vertically.
VerticalStackLayout	Stacks child elements vertically.

Table 4.2: *MAUI XAML layouts*

And finally, we will go through the individual views that MAUI supports. Those are listed in *table 4.3*:

View type	Description
ActivityIndicator	Uses animation to show that the app is busy.
BlazorWebView	Hosts a Blazor application inside MAUI.
Border	Draws either borders or backgrounds.
BoxView	Draws either squares or rectangles.
Button	A clickable button.
CarouselView	Displays a scrollable collection of items.
CheckBox	A box that can be checked.

View type	Description
CollectionView	Displays a scrollable collection of items based on layout specifications.
ContentView	Enables creation of custom reusable controls.
DatePicker	Allows to pick a specific date.
Editor	Accepts multi-line text input.
Ellipse	Draws either an ellipse or a circle.
Entry	Accepts single-line text input.

Table 4.3: Some MAUI XAML views

There are many views available in .NET MAUI, so it would be easier to show them at multiple tables. *Table 4.4* shows the additional views:

Layout type	Description
Frame	Wraps layout elements within a configurable border.
GraphicsView	A canvas for drawing 2D graphics.
Image	Displays an image.
ImageButton	A clickable image that can perform some action.
IndicatorView	Works in conjunction with CarouselView and displays the number of items on it.
Label	Displays read-only text.
Line	Displays a line.
ListView	Displays a scrollable list of selectable items.
Path	Displays complex curve-like shapes.
Picker	Displays a list of items where one can be selected.
Polygon	Displays an arbitrary 2D polygon.
Polyline	Displays a line with multiple vertexes.
ProgressBar	Displays the progress of a given long-running action.
RadioButton	Allows the user to toggle between multiple values.
Rectangle	Displays a rectangle or a square.
RefreshView	Enables pull-to-refresh functionality for scrollable content.
RoundRectangle	Displays either a rectangle or a square with rounded corners.
ScrollView	A container element that allows scrolling through its children.
SearchBar	Enables search functionality.
Slider	Enables the user to select a fractional numeric value from a range.

Layout type	Description
Stepper	Enables the user to select a fractional numeric value from a range of incremental values.
SwipeView	Enables a swipe gesture.
Switch	On/off style toggle.
TableView	Represents a table.
TimePicker	Allows to pick a specific time.
WebView	Allows the display of any arbitrary HTML that can be normally displayed in the browser.

Table 4.4: Additional MAUI XAML views

However, XAML is not the only way the views can be constructed in MAUI. Since every one of these elements is represented by a class in the code, you can write user interfaces by using pure C#. This is something that you could do in Xamarin.Forms too. However, since MAUI is fully integrated in the current version of .NET, there is also another way of writing a UI that was not available in Xamarin.Forms. You can do it by using Blazor.

Working with Blazor on .NET MAUI

Blazor is a collection of technologies that allows developers to compile .NET code into WebAssembly, which is binary code that can run in browsers. The benefits of Blazor are numerous, ranging from the ability to write front-end code in C# to the performance benefits of running low-level compiled code. Since both MAUI and Blazor are fully integrated in .NET, you can combine these two technologies together. Now you will learn how.

Although Blazor dependencies can be added to an MAUI project retroactively, there is a project template available for MAUI applications with Blazor UI. This makes it available. You will need to have both MAUI and ASP.NET core Web development workloads enabled on your development machine. You will need the latter because Blazor is primarily a Web development technology.

We will now create an MAUI project with Blazor UI by executing the following command:

```
dotnet new maui-blazor -o BlazorMauiApp
```

And now, we can have a look at the project structure, which should look like what *figure 4.6* demonstrates:

Figure 4.6: *Blazor MAUI project structure*

We have all our standard MAUI components, including **App.xaml**, **MauiProgram. cs**, and **MainPage.xaml**. But this time, our **MainPage.xaml** file contains **BlazorView** component in its markup. We also have Blazor-specific files with RAZOR extension. And we have **wwwroot** folder with JavaScript, HTML, and CSS files that you would normally see in a Web application.

So, the MAUI components just act as the foundation for our application. Since **BlazorView** is the dominant component of the UI, the entire UI is delegated to Blazor.

We will cover Blazor in more detail in *Chapter 7: Blazor and WebAssembly on .NET*. But for now, we will make some modifications to the existing code to see how it reflects in the app we are building. To do so, we will locate **Counter.razor** file inside **Pages** folder. This page is similar to the default Blazor UI, as it comes with a counter and a clickable button to increment it. And, just like before, we will add the ability to change the increment value by binding it to a variable. So, the content of the **Counter.razor** file will now look like the following:

```
@page "/counter"

<h1>Counter</h1>

<p role="status">Current count: @currentCount</p>

<input type="number" @bind="increment" />
```

```
<button class="btn btn-primary" @onclick="IncrementCount">Click me</
button>

@code {
    private int? increment = 1;

    private int currentCount = 0;

    private void IncrementCount()
    {
        currentCount += increment ?? 0;
    }
}
```

We will run this code on both desktop and mobile platforms later. But for now, we will have a look at another important feature of MAUI—support for various architectural patterns.

MAUI architectural patterns

With MAUI, you can just use the default coding pattern that comes with the project templates. But once your application becomes more complex, you will probably have to start using well-established architectural patterns. Otherwise, your code will become hard to maintain.

There are three main architectural patterns supported by MAUI: **Model-View-ViewModel (MVVM)**, **ReactiveUI (RxUI)**, and **Model-View-Update (MVU)**. MVVM is a pattern that is available in MAUI out of the box, so we will have a look at its implementation example. The other two patterns are enabled in MAUI via third-party libraries. But we will still go through an overview of each.

Model-View-ViewModel

MVVM design pattern consists of three primary components: Model, View, and ViewModel.

- Model is a component that represents some back-end data, such as a database record.

- View represents an individual page of the UI.

- ViewModel is an object that holds the data that is directly bound to the controls in a particular view.

To show an example of MVVM implementation, we will create a new MAUI project by executing the following command:

```
dotnet new maui -o MvvmMauiApp
```

We will then place **MainPageViewModel.cs** file into the project folder and populate it with the following content:

```
namespace MvvmMauiApp
{
    public class MainPageViewModel
    {
        public int IncrementBy { get; set; } = 1;
    }
}
```

Basically, we are building an app that has similar logic to what we had before. But this time, our increment value will be inside the view model, which will bind directly to the control in the UI. To make it work, we will need to insert the **ViewModel** into the constructor of our **MainPage** class. We will then map this **ViewModel** to the **BindingContext** property shown as follows:

```
namespace MvvmMauiApp;

public partial class MainPage : ContentPage
{
int count = 0;

public MainPage(MainPageViewModel viewModel)
{
        BindingContext = viewModel;
        InitializeComponent();
}

private void OnCounterClicked(object sender, EventArgs e)
{
count += ((MainPageViewModel)BindingContext).IncrementBy;

if (count == 1)
CounterBtn.Text = $"Clicked {count} time";
else
CounterBtn.Text = $"Clicked {count} times";
```

```
SemanticScreenReader.Announce(CounterBtn.Text);
}
}
```

And now, we will need to modify the markup inside the **MainPage.xaml** file. First, we will replace the opening **ContentPage** element with the following:

```
<ContentPage xmlns="http://schemas.microsoft.com/dotnet/2021/maui"
xmlns:x="http://schemas.microsoft.com/winfx/2009/xaml"
  xmlns:local="clr-namespace:MvvmMauiApp"
  x:Class="MvvmMauiApp.MainPage">


  <ContentPage.BindingContext>
    <local:MainPageViewModel />
</ContentPage.BindingContext>
```

In here, we have specified the type that will be used as the **BindingContext**. And how we will add the following element just before the **Button** element markup:

```
<Entry
x:Name="IncrementInput"
  Text="{Binding IncrementBy}"
  HorizontalOptions="Center" />
```

The text in this field is now bound directly to the **IncrementBy** property of the **MainViewModel**. But since this class now gets injected into the **MainPage** via its constructor, we need to register both these classes in the dependency injection container. To do so, we will open **MauiProgram.cs** file and add the following lines just before return **builder.Build()**:

```
builder.Services.AddTransient<MainPage>();
builder.Services.AddTransient<MainPageViewModel>();
```

Now, our application should be identical in its functionality to the first application that we created. But this time, the interaction between the UI and the back-end is done via **ViewModel** binding.

Now, we will briefly have a look at architectural patterns that can be applied in MAUI applications by using third-party frameworks.

Patterns supported by MAUI via third-party frameworks

Even though these patterns are not available in MAUI out-of-the-box, they can make the life of a MAUI developers a lot easier. Therefore, they are still worth going over.

ReactiveUI

ReactiveUI pattern combines MVVM with reactive programming. So, if you, as a developer, have used MVVM before, you will see many familiar concepts, such as ViewModels and data binding. However, this pattern also adds many techniques for quick and efficient updates to the UI, so the UI will feel much more responsive than it would be otherwise.

On MAUI, the ReactiveUI pattern is available by installing `ReactiveUI.Maui` NuGet package. And its API documentation is available via the following URL:

https://www.reactiveui.net/api/reactiveui.maui/

Model-View-Update

MVU pattern became popularized by Web development frameworks and libraries, such as React. Just like ReactiveUI, it is highly suitable for building responsive user interfaces. However, its structure is completely different.

As the name suggests, the pattern consists of three main components: View, Model, and Update.

View represents a user interface and all its data. So, it is analogous to both View and ViewModel from MVVM. Model represents the current state of the application. And Update is a function that creates a new copy of the application's state, that is, the Model.

The easiest way to enable MVU on MAUI is to use `Comet` library, which is represented by `Clancy.Comet` NuGet package. The code repository of the package can be found via the following link:

https://github.com/dotnet/Comet

Now, we will cover the process of running and publishing MAUI apps on specific platforms. We will start by covering the process of building desktop applications on Windows.

Using MAUI to build desktop applications

MAUI is available on two desktop operating systems, Mac and Windows. You can build MAUI apps for Linux as well. But this is a purely community-enabled feature that is not officially supported by Microsoft. Now we will discuss the process of running and publishing an MAUI app on a Windows PC.

Preparing desktop development environment

Before we can build and run an MAUI application on Windows, we need to switch the developer mode on. This can be found in your settings. Alternatively, if you try to run your application from an IDE, you will be prompted to switch the developer mode on. *Figure 4.7* demonstrates what this prompt looks like on Visual Studio:

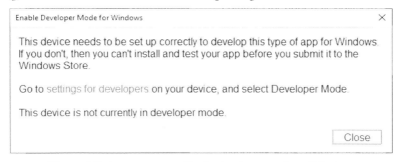

Figure 4.7: A prompt to enable the developer mode on Windows

Now your environment is ready for running MAUI apps on it. The first thing we will cover is running an MAUI app in debug mode.

Running a desktop app in a debug mode

As with any other type of app, you should be able to debug the MAUI codebase and set breakpoints in it. The process of doing so for MAUI apps is identical to what it would be with any other app type.

If you are running the MAUI app on Windows, the Windows profile should be enabled by default. Therefore, you will be able to run the application by either executing an appropriate command from .NET CLI or by clicking on **the Run** button from the IDE.

If we launch either the **SampleMauiApp** or the **MvvmMauiApp** application that we created earlier, we are expected to see the user interface as shown in *figure 4.8*:

Figure 4.8: MAUI user interface

If we launch our **BlazorMauiApp** and navigate to the **Counter** component, we should expect the UI shown in *figure 4.9*:

Figure 4.9: Blazor MAUI app UI

This concludes the overview of the process of launching an MAUI application on a desktop PC. Now, we will have a look at how we can publish it, so it can be deployable on other devices.

Publishing a desktop app

If you want to deploy any Windows application on any official app store or otherwise distribute it in professional settings, your application needs to be signed with a certificate. Otherwise, the operating system will complain that the application comes from an unknown publisher. However, it is not strictly necessary if you want to create a deployment package purely for evaluation and test purposes.

As with any other type of .NET application, the easiest way to publish an MAUI app is via an IDE. You can do it via the CLI too, but the process will be more involved. To publish your application from Visual Studio, all you have to do is select your main application project in **Solution Explorer**, right-click on it, and click **Publish**. You will then be prompted to select the distribution method, as shown in *figure 4.10*:

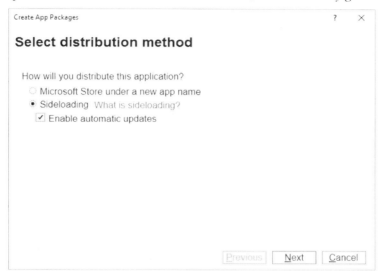

Figure 4.10: Selecting distribution mode while publishing a MAUI Windows app

Then, you will be presented with the option of selecting a package signing method, which you will need to perform to make your package production ready. Following this, you will be able to specify the CPU architecture for your package. And you can just follow all the steps to complete the package-generation process.

This covers the process of running and deploying MAUI applications on a Windows desktop. Next, we will have a look at how to build MAUI mobile apps for Android.

Using MAUI to build mobile apps

You can build MAUI apps for Android by using any machine with any operating system, as long as it supports either the ability to connect a real Android device to it and run it in developer mode or use emulators. So, let us now learn to set up our development environment so we can start building mobile applications on it.

Preparing mobile development environment

The easiest way to test your mobile application before publishing it is to use an emulator. Emulator is a virtual machine that closely mimics a real mobile device. The easiest way to set one up is by using an IDE. For example, in Visual Studio, you can click on **Tools** tab, select **Android** and click on **Android SDK Manager**, as demonstrated in *figure 4.11*:

Figure 4.11: Android SDK Manager menu option in Visual Studio

You will then be able to select any emulator from the list and install it. Choosing to install it will prompt you to accept the license agreement, as demonstrated in *figure 4.12*:

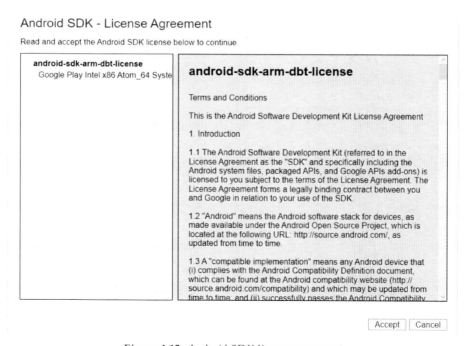

Figure 4.12: Android SDK license agreement

It will take a while for emulators to get installed. And then, we will be able to run our applications on it.

Running a mobile app on an Emulator

You will be able to select the emulator as the execution target from the **Run** menu of the IDE, as *figure 4.13* demonstrates:

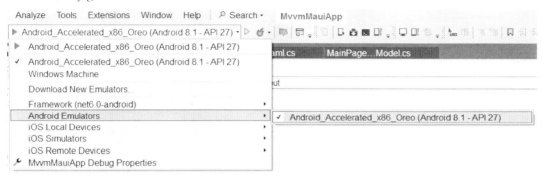

Figure 4.13: Selecting Android emulator from the Run menu of Visual Studio

The rest of the process is the same as running any other application type in Visual Studio. Once you click **Run** while an Android emulator is selected, the emulator will be launched, and your application will be launched on it. While it is running, you will be able to place breakpoints in the code.

This concludes the subject of running Android MAUI apps on a PC. Next, we will have a look at the process of publishing your app, so you will be able to distribute it via app stores.

Publishing a mobile app

The process of publishing MAUI apps for Android is not much different from publishing them for Windows. While Android is selected as the build target and the build configuration is selected as Release, all you have to do is right-click on your project in **Solution Explorer** and click **Publish**. It will then take you to the Android-specific publishing screen, as shown in *figure 4.14*:

Figure 4.14: Publishing an MAUI app for Android

This will produce an APK file that can install the app on Android devices. The file will reside inside the following location inside the project:

`bin/Release/net7.0-android`

Alternatively, the following command can be executed from the project folder via the CLI:

`dotnet build -f net7.0-android -c:Release`

This concludes the process of publishing MAUI apps for Windows and Android. Now, we will cover the process of running and publishing MAUI apps for Mac and iOS.

Limitations of developing for Mac OS and iOS

When we covered the process of building MAUI apps for Windows, you may have noticed that all the steps of it imply that we do it on a Windows device. There is no such thing as a Windows emulator. If you try to run a Windows app on a non-Windows machine, it simply will not work.

A similar limitation exists for Mac and iOS apps. You need an Apple device to run them. But even though iOS emulators are available, they can only be run on another Apple device. One reason for this is that you need an Apple account to be able to deploy your apps into any of Apple's app stores. But this is not the only reason. To be able to emulate iOS on your development machine, you will need some special tools. Apple refuses to publish any of these tools for any operating system other than Apple's own.

Extra tools required for publishing apps for iOS

Normally, if you would want to build standard native iOS apps, you would need an IDE called XCode. This IDE is only available on Mac. Unfortunately, you cannot emulate an iOS device without the tools that this IDE provides. And you cannot build a native iOS deployment package for your application either. So, even if you intend to develop iOS apps by using MAUI, you will still have to install XCode, which can be found via the following link:

https://developer.apple.com/xcode/

Once XCode is installed, you will need to either connect your existing development account to it or create a new one. To do so, you will need to open **the Preferences** dialog from the **XCode** menu. Then you will need to select the **Accounts** tab. From the dialog that appears, you can then select a plus (**+**) button to add a new account. What you can then do is link your Apple ID and follow the remaining instructions.

You will then need to add some metadata to your project file and sign the package. But the publishing tool should notify you if any of it is missing. Likewise, you can connect Visual Studio for Mac to your Mac build host to be able to use the IDE to work with MAUI code. You will need this if you still want to use full IDE capabilities, as XCode has not been designed to work with .NET and C#.

Then, to publish your application for iOS, you will need to execute the following command from your project folder:

```
dotnet publish -f net7.0-ios -c Release
```

Your application package will then be placed into the bin folder of the project.

Slightly lighter requirements for Mac OS apps

If you want to publish an MAUI application for Mac OS, the restrictions will be somewhat lighter. You will not need XCode or any other additional tools. You will not even need anything beyond any standard .NET IDE or a code editor. However, if you then intend to publish your app into any official app repositories, you will still need a developer account and need to sign your package.

Mac will still allow you to download and install packages that are not signed. But a security warning will be given. We have now completed the overview of .NET MAUI.

Conclusion

In this chapter, you have learned that .NET MAUI is an evolution of Xamarin.Forms that allows developers to write both desktop and mobile applications. Unlike its predecessor, MAUI is fully integrated with .NET 7 and has access to all the latest language features of C# 11. Likewise, its project structure is much more convenient to work with than that of Xamarin.Forms. It also supports a full range of mobile and desktop operating systems.

Since .NET MAUI is fully integrated with .NET 7, it can be combined with any .NET 7 libraries and frameworks. For example, you can build its UI by using Blazor WebAssembly.

.NET MAUI supports three main architectural patterns, MVVM, RxUI, and MVU. The latter pattern allows developers that had no prior experience of using MAUI to learn it quickly, as the pattern is incredibly easy to understand.

What makes MAUI particularly convenient is that you can write your application on any type of machine and compile it for any other supported operating system. However, there is one caveat. If you intend to develop applications for Mac or iOS, you will need Mac to do so. This is because Apple does not allow developers to publish software that was not developed on Mac, and it does not provide tooling for any other operating systems.

In the upcoming chapter, you will learn about the latest version of Entity Framework Core, which is used for accessing structural SQL data by abstracting it in the code.

Points to remember

- .NET MAUI can be used for building mobile and desktop applications.

- MAUI is an evolution of Xamarin.Forms.

- MAUI is fully integrated in .NET 7 and has full access to the latest language features.

- The primary markup language for MAUI user interfaces is XAML.

- MAUI can have its UI built by using other technologies, including Blazor WebAssembly.

- MAUI can use either of the following architectural patterns: MVVM, RxUI, and MVU.

- The applications built for either Mac or iOS can only be published from a Mac device due to restrictions imposed by Apple.

Multiple choice questions

1. **What operating systems can you run MAUI apps on?**

    a. Android

    b. iOS

    c. Windows

    d. All of the above

2. **What is the key difference between MAUI and Xamarin.Forms?**

    a. Xamarin.Forms does not have access to the latest C# language features, whereas MAUI does

    b. Xamarin.Forms cannot run Blazor WebAssembly, whereas MAUI can

    c. Xamarin.Forms was primarily intended for mobile, whereas MAUI is intended for both mobile and desktop

    d. All of the above

3. **Which architectural pattern is not supported by MAUI?**

   a. ReactiveUI

   b. MVVM

   c. MVC

   d. MVU

4. **What is the main language used by MAUI for defining user interface layouts?**

   a. XML

   b. XAML

   c. JSON

   d. HTML

Answers

1. d
2. d
3. c
4. b

Key terms

- **MAUI**: Multi-platform UI; a framework for developing native mobile and desktop applications on .NET.

- **Xamarin.Forms**: A predecessor of MAUI that was specifically designed for building cross-platform mobile applications.

- **MVVM: Model-View-ViewModel**; An architectural pattern that consists of a user interface component (view), back-end data abstraction (model), and the data that populates the user interface (ViewModel).

- **ReativeUI**: A framework that adds reactive programming components on top of MVVM.

- **MVU**: Model-View-Update, also known as Elm Architecture, is an architectural pattern that consists of the user interface (view), data abstraction (model), and a component that updates the model when some action is triggered in the UI (update).

Join our book's Discord space

Join the book's Discord Workspace for Latest updates, Offers, Tech happenings around the world, New Release and Sessions with the Authors:

https://discord.bpbonline.com

CHAPTER 5
Database Access with Entity Framework 7

Introduction

Entity Framework Core (**EF Core**) is an **object-relational mapper** (**ORM**) that is used by .NET platform. The purpose of an ORM is to allow application code to interact with a relational database by abstracting objects from the database as objects in the code (classes, records, and so on). There are other ORMs also available on .NET, but those are developed and maintained by third parties. EF Core is developed by the core Microsoft team alongside the rest of .NET.

In this chapter, we will cover the most fundamental features of EF Core. By the end of it, you will have learned how to use it inside your application code to manipulate data in a database. We will also cover the scenarios where we need to create EF Core code from an existing database and cover the process of creating a new database from EF Core objects.

Also, because ORMs work with relational databases, you will need to know the fundamentals of relational databases to fully understand ORMs. Therefore, this chapter will provide a brief overview of relational database concepts.

Finally, as the scope of this book is to cover the latest feature of C# 11 and .NET 7, we will have a look at what new features have been added to version 7 of EF Core, which is properly called EF7 rather than EF Core 7. So, not only will you know the fundamentals of EF Core, but you will also know how to use its cutting-edge features.

Structure

In this chapter, we will discuss the latest features of Entity Framework 7, which will include the following topics:

- Introducing fundamentals of relational databases
- Introducing Entity Framework 7
- Code-first approach in EF7
- Database-first approach in EF7
- The latest features of EF7

Objectives

By the end of this chapter, you will have learned how to integrate a .NET core application with a database by using EF7. You will also know how to apply the latest features of EF7.

Prerequisites

To follow this chapter, you will need the following:

- A machine running either Windows, MacOS, or Linux OS
- .NET 7 SDK
- A suitable IDE or a code editor
- Being familiar with C# fundamentals

If you do not have any of the preceding listed dependencies installed already, let us set up using the instruction provided in *Chapter 1: Getting Familiar with .NET 7 Application Structure*, which also provides a recap of C# fundamentals.

Introducing fundamentals of relational databases

Since EF7 is an ORM that is primarily designed to interoperate with relational databases, one needs to understand how relational databases work before attempting to learn how the ORM works. Fortunately, you do not need to be a database expert before you can start using EF7. But you will definitely need to understand the fundamentals.

Overview of relational database management systems and SQL

Relational databases are hosted inside **Relational Database Management Systems (RDBMS)**. There are several different RDBMS technologies manufactured by different vendors. Although there are some fundamental architectural differences between them, there are also some shared characteristics. Any RDBMS, regardless of the vendor, has the following components:

- Databases comprised of tables.

- Each table has a rigid schema, which means that it consists of a fixed number of columns, and each of these columns only accepts data of a specific type (integer, textual, binary/Boolean, and so on).

- Tables refer to each other via the so-called foreign keys, which enables relationships between tables.

- SQL language is used for retrieving data, manipulating data, and modifying the structure of the database itself.

Structured Query Language (SQL) is a universal language of database management. Different RDBMS vendors use different flavors (or dialects) of SQL, so a statement written for a particular type of RDBMS would not necessarily be compatible with another type of RDBMS manufactured by another vendor. The most fundamental commands will either be the same regardless of the vendor or very similar. For example, let us look at the following SQL expression:

```
SELECT * FROM USERS
```

Anyone who is familiar with SQL will be able to tell what this expression does. The **SELECT** keyword indicates that we are selecting some data. The ***** symbol means that we are selecting all fields. Alternatively, we could have written down specific fields that we wanted to return. FROM is the keyword that is used to specify the object that we want to return the data from, which would typically be a table. **USER** is the name of a specific object.

Typically, a SQL expression to retrieve data is known as a query. A SQL expression to modify the data, either inserting or updating it, is referred to as a command.

The most popular RDBMS types are the following:

- **SQL Server**: manufactured by Microsoft as a proprietary product primarily used for commercial projects

- **Oracle Database**: the main RDBMS product manufactured by Oracle as a proprietary product primarily used for commercial projects

- **MySQL**: lightweight free and open-source RDBMS maintained by Oracle that is frequently used for non-commercial projects

- **PostgreSQL**: free and open-source RDBMS with advanced features that are primarily used for commercial projects

Now, let us have a look at a typical structure of an RDBMS table.

Tables, relationships, and normalization

Since relational databases store data in tables, we will have a look at an example of such a table. Then, we will make some changes to it to highlight the fundamental features of an RDBMS.

Let us imagine that we have a system that manages data for a company that owns multiple factories. The database behind this system will store information on the factory's employees, their pay, their shifts, their job titles, and so on. Initially, we would store this information in a single table, which will have the following columns, as outlined in *table 5.1*:

Column name	Data type
First Name	Textual
Last Name	Textual
Job Title	Textual
Annual Salary	Decimal
Date of Birth	Date
Date of Joining the Company	Date
Employment Location	Textual
Factory Name	Textual
Shift Start	Time
Shift End	Time

Table 5.1: The structure of the initial flat table containing employee information

Even though there is nothing that stops us from storing data this way, there are many problems with this approach.

- First of all, it is just a flat table containing the entire employee data. It is something we could do easily in an *Excel* spreadsheet. So, why would we even need to set up an RDBMS?

- Second, storing all information on a single table makes it harder to apply any changes. For example, there is probably a very finite number of job titles with associated salaries. Also, there is a finite number of factories where the employee work. But what happens if one of the job titles gets the salary associated with it increased? Or what if a particular factory gets closed and its employees need to be transferred to a nearby factory? If you have the job title, salary, and site data stored on the same table as the employee information, you will then need to find and update every record that has outdated information. If you have a large organization with thousands of employees, then this process might take longer.

- Also, a single flat table makes it difficult to store employee shift information. We currently have shift start and end time. This is OK if a given employee is always doing the same shift and if the factory is open only on specific days. But what if this is not the case? What if the factory is open 24/7, and each employee may be doing a combination of different shifts? Or what if the same employee shifts in different factories? This would be very difficult to store in a flat table. You would either need to store this information in a free text field, which will be harder to query or you would need multiple redundant columns for multiple start and end times and days worked.

These are, perhaps, the most obvious disadvantage of storing a large amount of data inside a flat table. But a relational database will be able to address all these issues. All we need to do is turn this flat table into multiple tables linked to each other. And this is what we will do next.

Introducing primary keys

Before splitting our table, we will first add a primary key to it. The primary key is a column that has a unique value in each row. Or it can be a mixture of multiple columns, but the combination of the values in each row still must be unique.

Using a primary key has multiple advantages. But the main ones are as follows:

- A primary key acts as both a unique identifier of a record and its index, so a specific record becomes faster to retrieve.

- A primary key of one table can be used as the so-called *foreign key* in another table, enabling a relationship between two tables.

So, what could we use as a primary key in our table? Well, theoretically, we could use a combination of the first and the last name. But then, there is no guarantee that we will have a unique combination in every row, as unrelated people who share the same name exist. Perhaps we could add a date of birth to it. Even then, it would not necessarily guarantee uniqueness. Also, having different data types in our primary key will make it more complicated and harder to manage.

To address this, we will just do what is commonly done in this situation and add another column that will just store the primary key. It will be an integer column with auto-generated sequential values, so each record is guaranteed to have a unique value. This type of column is usually referred to as **identity**. Its name could either be **id** or **<table name>_id**, such as **employee_id**. Next, we will apply the technique known as normalization to split the table into multiple tables.

Normalization and foreign key relationships

Normalization is the process of removing repeated and redundant data from one table and moving it into separate tables, which the original table will still be able to refer to. This way, instead of being repeated, each value will be stored in its own table. Then, if another table needs to refer to this value, it will refer to the index of the record of the table where this value is stored. So, if you then need to change the value (such as the name of the factory or a job title), you will only have to change it in a single place.

Now, we will apply normalization to our own data. Since we have a finite number of job types, each having its own annual salary, we will move job information into a separate table, which will have a structure outlined in *table 5.2*:

Column name	Data type	Notes
Job ID	Integer (identity)	Primary key
Job Title	Textual	
Compensation	Decimal	

***Table 5.2**: The structure of the Jobs table*

Next, we can create a table containing information on factories, as outlined in *table 5.3*:

Column name	Data type	Notes
Factory ID	Integer (identity)	Primary key
Factory Name	Textual	
Factory Location	Textual	

***Table 5.3**: The structure of Factories table*

We will take care of the shift table later. For now, we will get back to our tables containing the remaining employee data, which will now be structured as shown in *table 5.4*:

Column name	Data type	Notes
Employee ID	Integer (identity)	Primary key
First Name	Textual	
Last Name	Textual	
Date of Birth	Date	
Date of Joining the Company	Date	
Job ID	Integer	Foreign key (matches a primary key of Jobs table)

Table 5.4: The structure of the employees' table

Here, we have our first example of a relationship between two tables via a foreign key. **Job ID** column in the **Employees** table refers to the **Job ID** column in the **Jobs** table. Here, we have a one-to-many relationship between a job and employees, as there can be multiple employees with the same job title. In the preceding example (and in any other instance of foreign key relationships), the value that you put into the **Job ID** column of the **Employees** table must match a value that exists in the **Job ID** column of the **Jobs** table.

Finally, we will add a **Shifts** table, which will be structured as shown in *table 5.5*:

Column name	Data type	Notes
Shift Id	Integer (identity)	Primary key
Weekday	Integer	Must be between 1 and 7
Start Time	Time	
End Time	Time	
Employee ID	Integer	Foreign key (primary key of Employees table)
Factory ID	Integer	Foreign key (primary key of Factories table)

Table 5.5: The structure of the shifts table

Now, we can easily store detailed enough information about the shifts employees are assigned to do. Now, it is also possible to associate an employee with multiple factories via the Shifts table. So, there is now a many-to-many relationship between employees and factories.

This concludes an overview of relational databases. Of course, the subject is much larger, especially as every type of RDBMS has its own nuances. But we have covered enough of the basics to be able to understand how EF7 works. So, let us set our environment up for using it.

Introducing entity framework 7

So far, we have briefly mentioned that relational databases rely on the language called SQL for data retrieval and manipulation. But if you are using an ORM, such as entity framework 7 (EF7), you would not have to use SQL directly in most cases. Your tables and relationships will be represented by objects in the code, which, in C#, would normally be either classes or records. The ORM will do all the necessary mapping for you.

To start working with EF7, you will need two things: EF CLI tools and a NuGet package representing a specific RDBMS provider.

EF7 supports the following providers:

- **Microsoft SQL Server**: Represented by **Microsoft.EntityFrameworkCore. SqlServer** NuGet package.

- **SQLight**: Represented by **Microsoft.EntityFrameworkCore.Sqlite** NuGet package.

- **Azure Cosmos DB**: Represented by **Microsoft.EntityFrameworkCore. Cosmos** NuGet package.

- **PostgreSQL**: Represented by **Npgsql.EntityFrameworkCore.PostgreSQL** NuGet package.

- **MySQL**: Represented by **Pomelo.EntityFrameworkCore.MySql** NuGet package.

- **In-memory database**: Represented **Microsoft.EntityFrameworkCore. InMemory** NuGet package.

Not all these providers represent true relational databases. For example, Azure Cosmos DB is a document store, a different type of database. Likewise, In-memory Database is not a real database. But nevertheless, a relational database is the primary database type, EF7, designed to work with.

To install EF CLI tools, you can execute the following command in your terminal:

```
dotnet tool install --global dotnet-ef
```

If you already have the tools installed, you can execute the following command to update them to the latest version:

```
dotnet tool update --global dotnet-ef
```

You can use EF7 on any OS that can work with .NET. But Visual Studio 2022 for Windows has the richest user experience. For example, Visual Studio 2022 comes with an inbuilt version of SQL Server called **LocalDB**, so you do not have to set up an instance of SQL Server manually. It just needs to be enabled via Visual Studio

Installer. All you need to do is open the Installer, click the **Modify** button next to the Visual Studio 2022 instance, and select to install **Data storage and processing** workload, as demonstrated by *figure 5.1*:

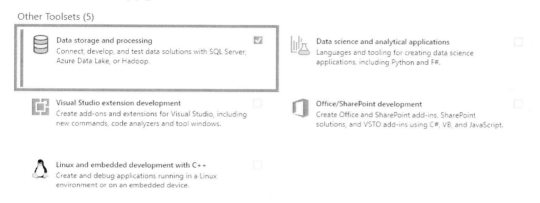

Figure 5.1: *Installation of Data storage and processing workload*

Once installed, we will be able to access SQL Server by selecting **SQL Server Object Explorer** option from the **View** tab, as demonstrated by *figure 5.2*:

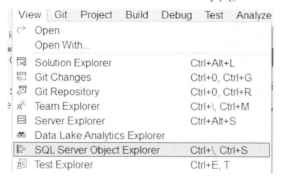

Figure 5.2: *Accessing SQL server object explorer*

This is everything you need to get started with EF7. Now, we will have a look at how to use EF7 in the code. We will start by applying one of its most powerful capabilities—being able to create a fresh database purely from the code. This is known as the **code-first approach**.

Code-first approach in EF7

Code-first approach, as well as giving you the ability to create a complete database from the code, also allows you to populate the database with the initial data. Now, we will go through the steps that are needed to set up Entity Framework in your application, get it to automatically generate a database for you, and then populate it with some data. We will start by going through the EF7 basics.

Adding Entity Framework code

Entity Framework is commonly used inside ASP.NET Core Model-View-Controller (MVC) apps. We will cover this type of apps in detail in *Chapter 6: Web Application Types on .NET*. But, for now, we will create an MVC Web application with database access by executing the following command:

```
dotnet new mvc -o MvcDataApp
```

Next, we will go into the **MvcDataApp** project folder and run the following command to install a NuGet package that contains EF7 diagnostics. Alternatively, you can install this package via the GUI of your IDE.

```
dotnet add package Microsoft.AspNetCore.Diagnostics.EntityFrameworkCore
```

Next, we will install the following NuGet package, which contains Entity Framework provider for SQL Server:

```
dotnet add package Microsoft.EntityFrameworkCore.SqlServer
```

Now, we are ready to add objects that will represent our database tables. We will use the same factory management solution that we have described earlier when we covered database normalization.

Adding entity objects

The first object we will add will represent an entry in the **Jobs** table. To add the object, we will add **Job.cs** file into the **Models** folder of the project and populate it with the following code:

```
using System.ComponentModel.DataAnnotations.Schema;

namespace MvcDataApp.Models;

public record Job
{
    [DatabaseGenerated(DatabaseGeneratedOption.Identity)]
    public int JobId { get; set; }
    public string JobTitle { get; set; }
    [Column(TypeName = "decimal(8, 2)")]
    public decimal Compensation { get; set; }
```

```
    public ICollection<Employee> Employees { get; set; }
}
```

We have used a record as our base type. This keyword has been added in C# 10. It is similar to a class but is primarily designed to represent a database record. However, the code would work with a class too.

This code contains some annotation attributes that we have added to demonstrate the capabilities of EF7. The first one is **DatabaseGeneratedAttribute**, which we have placed above the **JobId** property. This attribute is not strictly necessary, as this property will be recognized as the primary key identity column based on the naming conventions. But we have put it there to demonstrate how we can mark any arbitrary column as the primary key identity.

Decimal data type in SQL server requires precision and scale. Precision is the total number of digits that we are allowed to store. Scale is how many digits we can have after the decimal point. And to specify this information, we have added a **Column** attribute.

Entity Framework objects represent one-to-many relationships as collections. In our case, because we have a one-to-many relationship between a **Job** entity and **Employee** records, we have a collection of **Employee** objects inside our Job record.

Next, we will add the definition of an employee record. We will, once again, place the **Employee.cs** file into the **Models** folder and will populate it with the following code:

```
using System.ComponentModel.DataAnnotations;
using System.ComponentModel.DataAnnotations.Schema;


namespace MvcDataApp.Models;


public record Employee
{
    [DatabaseGenerated(DatabaseGeneratedOption.Identity)]
    public int EmployeeId { get; set; }
    [StringLength(20)]
    public string FirstName { get; set; }
    [StringLength(20)]
    public string LastName { get; set; }
    public DateTime DateOfBirth { get; set; }
    public DateTime StartDate { get; set; }
    public int JobId { get; set; }
```

```
public Job { get; set; }
public ICollection<Shift> Shifts { get; set; }

[NotMapped]
public string FullName => FirstName + " " + LastName;
}
```

Here, we have added some more useful attributes. The **stringLength** attribute will add a constraint on the database column to restrict it to a specific number of characters. **NotMapped** attribute is added to the properties that may be useful in the code but should not represent a database column.

Since each **Employee** entity can only relate to a single **Job** entity, we have added a singular **Job** property. But because an **Employee** can be associated with multiple **Shift** entities, we have a **Shifts** property representing a collection of **Shift** entities.

Next, we will add the **Factory.cs** file into the **Models** folder with the following content:

```
using System.ComponentModel.DataAnnotations.Schema;

namespace MvcDataApp.Models;

public record Factory
{
    [DatabaseGenerated(DatabaseGeneratedOption.Identity)]
    public int FactoryId { get; set; }
    public string FactoryName { get; set; }
    public string Location { get; set; }

    public ICollection<Shift> Shifts { get; set; }


}
```

Finally, we will add the following object representing a **Shift** entity:

```
using System.ComponentModel.DataAnnotations;
using System.ComponentModel.DataAnnotations.Schema;

namespace MvcDataApp.Models;
```

```
public record Shift
{
    [DatabaseGenerated(DatabaseGeneratedOption.Identity)]
    public int ShiftId { get; set; }
    [Range(1, 7)]
    public int WeekDay { get; set; }
    public TimeSpan StartTime { get; set; }
    public TimeSpan EndTime { get; set; }
    public int FactoryId { get; set; }
    public int EmployeeId { get; set; }

    public Employee Employee { get; set; }
    public Factory Factory { get; set; }
}
```

We now have entity objects representing all database tables that we have described earlier. The properties in this class map to SQL data types. We can also apply additional constraints on these data types like we are doing with the **Range** attribute on the **WeekDay** property. In our example, the only values we are allowing to be inserted into the corresponding integer column are between 1 and 7.

Now, we need to let the Entity Framework know that these objects represent entities in database tables. To do so, we will need to add the so-called **database** context and register it.

Adding database context

Database context is a custom class that is derived from **DbContext** base class of Entity Framework. This class allows us to register all the entity objects that we intend to map to database tables.

In our case, we will call our database context class **FactoryManagerContext**. To create it, we will create a **Data** folder inside the root folder of our project and add **FactoryManagerContext.cs** file to it with the following code:

```
using Microsoft.EntityFrameworkCore;
using MvcDataApp.Models;


namespace MvcDataApp.Data;
```

```csharp
public class FactoryManagerContext : DbContext
{
    public FactoryManagerContext(DbContextOptions<FactoryManagerContext>
options) : base(options)
    {
    }

    public DbSet<Employee> Employees { get; set; }
    public DbSet<Factory> Factories { get; set; }
    public DbSet<Job> Jobs { get; set; }
    public DbSet<Shift> Shifts { get; set; }
}
```

We have added a **DbSet** property for each of the entity types we added earlier.
Now, we need to register this database context object and associate it with a specific
connection string to a SQL Server instance. We will do so in the **Program.cs** file,
which would have the following content at the beginning:

```csharp
var builder = WebApplication.CreateBuilder(args);

// Add services to the container.
builder.Services.AddControllersWithViews();

var app = builder.Build();

CreateDbIfNotExists(app);

// Configure the HTTP request pipeline.
if (!app.Environment.IsDevelopment())
{
    app.UseExceptionHandler("/Home/Error");
    // The default HSTS value is 30 days. You may want to change this
for production scenarios, see https://aka.ms/aspnetcore-hsts.
    app.UseHsts();
}

app.UseHttpsRedirection();
app.UseStaticFiles();

app.UseRouting();
```

```
app.UseAuthorization();

app.MapControllerRoute(
    name: "default",
    pattern: "{controller=Home}/{action=Index}/{id?}");

app.Run();

static void CreateDbIfNotExists(IHost app)
{
    using var scope = app.Services.CreateScope();

    var services = scope.ServiceProvider;
    try
    {
        var context = services.
GetRequiredService<FactoryManagerContext>();
        DbInitializer.Initialize(context);
    }
    catch (Exception ex)
    {
        var logger = services.GetRequiredService<ILogger<Program>>();
        logger.LogError(ex, "Failed to create the DB.");
    }
}
```

We will start by adding the following using statements to the **Program.cs** file:

```
using Microsoft.EntityFrameworkCore;
using MvcDataApp.Data;
```

Then, we will add the following lines anywhere before **builder.Build()**:

```
builder.Services
    .AddDbContext<FactoryManagerContext>(options =>
        options
    .UseSqlServer(builder
    .Configuration
    .GetConnectionString("DefaultConnection")));
  builder.Services.AddDatabaseDeveloperPageExceptionFilter();
```

Here, we have registered the database context with the database connection string that has the key of **DefaultConnection**. The **AddDatabaseDeveloperPageException Filter** method call will help us to debug any errors with the database setup by outputting them as HTML. However, it would be bad practice to use this line in production.

To make the database connection work, we need to add this entry to the settings. To do so, we will add the **ConnectionStrings** section to our **appsettings.json** file with the **DefaultConnection** entry inside it. The following example shows the content of the **appsettings.json** file that uses an inbuilt **LocalDB** connection:

```
{
  "Logging": {
    "LogLevel": {
      "Default": "Information",
      "Microsoft.AspNetCore": "Warning"
    }
  },
  "AllowedHosts": "*",
  "ConnectionStrings": {
    "DefaultConnection": "Server=(localdb)\\
mssqllocaldb;Database=FactoryManager;Trusted_
Connection=True;MultipleActiveResultSets=true"
  }
}
```

Now, we have Entity Framework fully configured inside our application. Next, we will add some additional code to take full advantage of the code-first approach.

Adding database creation script

If we apply a code-first approach to our Entity Framework, a database will be generated at the location-specific by the connection string when we launch our application for the first time. To enable this, we can add **DbInitializer** class to our **Data** folder and add the following content to it:

```
using MvcDataApp.Models;


namespace MvcDataApp.Data;


public class DbInitializer
{
```

```
    public static void Initialize(FactoryManagerContext context)
    {
        context.Database.EnsureCreated();

        if (context.Jobs.Any())
        {
            return;
        }
    }
}
```

The **Initialize** method will create a database if it does not already exist. This is done by calling the **EnsureCreated** method on the **Database** property of the database context object. Also, this code will exit if the database already has some data in the **Jobs** table. This is needed so we can skip the data insertion steps if we already went through them.

To add data insertion steps, we will need to add some more code to the **Initialize** method. Since it will be a relatively long script, we will add it step-by-step. First, we will add the following code to add some entries to the **Jobs** table:

```
var jobs = new Job[]
{
new Job
    {
        JobTitle = "Manager",
        Compensation = 50000
    },
    new Job
    {
        JobTitle = "Laborer",
        Compensation = 25000
    }
};
foreach (var j in jobs)
{
  context.Jobs.Add(j);
}
context.SaveChanges();
```

Here, we are creating a collection of **Job** objects. Then, we are adding each of them to the Jobs dataset in the database context. Then, we are calling the **SaveChanges** method.

It is vitally important that we call the **SaveChanges** method once we are ready to insert the data. This is the method that performs the actual insertion of the data into the database. Until it is called, all the data will reside only in the memory.

Next, we will add some data to the **Employees** table:

```
var employees = new Employee[]
{
new Employee
{
FirstName="John",
      LastName="Smith",
      DateOfBirth=DateTime.Parse("1992-10-01"),
      StartDate=DateTime.Parse("2020-09-01"),
      JobId = 1,
   },
   new Employee
   {
      FirstName="Alexander",
      LastName="Marshall",
      DateOfBirth=DateTime.Parse("1982-09-12"),
      StartDate=DateTime.Parse("2017-09-01"),
      JobId = 2,
   },
   new Employee
{
FirstName="Michael",
      LastName="Davidson",
      DateOfBirth=DateTime.Parse("1989-05-11"),
      StartDate=DateTime.Parse("2010-09-01"),
      JobId = 2,
   },
};
foreach (var e in employees)
{
```

```
      context.Employees.Add(e);
}
context.SaveChanges();
```

Following this, we will add some **Factories** entities:

```
var factories = new Factory[]
{
new Factory
{
        FactoryName = "Best Cookies",
        Location = "New York"
    }
};
foreach (var f in factories)
{
  context.Factories.Add(f);
}
context.SaveChanges();
```

Then, we can apply the same principle to insert any number of arbitrary **Shifts** data, as per the following example:

```
var shifts = new Shift[]
{
new Shift
{
WeekDay = 1,
        StartTime = new TimeSpan(9,0,0),
        EndTime = new TimeSpan(17,0,0),
        FactoryId = 1,
        EmployeeId = 1
    },
    new Shift
    {
        WeekDay = 2,
        StartTime = new TimeSpan(9,0,0),
        EndTime = new TimeSpan(17,0,0),
        FactoryId = 1,
        EmployeeId = 1
```

```
    },
};
foreach (var s in shifts)
{
  context.Shifts.Add(s);
}
context.SaveChanges();
```

Please note that we are not manually inserting the identity columns. This is because the database will do it for us automatically. If we are inserting the data into a newly created database, then the identity value of the first record in each table will be 1. The next one will be 2, and each record will have its identity value auto-incremented by 1. This is the principle that we have based the values of our foreign key columns on. For example, since we only have two **Job** entities, the **JobId** column inside the **Employees** table can only have values of 1 and 2.

Now, we just need to add some code that will call this script when the application starts up. To do so, we will first add the following method to the **Program.cs** file:

```
static void CreateDbIfNotExists(IHost app)
{
    using var scope = app.Services.CreateScope();

    var services = scope.ServiceProvider;
    try
    {
        var context = services.
GetRequiredService<FactoryManagerContext>();
        DbInitializer.Initialize(context);
    }
    catch (Exception ex)
    {
        var logger = services.GetRequiredService<ILogger<Program>>();
        logger.LogError(ex, "Failed to create the DB.");
    }
}
```

Then, we will call this method by passing the app variable to it:

```
CreateDbIfNotExists(app);
```

Now, we are ready to launch the application and see how the database gets generated.

Creating the database by running the application

We can launch our application by either executing the dotnet run command from the console or by doing it via the IDE. Since we have not yet created a database, we should expect to see various SQL statements being displayed in the console. Then, when the application is up and running, we can open our SQL Server Object Explorer and have a look at the newly created database. *Figure 5.3* shows what we should expect the data in the **Jobs** table to look following:

JobId	JobTitle	Compens...
1	Manager	50000.00
2	Laborer	25000.00

Figure 5.3: Data in the Jobs table

Figure 5.4 demonstrates what you should expect to see inside the **Factories** table:

FactoryId	FactoryName	Location
1	Best Cookies	New York

Figure 5.4: Data in the Factories table

The data that we expect to see in the **Employees** table is shown in *figure 5.5*:

EmployeeId	FirstName	LastName	DateOfBirth	StartDate	JobId
1	John	Smith	01/10/199...	01/09/202...	1
2	Alexander	Marshall	12/09/198...	01/09/201...	2
3	Michael	Davidson	11/05/1989...	01/09/201...	2

Figure 5.5: Data in the Employees table

And finally, depending on what specific records we have added to the **Shifts** table, its data would look similar to what is shown in *figure 5.6*:

ShiftId	WeekDay	StartTime	EndTime	FactoryId	EmployeeId
1	1	09:00:00	17:00:00	1	1
2	2	09:00:00	17:00:00	1	1
3	3	09:00:00	17:00:00	1	1
4	4	09:00:00	17:00:00	1	1
5	5	09:00:00	17:00:00	1	1
6	1	09:00:00	17:00:00	1	2
7	2	09:00:00	17:00:00	1	2
8	3	09:00:00	17:00:00	1	2
9	4	09:00:00	17:00:00	1	2
10	5	09:00:00	17:00:00	1	2
11	1	09:00:00	17:00:00	1	3
12	2	09:00:00	17:00:00	1	3
13	3	09:00:00	17:00:00	1	3
14	4	09:00:00	17:00:00	1	3
15	5	09:00:00	17:00:00	1	3

Figure 5.6: Data in the Shifts table

This concludes the overview of the code-first approach in EF7. But you can also do things the other way around. You can auto-create your `Entity` objects by reverse-engineering an existing database. This is what we will have a look at next.

Database-first approach in EF7

EF7 CLI tools can create the entirety of Entity Framework code from an existing database connection. The tool is not perfect, and very frequently, you would need to refactor the auto-generated classes and remove redundant code from them. But the resulting entity objects would usually still represent the database table with a reasonable degree of accuracy.

Creating EF7 models from an existing database

Before we can start reverse-engineering an existing database, we need to add the following NuGet package to the project that we want to do it in:

`Microsoft.EntityFrameworkCore.Design`

Then, we need to add a NuGet package representing a specific database provider that we intend to work with. For example, to use an SQL Server provider, we would add the following NuGet package:

`Microsoft.EntityFrameworkCore.SqlServer`

Then, to trigger the reverse-engineering process, you would need to execute the following command from your project folder:

`dotnet ef dbcontext scaffold <database connection string> <the name of the database provider NuGet package>`

This will initiate the scaffolding process, which consists of reading the database schema and automatically generating code based on this schema. The EF objects that we created manually in the code-first approach, such as DB context and data models, are created automatically.

There are some additional parameters you can apply. For example, you can use `--table` parameter multiple times if you want to include only specific tables. Or you can use `--schema` parameter to include only the objects from a specific schema. For example, if we want to reverse-engineer the SQL Server database that we have created previously and only include the objects from the default **dbo** schema, we will execute the following command:

```
dotnet ef dbcontext scaffold "Server=(localdb)\
mssqllocaldb;Database=FactoryManager;Trusted_
Connection=True;MultipleActiveResultSets=true" Microsoft.
EntityFrameworkCore.SqlServer --schema dbo
```

We can also improve the security of this command by retrieving the connection string from .NET secrets instead of using an open text value. To do so, we will first need to add a secret entry by executing the following command:

```
dotnet user-secrets set ConnectionStrings:Default
"Server=(localdb)\mssqllocaldb;Database=FactoryManager;Trusted_
Connection=True;MultipleActiveResultSets=true"
```

And then, we can modify our original command by referencing the key of the secret rather than the actual value:

```
dotnet ef dbcontext scaffold Name=ConnectionStrings:Default Microsoft.
EntityFrameworkCore.SqlServer --schema dbo
```

Now, we can create another Web application project, add the necessary NuGet packages to it and run either of the preceding commands inside the project folder.

Looking at auto-generated code

Once we run these commands inside a new project folder, we should expect all the entity objects to be present in it, along with the database context, as demonstrated by *figure 5.7*:

Figure 5.7: *Auto-generated code inside a project folder*

If we open one of the files containing the entity objects, it will look similar to what is shown in *figure 5.8*:

```
1   using System;
2   using System.Collections.Generic;
3
4   namespace DatabaseFirstDataApp
5   {
6       public partial class Employee
7       {
8           public Employee()
9           {
10              Shifts = new HashSet<Shift>();
11          }
12
13          public int EmployeeId { get; set; }
14          public string FirstName { get; set; } = null!;
15          public string LastName { get; set; } = null!;
16          public DateTime DateOfBirth { get; set; }
17          public DateTime StartDate { get; set; }
18          public int JobId { get; set; }
19
20          public virtual Job Job { get; set; } = null!;
21          public virtual ICollection<Shift> Shifts { get; set; }
22      }
23  }
24
```

Figure 5.8: Auto-generated employee entity class

As you can see, the code may need some refactoring and removal of the redundant entries. For example, we can clearly see that we do not need either of the using statements in the previous example. But it would still save us a lot of time, as we do not have to write any of the entity classes manually.

This concludes the overview of the most fundamental features of Entity Framework. Now, we will have a look at the new features that were added to EF7.

The latest features of EF7

Version 7 of Entity Framework, just like every version that was released before it, comes with its own set of useful features. These go beyond simple bug fixes and performance improvements.

Controlling database-first via T4 templates

T4 templates were used by various Microsoft technologies for many years. These templates were used primarily for generating text based on specific rules. The formatting of T4 templates allowed developers to apply a complex mixture of text and control logic to generate documents of any complexity. Now, T4 templates can be used for defining complex configurations for applying database-first reverse engineering by EF7.

Not all databases are as simple as a collection of tables inside a single schema. There are many enterprise databases that use a large number of tables, multiple schemas, and complex business rules. Sometimes you do not want to represent them all in your ORM code. This is when T4 templates may be especially handy.

Guarded key

By default, entity objects used by Entity Framework use int data type to represent a primary key **identity** property. The property needs to have both the getter and the setter, which may cause some problems. Even though the value inside the **identity** column is meant to be immutable in the database, it is just a writeable int in the object that represents a database record. Therefore, there is nothing that stops you from accidentally modifying key values and getting unexpected results, such as updating the wrong record in the database.

To protect against these situations, EF7 has added the concept of a guarded key. A guarded key is a key wrapped in its own class. The value can be initiated via the constructor, so Entity Framework can still extract the value from the database into an entity object. But, once created, the value cannot be modified.

To apply a guarded key, we can make the following modification to our auto-generated **Employee** entity class:

```
namespace DatabaseFirstDataApp
{
    public partial class Employee
    {
        public Employee()
        {
            Shifts = new HashSet<Shift>();
        }

        public EmployeeKey EmployeeId { get; set; }
        public string FirstName { get; set; } = null!;
        public string LastName { get; set; } = null!;
        public DateTime DateOfBirth { get; set; }
        public DateTime StartDate { get; set; }
        public int JobId { get; set; }

        public virtual Job Job { get; set; } = null!;
        public virtual ICollection<Shift> Shifts { get; set; }
```

```
    }

    public class EmployeeKey
{
    public EmployeeKey(Func<int> generator) => EmployeeId = generator();
        public EmployeeKey(int id) => EmployeeId = id;
        public int EmployeeId { get; private set; }
    }
}
```

As we can see, instead of having the **EmployeeId** property as an int, we have it as **EmployeeKey** class that acts as a wrapper for a read-only **int** property. This class has two constructors. One accepts **int** value, whereas the other one accepts a function that returns an int value. So, it is compatible with any code that Entity Framework might call.

Table-per-concrete-type (TPC) mapping

The predecessor of EF7, EF Core 6, had two ways of dealing with entity objects that were inherited from one another:

- **Table-per-hierarchy** (**TPH**) mapping, where each complete inheritance hierarchy was represented by a single table.

- **Table-per-type** (**TPT**) mapping, where any types, including abstract types, were placed into their own individual tables that were referring to each other by foreign key relationships.

Now, a third type of mapping has been added, **table-per-concrete-type** (**TPC**), which creates a table based on each concrete type in the hierarchy.

To explain how different types of mappings work, let us modify our original code-first application. Let us add a **Person.cs** file to the **Models** folder and populate it with the following code:

```
using System.ComponentModel.DataAnnotations;
using System.ComponentModel.DataAnnotations.Schema;

namespace MvcDataApp.Models;

public abstract record Person
{
    public int Id { get; set; }
```

```
    [StringLength(20)]
    public string FirstName { get; set; }
    [StringLength(20)]
    public string LastName { get; set; }
    public DateTime DateOfBirth { get; set; }


    [NotMapped]
    public string FullName => FirstName + " " + LastName;
}
```

We will then modify our **Employee** record so it inherits from this base record:

```
namespace MvcDataApp.Models;


public record Employee : Person
{
    public DateTime StartDate { get; set; }
    public int JobId { get; set; }


    public Job Job { get; set; }
    public ICollection<Shift> Shifts { get; set; }
}
```

Then, we will add a **Supervisor.cs** file, which will contain a record that will inherit from an **Employee** record:

```
namespace MvcDataApp.Models;


public record Supervisor : Employee
{
    public int TeamSize { get; set; }
}
```

Here is how different mapping types will work. If we are to use TPH, we will have a single table in the database because we have only one inheritance hierarchy (**Person** to **Employee** to **Supervisor**). If we were to use TPT, we would have three tables, one for **Person**, one for **Employee**, and one for **Supervisor**. Each table will only have those fields that correspond to the properties of the original entity class, except for the Id column, which will be present in all tables. The tables will use this column to link to each other. If we use the newly added TPC mapping, we will have two tables: **Supervisors** and **Employees**. **Person** entity will not have a table associated with it because it is an abstract record. But each table will have all the fields present in the entire inheritance hierarchy.

To demonstrate how TPC works, we will delete our existing database and modify our **FactoryManagerContext** definition:

```
using Microsoft.EntityFrameworkCore;
using MvcDataApp.Models;


namespace MvcDataApp.Data;


public class FactoryManagerContext : DbContext
{

    public FactoryManagerContext(DbContextOptions<FactoryManagerContext>
options) : base(options)
    {
    }


    public DbSet<Employee> Employees { get; set; }
    public DbSet<Supervisor> Supervisors { get; set; }
    public DbSet<Factory> Factories { get; set; }
    public DbSet<Job> Jobs { get; set; }
    public DbSet<Shift> Shifts { get; set; }


    protected override void OnModelCreating(ModelBuilder modelBuilder)
    {
        modelBuilder.Entity<Person>().UseTpcMappingStrategy();
        modelBuilder.Entity<Employee>();
        modelBuilder.Entity<Supervisor>();
        modelBuilder.Entity<Factory>();
        modelBuilder.Entity<Job>();
        modelBuilder.Entity<Shift>();
    }
}
```

To apply TPC, we will need to register all our entity objects, including the abstract classes, inside an override of the **OnModelCreating** method. We will also need to call **UseTpcMappingStrategy** on the line that registers the base type of the hierarchy, which in our case is **Person**. TPT is enabled by default, or it can be enabled explicitly by calling the **UseTptMappingStrategy** method. TPH is enabled by calling the **UseTphMappingStrategy** method.

Now, after deleting the original database, we can apply TPC while creating a new database. To do so, will replace the script to insert **Employee** records inside the **DbInitializer** class with the following:

```
var employees = new Employee[]
{
    new Employee
{
    Id = 1,
        FirstName="Alexander",
        LastName="Marshall",
        DateOfBirth=DateTime.Parse("1982-09-12"),
        StartDate=DateTime.Parse("2017-09-01"),
        JobId = 2,
    },
    new Employee
{
    Id=3,
        FirstName="Michael",
        LastName="Davidson",
        DateOfBirth=DateTime.Parse("1989-05-11"),
        StartDate=DateTime.Parse("2010-09-01"),
        JobId = 2,
    },
};
foreach (var e in employees)
{
context.Employees.Add(e);
}
context.SaveChanges();
```

Then, we will add the following script to insert a **Supervisor** record:

```
var supervisors = new Supervisor[]
{
new Supervisor
```

```
{
    Id=1,
FirstName="John",
        LastName="Smith",
        DateOfBirth=DateTime.Parse("1992-10-01"),
        StartDate=DateTime.Parse("2020-09-01"),
        JobId = 1,
    },
};
foreach (var s in supervisors)
{
context.Employees.Add(s);
}
context.SaveChanges();
```

Now, our **Employees** table should look as shown in *figure 5.9*:

Id	FirstName	LastName	DateOfBirth	StartDate	JobId
2	Alexander	Marshall	12/09/198...	01/09/201...	2
3	Michael	Davidson	11/05/1989...	01/09/201...	2

Figure 5.9: *Data in Employees table*

Our **Supervisors** table should look like as shown in *figure 5.10*:

Id	FirstName	LastName	DateOfBirth	StartDate	JobId	TeamSize
1	John	Smith	01/10/199...	01/09/202...	1	0

Figure 5.10: *Data in Supervisors table*

Now, we will move on to the final notable new feature of EF7: the interceptors.

Interceptors

Interceptors are used by EF7 to apply some additional logic when a query is initiated. Such an interceptor needs to implement the **IMaterializationInterceptor** interface from **Microsoft.EntityFrameworkCore.Diagnostics** namespace. We will now add an example.

Let us create **EmployeeCachingInterceptor.cs** file inside the **Data** folder of our original project and populate it with the following content:

```
using Microsoft.EntityFrameworkCore.Diagnostics;
using MvcDataApp.Models;
using System.Collections.Concurrent;


namespace MvcDataApp.Data;


public class EmployeeCachingInterceptor : IMaterializationInterceptor
{
    private static readonly ConcurrentDictionary<string, Employee>
EmployeeCache = new();


    public InterceptionResult<object> CreatingInstance(
        MaterializationInterceptionData materializationData,
        InterceptionResult<object> result)
    {
        if (materializationData.EntityType.ClrType == typeof(Employee))
        {
            var employeeName = materializationData
.GetPropertyValue<string>(nameof(Employee.FullName));
            if (EmployeeCache.TryGetValue(employeeName, out var
employee))
            {
                Console.WriteLine($"Got employee '{
employee.FullName}' from the cache.");
                return InterceptionResult<object>
.SuppressWithResult(employee);
            }
        }


        return result;
    }
}
```

This interceptor uses a concurrent dictionary for caching **Employee** data. If a particular **Employee** record is present in the dictionary, we retrieve it. Otherwise, we retrieve it from the database.

Now, we need to register our interceptor. To do so, we will add the following override of the **OnConfiguring** method to our **FactoryManagementContext** class:

```
protected override void OnConfiguring(DbContextOptionsBuilder
optionsBuilder)
        => optionsBuilder.AddInterceptors(new
EmployeeCachingInterceptor());
```

This concludes the overview of EF7 and all of its new features.

Conclusion

In this chapter, we had an overview of relational databases. We also looked at SQL— the language used by relational databases to interact with the data. We have also covered various ways of how EF7 can be used. You should now be familiar with all the ways you can set up your relational database and connect EF7 to it, both code-first and database-first.

The code-first approach allows you to create a completely new database from the code. This approach allows a developer to focus on the code and allows the framework to automate the creation of data storage.

Database-first is more suited for scenarios where the ORM needs to be connected to an existing database. EF7 has tools that can read a database schema and generate the corresponding code abstractions.

We have also covered the latest features of EF7, such as guarded keys that hide implementation detail of key-generating logic and prevent developers from accidentally passing wrong keys to methods.

In the upcoming chapter, you will learn how to use ASP.NET Core, which is the main framework for building Web applications on .NET.

Points to remember

- Relational databases are defined by tables that are linked with other tables via the so-called foreign key relationships.

- **Structured Query Language** (**SQL**)'s purpose is to interact with relational databases.

- EF7 is the main (and the current) .NET ORM and has libraries to make it compatible with all major relational database types.

- EF7 is both capable of generating databases from the code and generating code from existing databases.

- Code-first approach is when you write the ORM code first and then create a relational database from it.

- Database-first approach is when you generate ORM code from an existing database.

Multiple choice questions

1. **What is the difference between a query and a command?**

    a. There is no difference, and these are interchangeable

    b. A query is for retrieving data, whereas a command is for manipulating data

    c. A query is for manipulating data, whereas a command is for retrieving data

    d. Queries are logged, whereas commands are not

2. **What is the difference between code-first and model-first approaches on EF7?**

    a. They are the same

    b. There is no code-first in EF7

    c. There is no model-first in EF7

    d. Code-first generates a new database, whereas model-first relies on an existing database

3. **What approach do you need to apply to generate EF7 models from an existing database?**

    a. Code-first

    b. Model-first

    c. Schema-first

    d. Database-first

4. **What is database normalization?**

    a. The process of eliminating redundant entries

    b. The process of making each table contain as few columns as possible

    c. All of the above

    d. None of these

Answers

1. b
2. c
3. d
4. c

Key terms

- **RDBMS**: Relational database management system.

- **SQL Server**: An RDBMS from Microsoft.

- **Oracle Database**: A commercial RDBMS from Oracle.

- **MySQL**: A semi-commercial lightweight RDBMS from Oracle.

- **PostgreSQL**: An advanced open-source RDBMS.

- **SQL**: Structured query language that is used for interacting with RDBMS.

- **ORM**: Object-relational mapper. A framework that mapped objects in the code (for example, classes) to objects in a database (for example, tables).

- **Entity Framework 7**: The main .NET ORM, which is developed by Microsoft alongside .NET itself.

- **Code-first**: An approach of setting up an ORM where the code is written first, and the database is generated afterward.

- **Database-first**: A technique of setting up an ORM by generating code from an existing database.

Join our book's Discord space

Join the book's Discord Workspace for Latest updates, Offers, Tech happenings around the world, New Release and Sessions with the Authors:

https://discord.bpbonline.com

CHAPTER 6
Web Application Types on .NET

Introduction

.NET has its own Web application development framework, which is called ASP. NET Core. **Active Server Pages** (**ASP**), and its initial version, which is now referred as ASP Classic, consisted of semi-static files that had a mixture of HTML markup and server-side code. Since then, an advanced version has been created and given the name ASP.NET. In this version, developers no longer had to combine client-side markup and server-side code in the same files. They could separate front-end and back-end components into separate files, which allowed them to maintain a clear separation of concerns and make the code more readable and maintainable. The new framework also came with its own implementations of commonly used architectural patterns, such as MVC, so developers no longer had to apply them manually.

One major disadvantage of ASP.NET was that it was only available on Windows, just like the rest of the .NET Framework at the time. But it all changed in 2016 when a cross-platform .NET Core was born. A new version of ASP.NET was created that was deployable on any major operating system and not just Windows. This new variant of the framework was given the name ASP.NET Core.

ASP.NET Core is a continuously evolving framework for Web application development. In this chapter, we will cover all application templates that are available on ASP.NET Core. While doing so, we will have a look at the latest features that were introduced in its version 7.

Structure

In this chapter, we will discuss the latest features of ASP.NET Core 7, which will include the following topics:

- ASP.NET Core basics
- Web API on ASP.NET Core
- MVC on ASP.NET Core
- Razor pages on ASP.NET Core

Objectives

By the end of this chapter, you will have learned how to use all main Web application types of ASP.NET Core and will be familiar with the latest features that have been added to version 7 of the framework.

Prerequisites

To follow this chapter, you will need the following:

- A machine running either Windows, MacOS, or Linux operating system
- .NET 7 SDK
- A suitable IDE or a code editor
- Being familiar with C# fundamentals

If you do not have any of these dependencies installed already, you can use the setup instructions provided in *Chapter 1: Getting Familiar with .NET 7 Application Structure*, which also provides a recap of C# fundamentals.

ASP.NET Core basics

ASP.NET Core project templates are available in the .NET SDK by default. However, if you are using Visual Studio 2022 and want to create ASP.NET Core projects from the GUI, you might have to enable the Web development workload via the Visual Studio Installer. To do so, you will need to open Visual Studio Installer, click the **Modify** button next to the Visual Studio 2022 instance and select ASP.NET and Web development workload to install, as *figure 6.1* demonstrates:

Figure 6.1: *Enabling ASP.NET Core workload in Visual Studio Installer*

Once the installation of all required components is completed, we can create a basic ASP.NET Core application, and we will get to know its structure.

Basic ASP.NET Core application structure

Let us create a project by using **ASP.NET Core Empty** project template and call it **BasicAspNetCoreApp**. If you are using .NET CLI, you can do so by executing the following command:

```
dotnet new web -o BasicAspNetCoreApp
```

Once created, your project will have the structure as displayed in *figure 6.2*:

- ▲ 🖥 **BasicAspNetCoreApp**
  - ▷ ⊙ Connected Services
  - ▷ 🔗 Dependencies
  - ▲ 🔍 Properties
    - + 🗋 launchSettings.json
  - ▲ + 🗋 appsettings.json
    - + 🗋 appsettings.Development.json
    - C# Program.cs

Figure 6.2: *The fundamental structure of an ASP.NET Core project*

The file called **appsettings.json** is the main file that holds the settings for the application. There can also be environment-specific varieties of it, such as **appsettings.Development.json**. An environment-specific file will override the main file if the application is running on a machine that has the **ASPNETCORE_ ENVIRONMENT** variable set to the same value as the suffix in the file name.

There is also a **Properties** folder with the **launchSettings.json** file. This file is primarily used in a development environment and sets the hosting rules for the application. For example, the settings in *figure 6.3* allow the application to be hosted on IIS Express and an inbuilt Web service called Kestrel:

```json
{
  "iisSettings": {
    "windowsAuthentication": false,
    "anonymousAuthentication": true,
    "iisExpress": {
      "applicationUrl": "http://localhost:12139",
      "sslPort": 44317
    }
  },
  "profiles": {
    "BasicAspNetCoreApp": {
      "commandName": "Project",
      "dotnetRunMessages": true,
      "launchBrowser": true,
      "applicationUrl": "https://localhost:7051;http://localhost:5051",
      "environmentVariables": {
        "ASPNETCORE_ENVIRONMENT": "Development"
      }
    },
    "IIS Express": {
      "commandName": "IISExpress",
      "launchBrowser": true,
      "environmentVariables": {
        "ASPNETCORE_ENVIRONMENT": "Development"
      }
    }
  }
}
```

Figure 6.3: An example of a launchSettings.json file

If hosted on IIS Express, the application is accessible on **http://localhost:12138** if no certificate is used and on **https://localhost:44317** if an SSL certificate is used. For a Kestrel-hosted application, the values are **http://localhost:5051** and **https://localhost:7051**, respectively.

To run an application with an SSL certificate on a development machine, you would need to set the development certificate as trusted. You can do it via the IDE or via the .NET CLI by executing the following command on either Mac OS or Windows:

```
dotnet dev-certs https --trust
```

The command will be different if you are using Linux and will depend on the specific distro you are using.

Finally, we have a **Program.cs** file, which is a standard .NET application entry point. Its content would look as follows:

```
var builder = WebApplication.CreateBuilder(args);
var app = builder.Build();
```

```
app.MapGet("/", () => "Welcome to ASP.NET Core!");


app.Run();
```

In this file, we have a **builder** variable, which allows us to configure various service dependencies for our application. Once we have configured everything we need, we then call the **Build** method on the **builder** variable and create the app variable from it. This variable allows us to add various steps to the request processing middleware. Since .NET6, we can also configure the HTTP endpoints for the application directly on the **app** variable in the **Program.cs** file. For example, we are calling **MapGet** to return a specific text when the root address of our application is called.

To see how it works, we can change this text, launch the application, open the browser, and navigate to the application URL, as defined in the **launchSettings. json** file. For example, if we replace the text with **Welcome to ASP.NET Core!**, the content of the file will be as follows:

```
var builder = WebApplication.CreateBuilder(args);
var app = builder.Build();


app.MapGet("/", () => "Welcome to ASP.NET Core!");


app.Run();
```

To launch an application in Kestrel, all we have to do is execute **dotnet run** command from inside the **application** folder. Then, we can navigate to its URL in the browser and verify that it displays **Welcome to ASP.NET Core!**.

Now, we will move on to more advanced Web application templates, starting with Web API.

Web API on ASP.NET Core

Web API application template on ASP.NET Core is designed primarily for building applications without user interfaces. Such applications are also known as Web services, and their purpose is to provide data to other authorized applications upon request.

Web API on ASP.NET Core primarily relies on **REpresentative State Transfer (REST)** as its external interface. It is integrated with tools, such as OpenAPI (also known as Swagger), which help visualize the application's REST endpoint in the browser.

In version 7 of ASP.NET Core, there are two kinds of Web API applications: Web API with controllers and Minimal API application. We will have a look at them both.

Web API with controllers

Web API with controllers relies on the so-called controller classes to define the endpoints accessible via HTTP. To demonstrate how it works, we will create a new application from the ASP.NET Core Web API template. If we are creating an application via an IDE, we need to ensure that the Use Controllers option is enabled. If you are using .NET CLI, you can create the application by using the following command:

```
dotnet new webapi -o WebApiAppWithControllers
```

Now, we have an application that has some additional options added to the **Program.cs** file. For example, it has **builder.Services.AddControllers()** call to add controller components, **builder.Services.AddSwaggerGen()** to enable Swagger support and **app.MapControllers()** to add the controller classes to the request processing pipeline and make them usable.

In fact, the template shows how a proper request processing middleware pipeline can be constructed. Most of the methods on the **app** variable ensure that certain steps are added to the pipeline in the order in which these methods are called. For example, calling **UseHttpsRedirection** before **UseAuthorization** and calling **MapControllers** afterwards ensure that the redirection to HTTPS happens first if the HTTP protocol was used in the original request. Then, we verify that the client is authorized to proceed any further. Only then the client is directed to a specific resource based on the path provided in the URL.

Let us now have a look at the **WeatherForecastController.cs** file, which is located inside the **Controllers** folder. We know that the class is an API controller because it has **ApiController** attribute and inherits from **ControllerBase**. Since it has **[controller]** set as its default route, the base path for any endpoints on this controller will match the controller class name minus the **Controller** suffix. It will be as follows:

```
{base URL}/WeatherForecast
```

To demonstrate some useful capabilities of ASP.NET Core, we will refactor this code. We will create a service that we will then inject into the controller by using dependency injection. This will allow us to maintain the so-called **thin controller principle**, which mandates that a controller should only be processing HTTP requests and returning responses to the clients. All business logic needs to happen inside separate services.

We will start by adding the **WeatherForecastService.cs** file to the project and adding the following interface to it:

```
namespace WebApiAppWithControllers;

public interface IWeatherForecastService
{
    IEnumerable<WeatherForecast> GetFiveDayForecast();
}
```

Then, we can add the class that implements this interface to the same file:

```
public class WeatherForecastService : IWeatherForecastService
{
    private static readonly string[] Summaries = new[]
    {
        "Freezing",
        "Bracing",
        "Chilly",
        "Cool",
        "Mild",
        "Warm",
        "Balmy",
        "Hot",
        "Sweltering",
        "Scorching"
    };


    public IEnumerable<WeatherForecast> GetFiveDayForecast()
    {
        return Enumerable.Range(1, 5).Select(index => new
WeatherForecast
        {
            Date = DateOnly.FromDateTime(DateTime.Now.AddDays(index)),
            TemperatureC = Random.Shared.Next(-20, 55),
            Summary = Summaries[Random.Shared.Next(Summaries.Length)]
        })
        .ToArray();
    }
}
```

Essentially, we have created a separate class that performs the same work that the controller used to do. Now, we can register this class in our dependency injection container. To do so, we just need to add the following line to the **Program.cs** file anywhere before the **Build** method is called on the **builder** variable:

```
builder.Services.AddTransient<IWeatherForecastService,
WeatherForecastService>();
```

This tells the underlying framework that if any file that is not directly referenced from the code, such as a controller, has a parameter of the type **IWeatherForecastService** passed into its constructor, it will be automatically resolved to a new instance of the **WeatherForecastService** class.

Since we have used **AddTransient**, we will have a new instance of this class per every request. But, if we wanted to use the same instance of the **WeatherForecastService** class throughout the application, we could use **AddSingleton** instead.

While we are in the **Program.cs** file, we can also configure logging to output into the console. To do so, we will add the following two lines before the **Build** method is called:

```
builder.Logging.ClearProviders();
builder.Logging.AddConsole();
```

Now, we will make the changes to our controller, so it will look like the following:

```
using Microsoft.AspNetCore.Mvc;

namespace WebApiAppWithControllers.Controllers;

[ApiController]
[Route("[controller]")]
public class WeatherForecastController : ControllerBase
{
    private readonly IWeatherForecastService _weatherForecastService;

    private readonly ILogger<WeatherForecastController> _logger;

    public WeatherForecastController(
        ILogger<WeatherForecastController> logger,
        IWeatherForecastService weatherForecastService)
    {
        _logger = logger;
        _weatherForecastService = weatherForecastService;
    }
}
```

We will then add the following method, which will replace the method we had before:

```
[HttpGet(Name = "GetWeatherForecast")]
public IActionResult Get()
{
    _logger.LogInformation("Obtaining 5-day weather forecast.");

    try
    {
        var forecast = _weatherForecastService.GetFiveDayForecast();
        return Ok(forecast);
    }
    catch (Exception ex)
    {
        _logger.LogError(ex, "Error obtaining weather forecast;");
        throw;
    }
}
```

The **HttpGet** attribute indicates that this method is called when a client submits a **GET HTTP** request. As this method does not have the path specified, it will be triggered when the base path of the controller is used.

This method relies on the **IWeatherForecastService** implementation that was injected into the constructor. But you can also apply dependency injection to the individual methods. Version 7 of ASP.NET Core will do it implicitly. To test it, you can add the following method:

```
[HttpGet("injected-service")]
public IActionResult GetFromService(
IWeatherForecastService weatherForecastService)
{
    _logger.LogInformation("Obtaining 5-day weather forecast.");

    try
    {
        var forecast = weatherForecastService.GetFiveDayForecast();
        return Ok(forecast);
    }
```

```
catch (Exception ex)
{
    _logger.LogError(ex, "Error obtaining weather forecast;");
    throw;
}
}
```

This method specifies injected-service as the path. So, the full path to trigger this endpoint will be as follows:

```
{base URL}/WeatherForecast/injected-service
```

Now, we will have a look at another feature that was newly added to version 7 of the framework—the ability to use **TryParse** functionality in **controller** method parameters. This functionality allows you to gracefully handle cases of clients sending you parameters of the wrong data type. To demonstrate how this functionality works, we will add **TryParseDemoController.cs** controller into the **Controllers** folder and will populate it with the following content:

```
using Microsoft.AspNetCore.Mvc;

namespace WebApiAppWithControllers.Controllers;

[ApiController]
[Route("[controller]")]
public class TryParseDemoController : ControllerBase
{
    [HttpGet(Name = "TryParseInt")]
    public IActionResult Get([FromQuery] IntParser parser)
    {
        if (parser?.Value == null)
            return NoContent();

        return Ok(parser.Value);
    }
}

public class IntParser
{
    public int? Value { get; set; }

    public static bool TryParse(int? input, out IntParser? result)
```

```
    {
        if (input is null)
        {
            result = default;
            return false;
        }


        result = new IntParser { Value = input };
        return true;
    }
}
```

To make this functionality work, we need a custom class with a static boolean **TryParse** method that returns an **output** parameter. This is the role of the **IntParser** class. Now, if we call this endpoint via the following URL, it will return **204** response code because there is no query string parameter supplied, and the parser will set the **Value** property to null.

```
{base URL}/TryParseDemo
```

However, if we supply the query string parameter as below, we will get the **200**-response code with the supplied integer value returned back to us:

```
{base URL}/TryParseDemo?Value=2
```

Now, we can launch our application and see how our newly added controller endpoints look like in Swagger. We have all the required Swagger middleware set up in the **Program.cs** file already, so all we need to do is navigate to the base URL of the application. We will expect to see a page similar to the one displayed in *figure 6.4*:

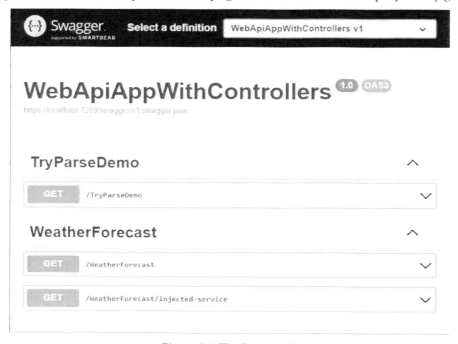

Figure 6.4: *The Swagger UI*

Now, we will cover another way of developing Web API applications on .NET 7— the minimal API.

Minimal API endpoints

Minimal API is a feature that allows you to add REST API endpoints to your Web application without controllers. This feature has only been added to ASP.NET Core version 6 and is very similar to how REST endpoints are configured in a Node.js application.

We briefly saw the use of minimal API when we have created our initial basic ASP. NET Core application. It was calling the **MapGet** method on the app variable in the **Program.cs** file. But there is also a more advanced minimal API template that you can use. All you need to do is create an application from the Web API and then either uncheck **Use Controllers** option if you are doing it from an IDE or add -minimal parameter if you are doing it from .NET CLI. So, our full command may look as follows:

```
dotnet new webapi -o WebApiAppWithMinimalApis -minimal
```

The application it will create will have all its HTTP endpoints mapped inside the **Program.cs** class. In version 7 of ASP.NET Core, a whole range of new features has been added specifically to the minimal API functionality. We will now have a look at them.

Adding open API metadata

In the **Program.cs** file of the newly added project, you can locate the call to **MapGet** of the **app** variable and insert the following statement before the semicolon at the end of the full statement:

```
.WithDescription("The endpoint for retrieving weather forecasts.")
```

This will add the description to the Open API document, which can be displayed on the Swagger page. Alternatively, you can add the same description by inserting the **EndpointSummary** attribute into the main call, like the following:

```
app.MapGet("/weatherforecast", [EndpointSummary("The endpoint for
retrieving weather forecasts.")]() => …
```

Or you can locate the **WithOpenApi** call and modify it as follows:

```
.WithOpenApi(operation => {
    operation.Summary = "The endpoint for retrieving weather
forecasts.";
    return operation;
});
```

Next, we will have a look at the recent improvements to how minimal API endpoints can accept parameters.

Improvements to minimal API parameters

If you are using multiple parameters of the same data type, you can now pass all parameters into your endpoint methods as a single array. But this only applies to arrays of primitive types, string arrays and **StringValues** objects. This is done as follows:

```
app.MapGet("/repeated-strings", (string[] names) =>
$"value 1: {names[0]} , value 2: {names[1]}, value 3: {names[2]}");
```

Likewise, instead of passing individual parameters into your endpoint methods, you can just create an object that will represent each parameter as a property and then pass this object. This can be done as follows. First, we would add this object:

```
internal struct ParamsRequest
{
    public int Id { get; set; }
    public int Page { get; set; }
}
```

Then, we can create an endpoint method that accepts this object as a set of parameters:

```
app.MapGet("/parameters-object",
([AsParameters] ParamsRequest request) =>
$"Id{request.Id}, Page: {request.Page}");
```

It will automatically recognize this object as a set of parameters because it is marked by **AsParameters** attribute.

Next, we will have a look at how to get your minimal API to return typed results.

Minimal API and typed results

Typed results allow you to return objects that have a strongly typed data payload and various metadata fields associated with it. To enable this, your endpoint method needs to return an implementation of the **IResult** interface. To demonstrate this, we will add **TypedResultsDemo.cs** file with the following content:

```
namespace WebApiAppWithMinimalApis;

public class Data
{
    public int Id { get; set; } = 1;
    public string Name { get; set; } = "test";
}

public static class TypedResultsDemo
{
    public static void MapTypedDataApi(this IEndpointRouteBuilder
routes)
    {
        routes.MapGet("/typed-data", ReturnTypedResult);
    }

    public static Task<IResult> ReturnTypedResult()
    {
        return Task.FromResult(Results.Ok(Task.FromResult(new Data())));
```

```
    }
}
```

We can now call the **MapTypedDataApi** extension method from our **Program.cs** class to register this endpoint. To do so, we will need to ensure that the namespace from this newly added file is referenced by the **Program.cs** file, like so:

```
using WebApiAppWithMinimalApis;
```

And then all we have to do is add the following line anywhere before **app.Run()**:

```
app.MapTypedDataApi();
```

Now, if we launch our application, open its Swagger page, and make a call to the endpoint we have just added, we can see that it has returned the JSON version of our **Data** object along with several metadata fields, as demonstrated in *figure 6.5*:

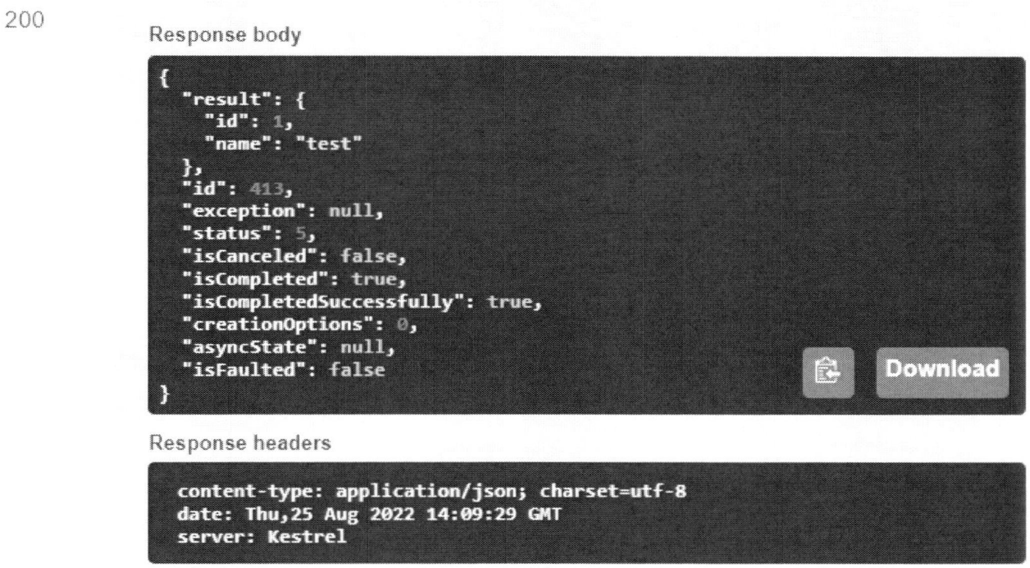

Figure 6.5: The JSON-serialize version of the IResult implementation

We can also configure our endpoints to return multiple types of results. To demonstrate this, we can add the following method to our **TypedResultsDemo** class:

```
public static Results<Ok<Data>, NotFound> ReturnSingeItem(int id)
{
    return id == 1
            ? TypedResults.Ok(new Data())
            : TypedResults.NotFound();
}
```

And then, add the following line to the **MapTypedDataApi** method:

```
routes.MapGet("/typed-data/{id}", (int id) => ReturnSingeItem(id));
```

The response object returned from this endpoint will look similar to this:

```
{
  "result": {
    "id": 1,
    "name": "test"
  },
  "id": 686,
  "exception": null,
  "status": 5,
  "isCanceled": false,
  "isCompleted": true,
  "isCompletedSuccessfully": true,
  "creationOptions": 0,
  "asyncState": null,
  "isFaulted": false
}
```

Now, we will move to another new capability of minimal API: the ability to upload files in a secure manner.

Uploading files to minimal API

Uploading a file to a server requires **POST HTTP** request rather than **GET**, so we will need to call **MapPost** method instead of **MapGet** to add an appropriate endpoint. Our endpoint may look like the following:

```
app.MapPost("/upload", async (IFormFile file) =>
{
    using var stream = File.OpenWrite("test.txt");
    await file.CopyToAsync(stream);
}).RequireAuthorization();
```

Here, we are getting the data that represents a file uploaded by the user and save it inside the test.txt file in the same folder where our application is hosted. In a real-life scenario, we would probably pass the data into blob storage.

We also have a **RequireAuthorization** call at the end of this call. This is something we can add to our endpoint mappings to ensure that only authorized users can access it. We can also pass some additional options into this method to specify more fine-grained access requirements (roles, policies, claims, and so on). But to make it work, we need to have authentication and authorization middleware configured.

Speaking about middleware, some new features have recently been added to it, which we will look at next.

The new in request processing middleware

Program.cs allows you to configure request-processing middleware via the builder variable and build a pipeline for it via the app variable. Now, we will examine the latest features that have been added to the ASP.NET Core middleware.

We will start with configuring the middleware via the builder. One of the newly added features is the ability to log custom header information in the server logs, known as W3C logs. This can be any arbitrary data with any arbitrary keys. For example, to log request information that contains custom keys of custom-header and another-custom-header headers, you can add the following code:

```
builder.Services.AddW3CLogging(logging =>
{
    logging.AdditionalRequestHeaders.Add("custom-header");
    logging.AdditionalRequestHeaders.Add("another-custom-header");
});
```

You can also configure custom problem information that you can record in your code. To do so, you will need to add the following code before **builder.Build()**:

```
builder.Services.AddProblemDetails();
```

This will register an implementation of the **IProblemDetailsService** interface. You can then resolve it from any place inside your application and call its **WriteAsync** method to record the details of the problem. This is how you can resolve this service from **IHttpContext**:

```
var problemDetailsService =
context.RequestServices.GetService<IProblemDetailsService>();
```

Then, we will add the following line that will register the appropriate provider that will allow us to decompress any compressed request data:

```
builder.Services.AddRequestDecompression();
```

Next, we will look at the actual middleware pipeline. The first thing we can add to it is the ability to automatically decompress compressed request data. To do so, we can add the following line after **builder.Build()**:

```
app.UseRequestDecompression();
```

Then, we can either get or set the value of the cookie that tracks whether the user has consented to the use of the cookie policy. This can be done via the **ConsentCookieValue** property of the **CookiePolicyOptions** class. This is how we can set this value in the request processing pipeline:

```
app.UseCookiePolicy(new CookiePolicyOptions
{
    ConsentCookieValue = "yes"
});
```

Some request processing steps are added to the endpoint mappings. For example, the **CacheOutput** method can be added to cache the results of the request, so the call does not have to make many round trips to the data storage or do a computationally expensive calculation. For example, the following endpoint will only calculate the date once. And then, if called again by the same client, it will just return the value that has already been calculated:

```
app.MapGet("/cached-date", () => DateTime.UtcNow.ToString()).
CacheOutput();
```

Next, there is some custom filtering that we can apply via the **AddEndpointFilter** method. For example, the following code demonstrates an endpoint that restricts access to the user with a particular name:

```
string GetGreetingMessage(string name) => $"User {name} is allowed to
access reource";

app.MapGet("/filter/invocation-context/{name}", GetGreetingMessage)
    .AddEndpointFilter(async (routeHandlerInvocationContext, next) =>
    {
        var name = (string)routeHandlerInvocationContext.Arguments[0];
        if (name == "Chris Davidson")
        {
            return Results.Problem("Access is not allowed for Chris
Davidson!");
        }
        return await next(routeHandlerInvocationContext);
    });
```

AddEndpointFilter method can also work with the **RouteHandlerContext** attribute or an implementation of the IRouteHandlerFilter interface.

This concludes an overview of the Web API and the most recent features that have been added to it. Next, we will have a look at Web application types that have user interfaces and start with the MVC template.

MVC on ASP.NET core

Model-View-Controller (**MVC**) is an architectural pattern that is specifically designed to enable efficient data manipulation via a user interface. This characteristic makes the MVC pattern specifically suitable for building enterprise applications.

As the name suggests, an MVC application consists of three types of components:

(1). **Model**, which represents the data in the back-end

(2). **View**, which represents a specific screen in the user interface

(3). **Controller**, which facilitates the connectivity between Views and Models

MVC controllers are conceptually similar to Web API controllers that we looked at earlier. But instead of merely returning some data, they are serving the views to the browsers.

We already had a look at examples of MVC models in *Chapter 5: Database access with Entity Framework Core*, and entity object, such as **Employee**, is a model in the MVC context. To demonstrate the fundamentals of ASP.NET Core MVC applications, we will just continue building upon the **MvcDataApp** application that we created in that chapter.

To make the demonstration simple, we will remove any interceptors that we have added. The easiest way to do it is to remove the **OnConfiguring** override from the **FactoryManagerContext** class.

Next, we will make some modifications to the **_Layout.cshtml** file, which is located in the **Shared** folder inside the **Views** folder. This is the file that provides the shared layout to all views inside the application. So, it enables features such as the common header, common navigation bar, common footer, and so on. It is written as a Razor template, which is a combination of raw HTML markup, C#, and various keywords and operators that glue the markup and the code together. The template executes on the server and renders an HTML page, which is then delivered to the client.

The first thing we will do is locate the title HTML element and replace it with the following:

```
<title>@ViewData["Title"] - Factory Manager</title>
```

Then, we will make some changes to our navigation bar. To do so, we will locate the **ul** element with the **navbar-nav** class attribute and will replace it with the following:

```
<ul class="navbar-nav flex-grow-1">
  <li class="nav-item">
    <a class="nav-link text-dark" asp-area="" asp-controller="Home" asp-action="Index">Home</a>
  </li>
  <li class="nav-item">
    <a class="nav-link text-dark" asp-area="" asp-controller="Home" asp-action="Privacy">Privacy</a>
  </li>
  <li class="nav-item">
    <a class="nav-link text-dark" asp-area="" asp-controller="Employees" asp-action="Index">Employees</a>
  </li>
</ul>
```

Now, we have three items on the navigation bar: **Home**, **Privacy**, and **Employees**. The **asp-controller** and **asp-action** elements indicate which controller and which action method (that is, view) each item represents. MVC controllers have the same naming convention as the Web API controllers we had a look at earlier. So, in this case, the first two items refer to the **HomeController** class. The first item refers to the action method called **Index**, whereas the second item refers to the Privacy action method. We can examine what these action methods look like by opening **HomeController.cs** class inside the **Controllers** folder. The views are located inside the **Home** folder of the **Views** folder. The third item refers to the **Index** action method of the **EmployeesController** class, which we have not added yet. So, we will now go ahead and add it.

Our **EmployeesController** class and corresponding views will give us the ability to view and manage **Employees** data from the database we have created earlier. If you are using Visual Studio 2022, the easiest way to add the appropriate controller and the view is to scaffold them. To do so, you will need to right-click on your project from the solution explorer, click **New** and select **Scaffolded Item**. In the dialog that appears, you will need to select **MVC Controller** with views using Entity Framework, as *figure 6.6* demonstrates:

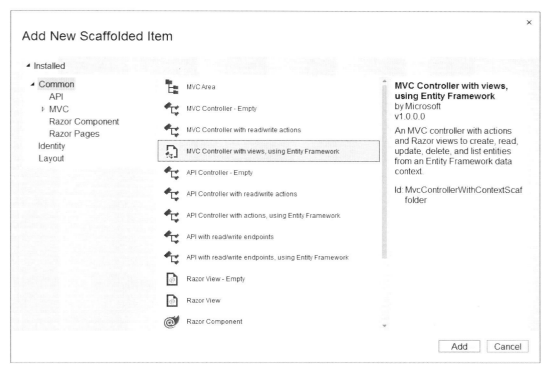

Figure 6.6: Scaffolding views and controller from the EF models

Then, you will need to select the appropriate database context class (**FactoryManagerContext** in our case), and the entity model (**Employee**), select all options for the views, and ensure that the controller's name is **EmployeesController**, as demonstrated in *figure 6.7*:

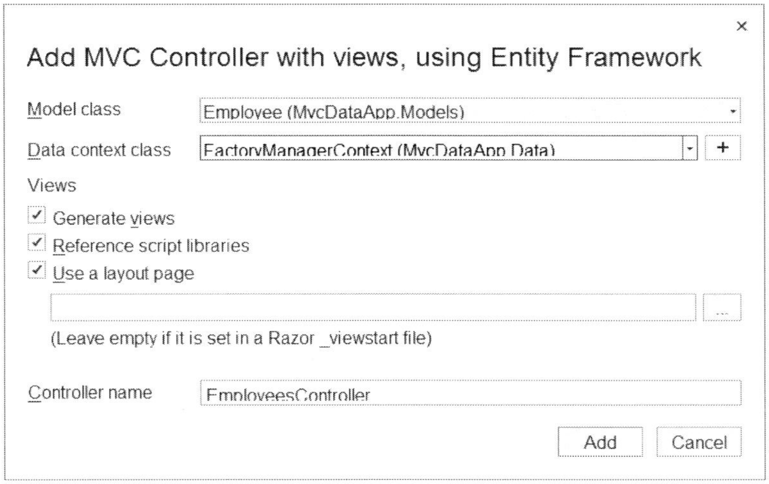

Figure 6.7: Configuring the items to scaffold

The scaffolding process may take a while, but once it is finished, you should see the **EmployeesControlelr.cs** file inside your **Controllers** folder of the project. You should also see the **Employees** folder inside the **Views** folder with a bunch of **CSHTML** files, as *figure 6.8* demonstrates:

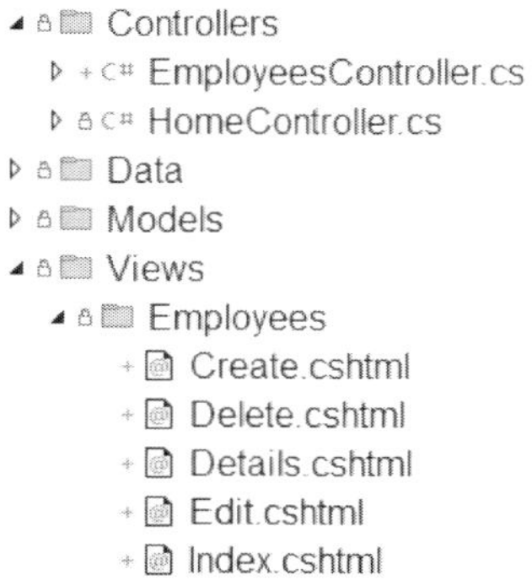

```
▲ ⌂ ▣ Controllers
    ▷ + C# EmployeesController.cs
    ▷ ⌂ C# HomeController.cs
▷ ⌂ ▣ Data
▷ ⌂ ▣ Models
▲ ⌂ ▣ Views
    ▲ ⌂ ▣ Employees
        + ▣ Create.cshtml
        + ▣ Delete.cshtml
        + ▣ Details.cshtml
        + ▣ Edit.cshtml
        + ▣ Index.cshtml
```

***Figure 6.8**: Newly created controller and views*

If you are not using Visual Studio 2022, we can add the controller and the views manually. We will start by adding **EmployeesControler.cs** file to our **Controllers** folder and populating it with the following content:

```
using Microsoft.AspNetCore.Mvc;
using Microsoft.AspNetCore.Mvc.Rendering;
using Microsoft.EntityFrameworkCore;
using MvcDataApp.Data;
using MvcDataApp.Models;

namespace MvcDataApp.Controllers;

public class EmployeesController : Controller
{
    private readonly FactoryManagerContext _context;

    public EmployeesController(FactoryManagerContext context)
    {
        _context = context;
    }

    private bool EmployeeExists(int id)
    {
```

```
        return (_context.Employees?.Any(e => e.Id == id)).
GetValueOrDefault();
    }
}
```

Then, we will add the **Index** action method, which will serve us the view that lists all the **Employees** entities we have in our database:

```
public async Task<IActionResult> Index()
{
    var factoryManagerContext = _context.Employees.Include(e => e.Job);
    return View(await factoryManagerContext.ToListAsync());
}
```

Then, we will add the **Details** action method, which will show us the details on any specific **Employee** entity based on its **Id**:

```
public async Task<IActionResult> Details(int? id)
{
    if (id == null || _context.Employees == null)
    {
        return NotFound();
    }

    var employee = await _context.Employees
        .Include(e => e.Job)
        .FirstOrDefaultAsync(m => m.Id == id);
    if (employee == null)
    {
        return NotFound();
    }

    return View(employee);
}
```

We will also add two action methods that will give us the ability to create a new **Employee** entity. One of them will be accessed by **GET** request and will give us the creation form. The other will be accessed by **POST** request that allows us to submit the form:

```
public IActionResult Create()
{
    ViewData["JobId"] = new SelectList(_context.Jobs, "JobId", "JobId");
return View();
}


[HttpPost]
    [ValidateAntiForgeryToken]
public async Task<IActionResult> Create(
[Bind("StartDate,JobId,Id,FirstName,LastName,DateOfBirth")]
Employee employee)
{
    if (ModelState.IsValid)
    {
        _context.Add(employee);
        await _context.SaveChangesAsync();
        return RedirectToAction(nameof(Index));
    }
ViewData["JobId"] =
new SelectList(_context.Jobs, "JobId", "JobId", employee.JobId);
    return View(employee);
}
```

Then, we will add **GET** and **POST** action methods to give us the ability to edit the existing **Employee** entities. Please note that the action endpoints are accessible via a **GET** HTTP verb by default. If we need to apply a different verb, we need to add an attribute to the method, such as **HttpPost** or **HttpDelete**.

```
public async Task<IActionResult> Edit(int? id)
{
    if (id == null || _context.Employees == null)
    {
        return NotFound();
    }

    var employee = await _context.Employees.FindAsync(id);
    if (employee == null)
    {
```

```
            return NotFound();
    }
ViewData["JobId"] =
new SelectList(_context.Jobs, "JobId", "JobId", employee.JobId);
    return View(employee);
}


[HttpPost]
[ValidateAntiForgeryToken]
public async Task<IActionResult> Edit(int id,
[Bind("StartDate,JobId,Id,FirstName,LastName,DateOfBirth")]
Employee employee)
{
    if (id != employee.Id)
    {
        return NotFound();
    }

    if (ModelState.IsValid)
    {
        try
        {
            _context.Update(employee);
            await _context.SaveChangesAsync();
        }
        catch (DbUpdateConcurrencyException)
        {
            if (!EmployeeExists(employee.Id))
            {
                return NotFound();
            }
            else
            {
                throw;
            }
        }
```

```
        return RedirectToAction(nameof(Index));
    }
ViewData["JobId"] =
new SelectList(_context.Jobs, "JobId", "JobId", employee.JobId);
    return View(employee);
}
```

Finally, we will add **GET** and **POST** action methods to delete an **Employee** entity:

```
public async Task<IActionResult> Delete(int? id)
{
    if (id == null || _context.Employees == null)
    {
        return NotFound();
    }

    var employee = await _context.Employees
        .Include(e => e.Job)
        .FirstOrDefaultAsync(m => m.Id == id);
    if (employee == null)
    {
        return NotFound();
    }

return View(employee);
}


[HttpPost, ActionName("Delete")]
[ValidateAntiForgeryToken]
public async Task<IActionResult> DeleteConfirmed(int id)
{
    if (_context.Employees == null)
    {
        return Problem("Entity set 'FactoryManagerContext.Employees'  is
null.");
    }
    var employee = await _context.Employees.FindAsync(id);
    if (employee != null)
```

```
    {
        _context.Employees.Remove(employee);
    }


    await _context.SaveChangesAsync();
    return RedirectToAction(nameof(Index));
}
```

So now, we will need to create a Razor view for each **GET** action method we have added to the controller. For this, we will create the **Employees** folder inside the **Views** folder. The first file we will insert will be **Index.cshtml**, the first part of which will look like the following:

```
@model IEnumerable<MvcDataApp.Models.Employee>


@{
    ViewData["Title"] = "Index";
}


<h1>Index</h1>


<p>
    <a asp-action="Create">Create New</a>
</p>
<table class="table">
    <thead>
        <tr>
            <th>
                @Html.DisplayNameFor(model => model.StartDate)
            </th>
            <th>
                @Html.DisplayNameFor(model => model.Job)
            </th>
            <th>
                @Html.DisplayNameFor(model => model.FirstName)
            </th>
            <th>
                @Html.DisplayNameFor(model => model.LastName)
```

```
        </th>
        <th>
            @Html.DisplayNameFor(model => model.DateOfBirth)
        </th>
        <th></th>
    </tr>
</thead>
<tbody>
```

Then, to construct the rows for the table, we can execute the following **foreach** loop:

```
@foreach (var item in Model) {
        <tr>
            <td>
                @Html.DisplayFor(modelItem => item.StartDate)
            </td>
            <td>
                @Html.DisplayFor(modelItem => item.Job.JobId)
            </td>
            <td>
                @Html.DisplayFor(modelItem => item.FirstName)
            </td>
            <td>
                @Html.DisplayFor(modelItem => item.LastName)
            </td>
            <td>
                @Html.DisplayFor(modelItem => item.DateOfBirth)
            </td>
            <td>
                <a asp-action="Edit" asp-route-id="@item.Id">Edit</a> |
                <a asp-action="Details" asp-route-id="@item.Id">Details</a> |
                <a asp-action="Delete" asp-route-id="@item.Id">Delete</a>
            </td>
        </tr>
}
    </tbody>
</table>
```

Then, we will insert **Create.cshtml** file, which will have the following content:

```
@model MvcDataApp.Models.Employee

@{
    ViewData["Title"] = "Create";
}


<h1>Create</h1>

<h4>Employee</h4>
<hr />
<div class="row">
    <div class="col-md-4">
        <form asp-action="Create">
            <div asp-validation-summary="ModelOnly" class="text-
danger"></div>
            <div class="form-group">
                <label asp-for="StartDate" class="control-label"></
label>
                <input asp-for="StartDate" class="form-control" />
                <span asp-validation-for="StartDate" class="text-
danger"></span>
            </div>
            <div class="form-group">
                <label asp-for="JobId" class="control-label"></label>
                <select asp-for="JobId" class ="form-control" asp-
items="ViewBag.JobId"></select>
            </div>
            <div class="form-group">
                <label asp-for="FirstName" class="control-label"></
label>
                <input asp-for="FirstName" class="form-control" />
                <span asp-validation-for="FirstName" class="text-
danger"></span>
            </div>
            <div class="form-group">
                <label asp-for="LastName" class="control-label"></label>
```

```
                    <input asp-for="LastName" class="form-control" />
                    <span asp-validation-for="LastName" class="text-
danger"></span>
                </div>
                <div class="form-group">
                    <label asp-for="DateOfBirth" class="control-label"></
label>
                    <input asp-for="DateOfBirth" class="form-control" />
                    <span asp-validation-for="DateOfBirth" class="text-
danger"></span>
                </div>
                <div class="form-group">
                    <input type="submit" value="Create" class="btn btn-
primary" />
                </div>
            </form>
        </div>
</div>

<div>
    <a asp-action="Index">Back to List</a>
</div>

@section Scripts {
    @{await Html.RenderPartialAsync("_ValidationScriptsPartial");}
}
```

Please note that the name of each of these files is the same as the name of one of the **GET** action methods on the controller, plus the **CSHTML** extension. So, the file for the **Details** action method will look like the following:

```
@model MvcDataApp.Models.Employee

@{
    ViewData["Title"] = "Details";
}


<h1>Details</h1>
```

```
<div>
    <h4>Employee</h4>
    <hr />
    <dl class="row">
        <dt class = "col-sm-2">
            @Html.DisplayNameFor(model => model.StartDate)
        </dt>
        <dd class = "col-sm-10">
            @Html.DisplayFor(model => model.StartDate)
        </dd>
        <dt class = "col-sm-2">
            @Html.DisplayNameFor(model => model.Job)
        </dt>
        <dd class = "col-sm-10">
            @Html.DisplayFor(model => model.Job.JobId)
        </dd>
        <dt class = "col-sm-2">
            @Html.DisplayNameFor(model => model.FirstName)
        </dt>
        <dd class = "col-sm-10">
            @Html.DisplayFor(model => model.FirstName)
        </dd>
        <dt class = "col-sm-2">
            @Html.DisplayNameFor(model => model.LastName)
        </dt>
        <dd class = "col-sm-10">
            @Html.DisplayFor(model => model.LastName)
        </dd>
        <dt class = "col-sm-2">
            @Html.DisplayNameFor(model => model.DateOfBirth)
        </dt>
        <dd class = "col-sm-10">
            @Html.DisplayFor(model => model.DateOfBirth)
        </dd>
    </dl>
</div>
```

```
<div>
    <a asp-action="Edit" asp-route-id="@Model?.Id">Edit</a> |
    <a asp-action="Index">Back to List</a>
</div>
```

The **Edit** view will look like the following:

```
@model MvcDataApp.Models.Employee

@{
    ViewData["Title"] = "Edit";
}


<h1>Edit</h1>


<h4>Employee</h4>
<hr />
```

Then, we will have the following form:

```
<div class="row">
    <div class="col-md-4">
        <form asp-action="Edit">
            <div asp-validation-summary="ModelOnly" class="text-
danger"></div>
            <div class="form-group">
                <label asp-for="StartDate" class="control-label"></
label>
                <input asp-for="StartDate" class="form-control" />
                <span asp-validation-for="StartDate" class="text-
danger"></span>
            </div>
            <div class="form-group">
                <label asp-for="JobId" class="control-label"></label>
                <select asp-for="JobId" class="form-control" asp-
items="ViewBag.JobId"></select>
                <span asp-validation-for="JobId" class="text-danger"></
span>
            </div>
            <input type="hidden" asp-for="Id" />
```

```
            <div class="form-group">
                <label asp-for="FirstName" class="control-label"></
label>
                <input asp-for="FirstName" class="form-control" />
                <span asp-validation-for="FirstName" class="text-
danger"></span>
            </div>
            <div class="form-group">
                <label asp-for="LastName" class="control-label"></label>
                <input asp-for="LastName" class="form-control" />
                <span asp-validation-for="LastName" class="text-
danger"></span>
            </div>
            <div class="form-group">
                <label asp-for="DateOfBirth" class="control-label"></
label>
                <input asp-for="DateOfBirth" class="form-control" />
                <span asp-validation-for="DateOfBirth" class="text-
danger"></span>
            </div>
            <div class="form-group">
                <input type="submit" value="Save" class="btn btn-
primary" />
            </div>
        </form>
    </div>
</div>
```

Then, we would finish off with the following footer:

```
<div>
    <a asp-action="Index">Back to List</a>
</div>

@section Scripts {
    @{await Html.RenderPartialAsync("_ValidationScriptsPartial");}
}
```

The **Delete** view will look like the following:

```
@model MvcDataApp.Models.Employee

@{
    ViewData["Title"] = "Delete";
}


<h1>Delete</h1>

<h3>Are you sure you want to delete this?</h3>
<div>
    <h4>Employee</h4>
    <hr />
    <dl class="row">
        <dt class = "col-sm-2">
            @Html.DisplayNameFor(model => model.StartDate)
        </dt>
        <dd class = "col-sm-10">
            @Html.DisplayFor(model => model.StartDate)
        </dd>
        <dt class = "col-sm-2">
            @Html.DisplayNameFor(model => model.Job)
        </dt>
        <dd class = "col-sm-10">
            @Html.DisplayFor(model => model.Job.JobId)
        </dd>
        <dt class = "col-sm-2">
            @Html.DisplayNameFor(model => model.FirstName)
        </dt>
        <dd class = "col-sm-10">
            @Html.DisplayFor(model => model.FirstName)
        </dd>
        <dt class = "col-sm-2">
            @Html.DisplayNameFor(model => model.LastName)
        </dt>
        <dd class = "col-sm-10">
```

```
            @Html.DisplayFor(model => model.LastName)
        </dd>
        <dt class = "col-sm-2">
            @Html.DisplayNameFor(model => model.DateOfBirth)
        </dt>
        <dd class = "col-sm-10">
            @Html.DisplayFor(model => model.DateOfBirth)
        </dd>
    </dl>

    <form asp-action="Delete">
        <input type="hidden" asp-for="Id" />
        <input type="submit" value="Delete" class="btn btn-danger" /> |
        <a asp-action="Index">Back to List</a>
    </form>
</div>
```

A basic MVC application is now complete and is fully capable of manipulating **Employee** data. To test it, we can launch the application and navigate to the **Employees** tab. We should see the page shown in *figure 6.9*. If we click on any links, we should be taken to an appropriate view, whether it is **Edit**, **Details**, or **Delete**.

MvcDataApp   Home   Privacy   Employees

Index

Create New

StartDate	Job	FirstName	LastName	DateOfBirth	
01/09/2020 00:00:00	1	John	Smith	01/10/1992 00:00:00	Edit | Details | Delete
01/09/2017 00:00:00	2	Alexander	Marshall	12/09/1982 00:00:00	Edit | Details | Delete
01/09/2010 00:00:00	2	Michael	Davidson	11/05/1989 00:00:00	Edit | Details | Delete

Figure 6.9: The Index view of the Employees controller

This concludes the overview of the ASP.NET Core MVC application template. Next, we will have a look at the final ASP.NET Core application template that has a user interface—Razor Pages.

Razor Pages on ASP.NET Core

Unlike MVC, Razor Pages applications are not specifically designed for working with data. While they can work with data, they are more flexible than MVC, as each page is a semi-autonomous unit that has its own back-end logic. So, while Razor Pages allow more flexibility, they probably are not as easy to work with as MVC when an application needs to be specifically designed for facilitating **Create, Read, Update, Delete (CRUD)** operations via the user interface.

To create a Razor Pages application, we can either select the ASP.NET Core Razor Pages template while creating a new project via the GUI or execute the following command via the CLI:

```
dotnet new web -o RazorPagesApp
```

The structure of our project will be similar to what is displayed in *figure 6.10*:

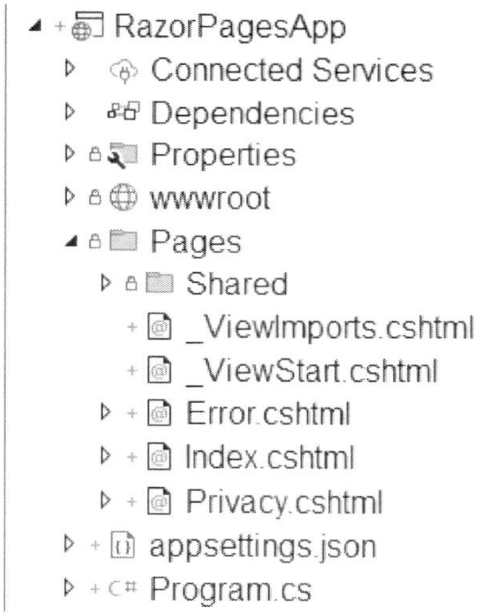

```
◢ + 🗔 RazorPagesApp
   ▷   ⊛ Connected Services
   ▷   🗗 Dependencies
   ▷ 🔒🗔 Properties
   ▷ 🔒⊕ wwwroot
   ◢ 🔒🗀 Pages
      ▷ 🔒🗀 Shared
         + 🗟 _ViewImports.cshtml
         + 🗟 _ViewStart.cshtml
      ▷ + 🗟 Error.cshtml
      ▷ + 🗟 Index.cshtml
      ▷ + 🗟 Privacy.cshtml
   ▷ + 🗓 appsettings.json
   ▷ + C# Program.cs
```

Figure 6.10: The structure of a Razor Pages project

In this project type, instead of having **Models**, **Views**, and **Controllers** folders, we have a folder called **Pages**. Just like in the MVC template, we have some common layout components that are located in the **Shared** folder inside the **Pages** folder. Just like with the MVC views, the files representing pages have the CSHTML extension and use Razor syntax. But this is where the similarities end. In Razor Pages, a page can have the so-called **code-bihind** file, which has the same name as the file representing the page but has an extra CS extension. So, for the **Index.cshtml** file, the code-behind file is called **Index.cshtml.cs**.

Code-behind file is a pure C# file, so you can do anything in it that you can do in any other C# class, such as pass dependencies to it via the constructor and have any kind of business logic. In the context of Razor Pages, such a class that inherits from **PageModel** can be fully referenced from the Razor code in the page.

When a client requests a page in a Razor Pages application, certain events get triggered in code-behind files in a particular order. There are also some methods that get executed by convention. These methods have the following names:

```
On<Pascal-case version of a HTTP verb>
```

So, if a **GET** request gets submitted to the page, the **OnGet** method will be triggered. If a **POST** request is submitted, the **OnPost** method is triggered, and so on. We can apply some additional logic to these methods. For example, if we would replace the content of the **Index.cshtml.cs** file with this, a session Id will be recorded as a debug message in the logs:

```
using Microsoft.AspNetCore.Mvc.RazorPages;

namespace RazorPagesApp.Pages;

public class IndexModel : PageModel
{
    private readonly ILogger<IndexModel> _logger;

    public IndexModel(ILogger<IndexModel> logger)
    {
        _logger = logger;
    }

    public void OnGet()
    {
        _logger.LogDebug($"Homepage requested. Session id: {HttpContext.Session.Id}");
    }
}
```

Please note that the implementation of the **ILogger** constructor parameter is configured in the dependency injection pipeline. This object allows us to log the information. We can register our own implementation if we need to.

This concludes the overview of all ASP.NET Core templates. Let us summarize what we have learned in this chapter.

Conclusion

In this chapter, we have learned all the fundamentals of ASP.NET Core. We have covered all available project templates of ASP.NET Core: empty, MVC, Web API, and Razor pages. We have covered the fundamental structure of ASP.NET Core applications, such as its start-up script, which includes dependency registration and request processing middleware. We have also covered the ASP.NET Core hosting model and the process of hosting it in a development environment.

We had a look at MVC project templates that allow developers to build display components separately from the back-end business logic and the database access. We also had a look at Web API templates, which are used for building Web services with REST API endpoints. Finally, we had a look at Razor Pages, which allows developers to have individual back-end logic for every page.

We have also covered the new features that have been added to version 7 of ASP.NET Core, such as improvements to the caching mechanism.

In the upcoming chapter, we will cover Blazor, which allows developers to build compiled .NET applications that can run inside browsers.

Points to remember

- ASP.NET Core is the main Web application development framework available on .NET.

- Any ASP.NET Core will have dependency registration and chained request processing middleware in its start-up code.

- ASP.NET Core comes with four main project templates by default: empty, MVC, Web API, and Razor Pages.

- Empty project template provides just the most bare-bone plumbing for Web application development, allowing the developers to add only those components that they would strictly need.

- MVC template uses Model-View-Controller architectural pattern.

- Web API template is primarily designed for building REST APIs.

- Razor Pages template comprises of Web page templates, each of which may also have the so-called code-behind file associated with it.

Multiple choice questions

1. **What is the difference between controllers in Web API and controllers in MVC?**

    a. There is no difference, and they are fully equivalent

    b. MVC controllers are designed for serving views, while Web API controllers will only return data

    c. There are no controllers in Web API

    d. Web API controllers can return data, whereas MVC controllers cannot

2. **What is Razor in the context of razor pages?**

    a. A language that can be used in the back-end of the application instead of C#

    b. The name of the dependency injection framework used by Razor pages

    c. A language that is designed for writing front-end templates

    d. It is just an arbitrary name of the application template

3. **What is the Services property of the builder object is used for in the ASP. NET Core start-up script?**

    a. To register required services, that is, objects that other objects depend on

    b. To provide the request processing middleware

    c. To connect the application to any external Web services

    d. To initiate background tasks

4. **What is the request processing middleware of ASP.NET Core is used for?**

    a. To enforce authentication

    b. To enforce authorization

    c. To provide a chain of processing steps that the request must go through before reaching its intended target

    d. All of the above

Answers

1. b
2. c
3. a
4. d

Key terms

- **ASP.NET Core**: The main Web application development framework on .NET.

- **Model-View-Controller (MVC)**: An architectural pattern where Views are responsible for display logic, Models are responsible for business logic and back-end data manipulation, and Controllers are responsible for bringing these types of components together.

- **Representational state transfer (REST)**: A type of Web services interface that allows the client applications to exchange data with Web services, typically by using JSON.

- **Web API**: An ASP.NET Core application template designed for building Web services with REST API.

- **Minimal API**: A type of Web API application development practice that does not use Controller classes.

- **Razor pages**: An ASP.NET Core application template that allows developers to build individual Web page templates with individual back-end logic.

- **Dependency injection**: The process of registering required services (such as classes) when the application starts up.

- **Request processing middleware**: A configurable chain of processing steps applied to an incoming request in a specific order before it can reach its intended target.

Join our book's Discord space

Join the book's Discord Workspace for Latest updates, Offers, Tech happenings around the world, New Release and Sessions with the Authors:

https://discord.bpbonline.com

CHAPTER 7

Blazor and WebAssembly on .NET

Introduction

Not very long ago, the only way to run a compiled high-performance application in your browser was to install a special plugin. Even then, the plugin would only be compatible with a specific application type. For instance, you needed a Java plugin to run Java applications, an Adobe Flash plugin to run Flash applications, and Microsoft Silverlight to run .NET Framework applications. The only other option was to run JavaScript code, which is interpreted rather than compiled, so it cannot reach the level of compiled code in terms of performance.

But it all changed with the introduction of WebAssembly, which became a standard feature of all browsers. WebAssembly is a binary instruction format for compiled applications. Essentially, just like with the standard Assembly language, the source code gets compiled into this format ahead of time. Because the application consists of low-level instructions, it is faster to execute than JavaScript, which is stored in its textual form and gets interpreted into executable instructions as it is being read.

.NET has its own implementation of WebAssembly called Blazor. This allows developers to write in-browser applications in C#. So, while having the ability to build high-performance applications for browsers, .NET developers can also do full-stack development without having to learn JavaScript and its countless modern frameworks.

But Blazor is bigger than just a technology that facilitates the process of turning .NET code into WebAssembly. It also provides an easy way of hosting your WebAssembly apps inside the standard ASP.NET Core applications. There is also a variety of Blazor known as Blazor Server. If you choose to use it, your code will be identical to Blazor WebAssembly code. But the compiler will do something different with it. Your compiled code will be running on the server, but the browser and the server will be communicating with each other in real-time, so the elements on the page will instantly react to the events happening on the server. And the code on the server can be instantly triggered by events in the browser.

In this chapter, we will cover all these concepts. We will also highlight the new Blazor features that were added in .NET 7.

Structure

In this chapter, we will discuss the latest features of Blazor on ASP.NET Core 7 and cover the following topics:

- Introducing Blazor
- Blazor WebAssembly overview
- Hosting Blazor WebAssembly in ASP.NET Core
- Setting up Blazor Server

Objectives

By the end of this chapter, you will have learned how to use .NET Blazor in all its form. You will be familiar with building stand-alone Blazor WebAssembly applications. You will also learn how to host a Blazor WebAssembly application inside a standard ASP.NET Core application. You will know how and when to use Blazor Server and will be familiar with the most recent features of Blazor.

Prerequisites

To follow this chapter, you will need the following:

- A machine running either Windows, MacOS, or Linux OS
- .NET 7 SDK
- A suitable IDE or a code editor
- Being familiar with C# fundamentals

If you do not have any of the preceding listed dependencies installed already, refer to the setup instruction provided in *Chapter 1: Getting Familiar with .NET 7 Application Structure*, which also provides a recap of C# fundamentals.

Introducing Blazor

Blazor comes in two flavors—Blazor WebAssembly and Blazor Server. Each has its own distinct project template and compiles differently. While Blazor Server is nothing more than a server-hosted ASP.NET Core Web application with some additional libraries, Blazor WebAssembly compiles into an executable that is hosted entirely in a browser.

But, despite the differences in the application structure, both flavors of Blazor share exactly the same syntax in its modules, which are referred as Razor Components. These are not to be confused with Razor Pages. Both are used to generate HTML that gets then rendered in the browser. But while Razor Pages have **.cshtml** file extension, the extension of Razor Components is .razor. Also, even though both types of modules work with Razor syntax, there are some keywords that only work in Razor Components and do not work in Razor Pages. The reverse is also true for some other keywords. For example, the **@code** keyword is only applicable to Razor Components, whereas the **@model** keyword is only applicable to Razor Pages.

Razor Components refer to other Razor Components in a similar manner as how HTML elements are referenced. There are opening and closing tags, and you can put some further content inside the elements like you can do with HTML and XML. You can also use properties of elements in a similar manner to HTML attributes. But the naming conventions are different. If you would normally use lowercase letters to write HTML elements, Razor Components use PascalCase, that is, every word starting with a capital letter while all other letters remain the same. For example, if there was a Razor Component called **Counter** and it had a property called **IncrementBy**, then it would be referenced inside other Razor Components as follows:

```
<Counter IncrementBy="5" />
```

Let us now have a look at some examples of Razor components to see how they are structured.

Razor component example

When you create a new application project from either Blazor WebAssembly or Blazor Server template, it will have some Razor components already present as examples. Both projects will have **Counter.razor** file inside the **Pages** folder, which will have the following content:

```
@page "/counter"

<PageTitle>Counter</PageTitle>

<h1>Counter</h1>

<p role="status">Current count: @currentCount</p>

<button class="btn btn-primary" @onclick="IncrementCount">Click me</
button>

@code {
    private int currentCount = 0;

    private void IncrementCount()
    {
        currentCount++;
    }
}
```

Let us break it down.

@page

The first thing that we have is the **@page** directive. This directive represents the path that the component is reachable on by default. So, in this case, if you would type the base application URL followed by the /counter path, your browser will take you to this component.

Next, we have a reference to the **PageTitle** Razor component with its inner content set to **Counter**. We can tell that it is a Razor component based on the fact that it looks similar to an HTML/XML element while it has a name in PascalCase.

Next, we have a paragraph element that has part of its text bound to the **currentCount** field. If we have a look inside the **@code** directive further down, there is a private integer field with this name. Please note that the markup in a Razor Component has full access to private members of its code. So, whenever the value of the **currentCount** will be changed in the code, the content inside the paragraph element will be updated too.

@onclick

Next, we have a button with the **@onclick** event handler. As before, we can tell that this is a Razor event handler because it starts with the @ symbol. This event handler refers to the **IncrementCount** method inside the **@code** directive. When this button is clicked, the method is triggered.

@code

Finally, we have the @code directive, which represents the C# code that we can trigger from our markup. If we had any members with public access modifier and **[Parameter]** attribute, then we could access those members from other Razor components. However, we can also access this code from our normal C# code. Each Razor component is represented as a class that inherits from **ComponentBase** from **Microsoft.AspNetCore.Components** namespace. The class will have the same name as the file. In this case, since the file is called **Counter.razor**, the class will be accessible as **Counter**. Inside other Razor components, you can reference it as **<Counter />**.

A Razor Component does not represent the entire page. Just like Razor Pages and MVC views, it is wrapped in a shared layout. It is the layout that has all the remaining page elements, such as HTML headers and navigation menu. However, the format of the layouts is different depending on whether you are using Blazor WebAssembly or Blazor Server project template. We will go over both variants later in the chapter. For now, let us go through all keywords that are used in Razor components.

Razor keywords in Razor components

We already covered **@page**, **@onclick**, and **@code** directives. We also had a look at how a single @ character can reference something inside plain C# code. So let us have a look at some other keywords you can use inside Razor components.

@using

In the context of Razor components, this keyword is used for inserting namespaces into the **@code** block in the same manner as using keyword is used for inserting namespace references into C# classes. The statements with this directive go just under the **@page** directive. Here is an example of such a statement:

```
@using HostedBlazorWasmDemo.Client.Models;
```

@implements

This directive is used if you want your Razor component to implement an interface. For example, you will use this directive as follows if you want to implement an

IDisposable interface:

@implements IDisposable

@inherits

You can use this directive if you want to inherit your Razor component from a specific C# class. This is how it can be applied:

@inherits SomeBaseClass

@inject

This directive is used for adding any dependencies into a Razor component that is registered in **Program.cs** file when the application starts up. The following example injects a **NavigationManager** instance into the component:

@inject NavigationManager

@layout

This directive specifies a layout component that can be applied to the Razor component. Even though there is an application-wide layout typically configured, this directive allows to apply a specific set of reusable elements to a specific Razor component. This is how this directive is used on top of a Razor component:

@layout CustomLayout

@namespace

This directive allows us to override the default namespace of a Razor component (which corresponds to the project folder structure) and set a specific namespace for it. This is how it can be used:

@namespace SomeNamespace

@preservewhitespace

By default, Blazor trims unnecessary whitespaces from the HTML markup to increase the performance. However, if whitespaces need to be preserved, this is how it can be achieved:

@preservewhitespace true

@attributes

This directive allows the dynamic insertion of any arbitrary HTML attributes into an HTML element from a C# dictionary. For example, we may have the following element:

```
<input id="mainText" @attributes="Attributes" />
```

We can have a dictionary field that looks similar to the following:

```
private Dictionary<string, object> Attributes { get; set; } =
        new()
        {
            { "maxlength", "10" },
            { "placeholder", "Default value" },
            { "required", "required" },
            { "class", "green-textbox" }
        };
```

@bind

This keyword allows you to bind an HTML element to a variable from C# code. If you apply it, changing the input value will change the value of the variable and vice versa. For example, if you have a **string** variable called name, you can bind it to an input element as follows:

```
<input @bind="name" />
```

@ref

This directive is used when you want to send commands to a specific reference of another Razor component. To use it, you will need to use the target Razor component as a variable in your code and then use the name of the variable with the keyword in your markup.

For example, if you had a Razor Component called **ChildComponent**, you could declare it as a private field inside your **@code** directive as follows:

```
private ReferenceChild? child;
```

Then, declare it in the markup to make sure that you refer to this specific field rather than a new instance of this component:

```
<ReferenceChild @ref="child" />
```

@typeparam

This directive allows you to use generics inside your Razor components. This is an example of its usage:

```
@typeparam TEntity where TEntity : class
```

This concludes the basic overview of features that are applicable to both Blazor WebAssembly and Blazor Server. Now, we will have a look at the process of setting up a Blazor WebAssembly project.

Blazor WebAssembly overview

We can create a new Blazor WebAssembly project either from the corresponding template in the IDE or by running the following command, which will create a project with the name of **BlazorWasmDemo**:

```
dotnet new blazorwasm -o BlazorWasmDemo
```

WASM is a commonly used abbreviation for WebAssembly. So, this is why we used it in the proceeding command.

Once the project is created, let us have a look at its structure. The first thing that we will look at is the topmost layout, which is provided by the **index.html** file inside the **wwwroot** folder. This plain HTML file provides the structure to the Blazor WebAssembly application; it is used as an outer shell by all Blazor Components. This is where HTML headers are defined, along with any placeholder elements, additional scripts, and style references.

A noteworthy script reference is a reference to the **_framework/blazor. webassembly.js** file. This file provides all JavaScript that is needed for rendering client-side Razor Components and providing interop functionality between them and plain JavaScript. Therefore, if you need to add any JavaScript that is meant to work alongside Blazor, you will need to add this code (or a reference to a JS file) after this scrip file reference.

Next, we have **_Imports.razor** file in the root of the project folder. This file is needed for listing any namespaces that we want to make available for import into Razor Components.

Then, there is **App.razor** file, which acts as the root element of the Blazor application itself. This is the file which determines what layout file is used and what to display if the path specified in the browser does not match with any Razor Component. Additionally, this is the file where you would add custom logic for other error responses, such as the user not being authorized. This file is registered inside **Program.cs** file and is inserted into an appropriate HTML element on the following line:

```
builder.RootComponents.Add<App>("#app");
```

By default, this will be an element where the id attribute is set to the app inside the index.html file.

By default, the **App.razor** file points at the **MainLayout** as the layout component. This layout can be found in the **MainLayour.razor** file inside the **Shared** folder. This will be the default layout Razor components will use unless it is overwritten with the **@layout** directive. The layout has some top-level HTML and Razor elements. The content of the Razor component that we navigate to will be replace the **@Body** directive in the layout.

Then, we have the individual Razor components. These are placed inside the **Pages** folder and have a Razor extension. Other than that, the **entrypoint** into the compiled part of a Blazor WebAssembly app is **Program.cs**, just like in most .NET application types.

This concludes the overview of the basic Blazor WebAssembly project structure. So far, we have covered scenarios where both the markup and the code are placed in the same file. But when you have a complex markup and complex code, this arrangement does not necessarily ensure the best readability. So, Blazor allows you to split the markup and the code into separate files. This is known as code-behind approach. This is what we will have a look at next.

Using code-behind approach

If you want to move the C# code from the Razor file into a separate file, you will need to create the file with the same name as your Razor file but give it an additional CS extension. To demonstrate this, we will split the content of the **FetchData.razor** file into two separate files. To do so, we will create **FetchData.razor.cs** file alongside our original **FetchData.razor** file and will populate it with the following content:

```
using Microsoft.AspNetCore.Components;
using System.Net.Http.Json;


namespace BlazorWasmDemo.Pages;


public class FetchDataBase : ComponentBase
{
    [Inject] HttpClient Http { get; set; }

    protected WeatherForecast[]? forecasts;

    protected override async Task OnInitializedAsync()
    {
        forecasts =
await Http.GetFromJsonAsync<WeatherForecast[]>
("sample-data/weather.json");
```

```
    }

    public class WeatherForecast
    {
        public DateOnly Date { get; set; }

        public int TemperatureC { get; set; }

        public string? Summary { get; set; }

        public int TemperatureF => 32 + (int)(TemperatureC / 0.5556);
    }
}
```

We are inheriting from **ComponentBase** class because every Razor component must inherit from **ComponentBase**. Please note that we have also called our class **FetchDataBase**, which is different from our original **FetchData** component. This is because Blazor would still treat these two files as two separate classes. The implementation of code-behind functionality is performed via inheritance. This is also why we have changed the access modifier on all members from private to protected.

Please note the field with the **[Inject]** attribute. This attribute is used for injecting services into code-behind files of Razor components instead of using the constructor injection. This attribute is equivalent to using **@inject** in Razor components.

In this class, we are loading some data from the **weather.json** file that can be found in the **sample-data** folder when the component is initiated. The content of the file is as follows:

```
[
  {
    "date": "2022-01-06",
    "temperatureC": 1,
    "summary": "Freezing"
  },
  {
    "date": "2022-01-07",
    "temperatureC": 14,
    "summary": "Bracing"
```

```
  },
  {
    "date": "2022-01-08",
    "temperatureC": -13,
    "summary": "Freezing"
  },
  {
    "date": "2022-01-09",
    "temperatureC": -16,
    "summary": "Balmy"
  },
  {
    "date": "2022-01-10",
    "temperatureC": -2,
    "summary": "Chilly"
  }
]
```

Now, we will replace the content of the **FetchData.razor** file with the following:

```
@page "/fetchdata"
@inherits FetchDataBase

<PageTitle>Weather forecast</PageTitle>

<h1>Weather forecast</h1>

<p>This component demonstrates fetching data from the server.</p>

@if (forecasts == null)
{
    <p><em>Loading...</em></p>
}
else
{
    <table class="table">
        <thead>
```

```
        <tr>
            <th>Date</th>
            <th>Temp. (C)</th>
            <th>Temp. (F)</th>
            <th>Summary</th>
        </tr>
    </thead>
    <tbody>
        @foreach (var forecast in forecasts)
        {
            <tr>
                <td>@forecast.Date.ToShortDateString()</td>
                <td>@forecast.TemperatureC</td>
                <td>@forecast.TemperatureF</td>
                <td>@forecast.Summary</td>
            </tr>
        }
    </tbody>
</table>
}
```

As we can see, the entire **@code** section has been removed. And the file now inherits from the **FetchDataBase** class. Otherwise, it is functionally identical to what it was before.

Another interesting feature of Blazor is its ability to interoperate with JavaScript on your Web page, which we will have a look at next.

JavaScript Interop

JavaScript interop functionality in Blazor allows both the C# code to call JavaScript methods and the JavaScript code to call C# methods. Let us demonstrate how it works. First, we will add the following script element to the **index.html** file from the **wwwroot** folder anywhere below the reference to the Blazor JavaScript library:

```
<script>
window.displayAlert = () => {
    alert('Counter successfully increased');
}
</script>
```

Please note that the **displayAlert** method is added to the scope of the window. This is the scope Blazor works with. Otherwise, the method would be unreachable to Blazor code.

Then, we will open the **Counter.razor** file in the **Pages** folder and will replace its content with the following:

```
@page "/counter"
@inject IJSRuntime JS


<PageTitle>Counter</PageTitle>


<h1>Counter</h1>


<p role="status">Current count: @currentCount</p>


<button class="btn btn-primary" @onclick="IncrementCount">Click me</button>


@code {
    private int currentCount = 0;

    private async Task IncrementCount()
    {
        currentCount++;

        await JS.InvokeVoidAsync("displayAlert");
    }
}
```

To make the JavaScript interop work, we have injected an **IJSRuntime** object, which is registered automatically alongside all other Blazor dependencies. This service allows us to call any suitable JavaScript method. In our case, we are calling the **displayAlert** method via **InvokeVoidAsync** because it does not return any value. However, if we wanted to extract a value from a JavaScript method, we would use **InvokeAsync** instead. Also, if the JavaScript method accepts any parameters, we would pass them after the method name. For example, if we had a method called **getFullName** that accepted two string parameters and returned a string, we would call it in the following manner:

```
var fullName = await JS.InvokeAsync<string>("getFullName", "John",
"Smith");
```

To call a C# method from JavaScript, the method must be a public static task with **[JSInvokable]** attribute. Then, to invoke this method from JavaScript, you will need to use **DotNet** object, which is available in the Blazor JavaScript library. The call needs to be constructed as follows:

```
DotNet.invokeMethodAsync('{Namespace Name}', '{.NET Method Name}',
{parameters});
```

Next, we will have a look at how to pass parameters from a Razor component to its child components.

Passing parameters to Razor components

To pass parameters from one Razor Component to its child component, the type representing the child component needs to be public and marked with the **[Parameter]** attribute. For example, we can change the increment logic in our **Counter** component. Instead of getting it to increment by one, we can make it increase by a custom number when the button is clicked. To do so, we have modified the content of the component by adding the **IncrementBy** property to it, which is marked with the **[Parameter]** attribute:

```
<PageTitle>Counter</PageTitle>


<h1>Counter</h1>


<p role="status">Current count: @currentCount</p>


<button class="btn btn-primary" @onclick="IncrementCount">Click me</
button>

@code {
    private int currentCount = 0;

    private async Task IncrementCount()
    {
        currentCount += IncrementBy;


        await JS.InvokeVoidAsync("displayAlert");
    }
```

```
    [Parameter]
    public int IncrementBy { get; set; } = 1;
}
```

Now, all we need to do is just set the value of this property the same way we set attribute values in HTML. To demonstrate this, we will change the content of our **Index.razor** file to the following:

```
@page "/"


<Counter IncrementBy="5" />
```

Now, if we launch our application, the **Counter** component will be displayed on the homepage. And if we click the button, the number will increase by one.

So far, we have only looked at the examples that used the default compilation mechanism for Blazor WebAssembly: compilation into .NET **Intermediate Language (IL)**, which uses **just-in-time (JIT)** compilation into the machine instructions when the code is run. So, when the application runs, every piece of its logic is interpreted into low-level machine instruction as it is being read.

But there is also another compilation mechanism that can be used in Blazor WebAssembly: **Ahead-of-Time (AoT)** compilation, which we will look at next.

Ahead-of-time compilation

Ahead-of-time compilation ensures that the application is pre-compiled into a set of hardware-specific instructions. So, there is no intermediate language and no per-instruction interpretation. The hardware already understands how to run everything inside the executable directly.

Because there is no intermediate interpretation step, the execution of such an application is quicker. However, there is also a downside. The process of preparing the executable for specific hardware will make the file larger. Hence, the initial download of the file will be longer.

To prepare your development environment, you will need to install **wasm-tools** workload, which can be done by executing the following command in the terminal:

```
dotnet workload install wasm-tools
```

Next, we will need to add the following section to the **.csproj** file:

```
<PropertyGroup>
  <RunAOTCompilation>true</RunAOTCompilation>
</PropertyGroup>
```

Since AoT compilation creates a self-contained executable that no longer relies on any external .NET dependencies, you cannot run it in **Debug** mode. Therefore, to compile your project into an executable, you will need to publish it in **Release** mode. This can be done by executing the following command from the project folder:

```
dotnet publish -c Release
```

Next, we will briefly cover an alternative Blazor WebAssembly project template that you can use.

Empty Blazor WebAssembly template

If you use the default Blazor WebAssembly project template, it will give you all the dependencies and examples that you need. But then you will have to remove all the default Razor Components because they have been intended purely for demonstration purposes and do not provide any useful functionality.

But, if you are already familiar with Blazor, you can just initiate an empty Blazor project that does not have any of these demo components. The template is called **blazorwasm-empty** and can be applied to a new project by executing the following command:

```
dotnet new blazorwasm-empty -o EmptyBlazorWasm
```

Once created, the project will have fewer files than the original Blazor WebAssembly project. The difference is demonstrated in *figure 7.1*:

Figure 7.1: *The difference between the default Blazor WebAssembly project and an empty project*

So far, we have covered Blazor WebAssembly as a stand-alone, self-contained application. But we can also host it inside an ASP.NET Core application and make it load automatically as one of its views.

Hosting Blazor WebAssembly in ASP.NET Core

It is possible to create a Blazor WebAssembly project that will be hosted in an ASP.NET Core application. All you have to do is select such an option while creating a project from this template. Or you can specify **--hosted** flag to the CLI command. For example, to create a hosted Blazor WebAssembly application called **HostedBlazorWasmDemo**, we can execute the following command:

```
dotnet new blazorwasm -o HostedBlazorWasmDemo --hosted
```

This command will create a solution called **HostedBlazorWasmDemo**. There will be three project folders placed inside these folders: **Client**, **Server**, and **Shared**:

- Client is our Blazor WebAssembly application.

- Sever is the ASP.NET Core application that hosts WebAssembly.

- Shared is a class library that contains components used by both applications.

When a Blazor WebAssembly is hosted by ASP.NET Core, it is the ASP.NET Core project that you will need to bring up to see the entire setup in action. You will no longer need to run the Blazor application on its own. So, in our specific case, it is the project inside the Server folder that needs to be run to bring up both the server and the WebAssembly.

We can also add a hosted Blazor WebAssembly application to an existing ASP.NET Core application. We can have a look at our project structure to find out how to do it.

Adding a hoster Blazor WebAssembly to an existing ASP.NET core application

To host a Blazor WebAssembly application, you need to have the following NuGet package installed in your ASP.NET Core application:

```
Microsoft.AspNetCore.Components.WebAssembly.Server
```

Then, you will need to reference the Blazor WebAssembly project from the ASP. NET Core application to ensure that the WebAssembly is available before the server application is ready. For example, our **HostedBlazorWasmDemo.Server.csproj** file has a reference to **HostedBlazorWasmDemo.Client** project.

Then, you will need to enable WebAssembly hosting by adding the following line to the **Program.cs** file of the ASP.NET Core project:

```
app.UseBlazorFrameworkFiles();
```

Then, if you do not have any default index page configured in your server application, Blazor WeBAssembly will take over and will be your index page. Otherwise, if the Blazor application is not meant to be on the homepage, you will need to add a `.cshtml` file for the Razor Page or the MVC view that you want to host your Blazor application in and add the following content to it:

```
@using { name of the Blazor application namespace that hosts the
component that you need };

  <component type="typeof({ name of the Razor Component you want to host
})"
                  render-mode="WebAssemblyPrerendered" />
  <script src="_framework/blazor.webassembly.js"></script>
```

This concludes the basic overview of hosting a Blazor application inside an ASP. NET Core project. Since such a setup uses both the client-side and the server-side components, now is an appropriate time to talk about Blazor forms and their validation.

Form validation in Blazor

In Blazor, you can use forms to post editable data to the server, just like you can do so in standard HTML pages. The data can also be validated with validation attributes, which are custom classes that can perform any validation logic. These classes inherit from **ValidationAttribute** class of the **System.ComponentModel. DataAnnotations** namespace. Since .NET 7, you can also pass services into these classes from dependency injection.

Let us create a **MaxIncrementValidator.cs** file inside our **Client** project folder and populate it with the following content:

```
using System.ComponentModel.DataAnnotations;

namespace HostedBlazorWasmDemo.Client;

public class MaxIncrementValidator : ValidationAttribute
{
    protected override ValidationResult? IsValid(object? value,
ValidationContext validationContext)
    {
        var paramValuesConfig = validationContext.
GetRequiredService<ParamValuesConfig>();

        if ((int)value > paramValuesConfig.MaxIncrementValue)
            return new ValidationResult($"Values greater than
```

```
{paramValuesConfig.MaxIncrementValue
                } are not allowed!", new[] { validationContext.
MemberName });

        return ValidationResult.Success;
    }
}


public class ParamValuesConfig
{
    public int MaxIncrementValue { get; set; } = 5;
}
```

In this class, we are checking that an integer value is not greater than a specific amount. The amount we compare it against is extracted from an instance of the **ParamValuesConfig** service and is 5 by default. We resolve this service via the **ValidationContext** parameter. To register this service, we just need to add the following line to the **Program.cs** file:

```
builder.Services.AddScoped<ParamValuesConfig>();
```

Next, we will need to add a model to our form so we can then apply this attribute to. In our example, we will create a **Models** folder inside the project and add **CounterModel.cs** file to it with the following content:

```
namespace HostedBlazorWasmDemo.Client.Models;


public class CounterModel
{
    [MaxIncrementValidator]
    public int IncrementBy { get; set; } = 1;
}
```

As you can see, we have an integer field called **IncrementBy**. This is the field to which we are applying the attribute.

Next, we will replace the content of the **Counter.razor** file with the following:

```
@page "/counter"
@using HostedBlazorWasmDemo.Client.Models;


<PageTitle>Counter</PageTitle>
```

```
<h1>Counter</h1>

<p role="status">Current count: @currentCount</p>

<button class="btn btn-primary" @onclick="IncrementCount">Click me</button>

<EditForm Model="@counterModel" >
    <DataAnnotationsValidator />
    <ValidationSummary />
    <label for="incrementBy">Increment by:</label>
    <InputNumber id="incrementBy" @bind-Value="counterModel.IncrementBy" />
</EditForm>
```

In here, we have **EditForm** Razor component, which represents a Blazor form. Inside of it, we have **DataAnnotationsValidator** and **ValidationSummary** components, which provide the ability to validate the form and display the validation error. There is an **InputNumber** Razor component, which we are binding to the **IncrementBy** field of the **CounterModel** instance.

Now, we will need to make some changes to our **@code** block. It will need to look as follows:

```
@code {

    private CounterModel counterModel = new();

    private int currentCount = 0;

    private async Task IncrementCount()
    {
        currentCount += counterModel.IncrementBy;
    }
}
```

Now, if we build and launch our **Server** project and navigate to the **Counter** page, we can test our validation logic. If we enter any number into the **IncrementBy** field higher than 5, we should see a validation error, as shown in *figure 7.2*:

Figure 7.2: Validation error on Blazor form

This concludes the overview of form validation in Blazor. Now, we will have a look at its navigation functionality and the ability to pass state from one Razor component to the next.

NavigationManager and passing state between pages

Blazor comes with **NavigationManager** class, which allows to navigate from one page to another. As of .NET version 7, you can also use it to pass information between the pages.

To demonstrate it, we have replaced the content of the **Index.razor** component with the following:

```
@page "/"
@inject NavigationManager NavigationManager

<button class="btn btn-primary" @onclick="NavigateToCounterComponent">
    Go to Counter
</button>

@code {

    private void NavigateToCounterComponent()
    {
        NavigationManager.NavigateTo("counter",
            new NavigationOptions
```

```
{
HistoryEntryState = "Navigated here from Index page"
});
    }

}
```

So, our index page now has a button that will redirect to the **Counter** page. The **Counter** page is expected to receive the message that says Navigated here from the Index page.

Now, we would make some changes to the **Counter.razor** file to see if it worked. First, we will inject the **NavgiationManager** instance into it by placing the following statement immediately underneath the **@using** directive:

```
@inject NavigationManager NavigationManager
```

Then, we will add the following element anywhere in the markup area:

```
<p>History entry state: @NavigationManager.HistoryEntryState</p>
```

Now, if we launch the **Server** application and click on the newly added navigation button on the homepage, we should see the **Counter** element with the message passed from the **Index** page, as demonstrated in *figure 7.3*:

Counter

History entry state: Navigated here from Index page

Current count: 0

[Click me]

Increment by: 1

Figure 7.3: Navigation state passed from another Razor component

This concludes the overview of a hosted Blazor WebAssembly. Now, we will go through the basics of Blazor Server and will demonstrate some additional Blazor features.

Setting up Blazor Server

We will now create a Blazor Server project called BlazorServerDemo. We can either do so via the Blazor Server project template in the IDE or by executing the following CLI command:

```
dotnet new blazorserver -o BlazorServerDemo
```

Once created, we can have a look at how this project is different from our Blazor WebAssembly in its structure. The first thing we should note is that this project is nothing more than a standard ASP.NET Core application with some additional Blazor dependencies added to it. It runs from the server. You can add any standard ASP.NET Core components to it, such as MVC components, Razor Pages, API controllers, and so on.

The Blazor Server components are configured by adding the following line to the **Program.cs** file:

```
builder.Services.AddServerSideBlazor();
```

And adding the following steps to the middleware pipeline:

```
app.MapBlazorHub();
app.MapFallbackToPage("/_Host");
```

There are some other differences in the project structure too. As you may have noticed, there is no **index.html** file inside the **wwwroot** folder. Instead, the base-level HTML is located inside the **_Host.cshtml** file, which is located inside the **Pages** folder. As you may have noticed, the name of this file is the default parameter inside the **app.MapFallbackToPage** call from the **Program.cs** file.

The rest of the structure is similar to that in a Blazor WebAssembly project. **App. razor** is the **root** element of the Blazor application. **MainLayout.razor** in the **Shared** folder is the default layout, and so on.

The Razor Components themselves use the same syntax as they do in a Blazor WebAssembly project. This is why you can reference Blazor class libraries from both Blazor application types. But these components are no longer compiled into browser-executable assemblies. They are compiled into the server-side classes, and additional work is done by the compiler to generate the HTML and JavaScript that will interact with these classes. **SignalR** is used as the communication mechanism between the browser and the server. We will cover it in more detail in Chapter 8: SignalR and *Two-way Communication*.

Since you are familiar with the project structure of both Blazor WebAssembly and Blazor Server, we will have a look at Blazor's ability to generate custom HTML elements, which is slightly different depending on what type of Blazor application you are using.

Custom elements in Blazor

HTML specification allows you to add custom elements to the document. You can convert Blazor Components into pure custom HTML elements. To do so, you will need to install the following NuGet package:

```
Microsoft.AspNetCore.Components.CustomElements
```

Then, you will need to add the following script reference to either index.html file if you are using Blazor WeBAssembly or **_Host.cshtml** if you are using Blazor Server:

```
<script src="/_content/Microsoft.AspNetCore.Components.CustomElements/
BlazorCustomElements.js"></script>
```

Please note that, just like any other script that interoperates with Blazor, this reference needs to be inserted after the reference to the main Blazor JavaScript library.

Then, what you do will differ depending on which type of Blazor project you use. If we want to turn our **Counter** Razor component into an HTML element called **custom-counter**, this is how we would do it in the **Program.cs** file of a Blazor Server application:

```
builder.Services.AddServerSideBlazor(options =>
{
    options.RootComponents.RegisterCustomElement<Counter>("custom-counter");
});
```

Also, this is what we would do instead in the **Program.cs** file of a Blazor WebAssembly application:

```
builder.RootComponents.RegisterCustomElement<Counter>("custom-counter");
```

Then, to apply this custom HTML element, we just need to insert it into the markup of any of our pages, just like we would insert any standard HTML element:

```
<custom-counter></custom-counter>
```

Next, we will cover the Razor component lifecycle and the methods that represent lifecycle events that you can override.

Razor component lifecycle

The **ComponentBase** class has overridable methods that get triggered during specific lifecycle events. By overriding them, you can add some custom logic to various loading stages. These methods have synchronous and asynchronous variants.

The first of such methods is **SetParameters**. In there, you have access to the **ParemeterView** input parameter, which allows you to intercept and modify the parameters that are being set on the Razor component.

The next method is **OnInitialized**. It gets triggered when the code inside the component has been initialized, but the component has not been rendered yet.

The next method is **OnParametersSet**. It allows you to apply any custom logic once the members of your component class have been populated with the values delivered to them as parameters.

And finally, there is a method called **OnAfterRender**. At this stage, the component is fully ready and has been rendered, and you can apply any further custom logic to it before the user can start interacting with it.

To demonstrate it, we can pass the following **@code** block to the **Index.razor** file of the Blazor Server application. We are doing it on Blazor Server because this will allow us to easily read console output on the machine that the application runs on, and we will be able to see what order the events are triggered in:

```
@code {

    public override async Task SetParametersAsync(ParameterView
parameters)
    {
        Console.WriteLine($"Started setting parameters at {DateTime.
Now}.");
        await base.SetParametersAsync(parameters);
    }

    protected override void OnInitialized()
    {
        Console.WriteLine($"Initialized at {DateTime.Now}.");
        base.OnInitialized();
    }

    protected override void OnParametersSet()
    {
        Console.WriteLine($"Parameters set at {DateTime.Now}.");
        base.OnParametersSet();
    }

    protected override void OnAfterRender(bool firstRender)
    {
        Console.WriteLine($"Completed rendering at {DateTime.Now}.");
        base.OnAfterRender(firstRender);
    }
}
```

This concludes the overview of Blazor Server fundamentals. Now we will have a look at the empty Blazor Server template.

Empty Blazor server template

Just like with Blazor WebAssembly, you can create an empty Blazor Server template. To create a project from such a template via the CLI, we could execute the following command:

```
dotnet new blazorserver-empty -o EmptyBlazorServer
```

Now, we can have a look at the differences between the standard Blazor Server template and an empty one. The key difference is that in the empty template, there are no sample Razor components. There is just a barebone collection of the most basic components needed for building a Blazor application, as demonstrated in *figure 7.4*:

Figure 7.4: *The difference between the default and empty Blazor Server templates*

This concludes the overview of Blazor, its main variants, and its capabilities.

Conclusion

In this chapter, you have learned the fundamental features of Blazor. We began by covering WebAssembly and its benefits. We have also covered the benefits and disadvantages of using AoT compilation in Blazor.

You are now familiar with the process of hosting Blazor WebAssembly applications inside standard ASP.NET Core applications and setting up the standard project templates for hosted Blazor applications. You must also be familiar with the process of retroactively adding Blazor applications to ASP.NET Core.

Finally, we have examined the pros and cons of Blazor Server applications, which make Blazor code work without using WebAssembly.

In the upcoming chapter, we will cover the use of gRPC on .NET—an efficient communication mechanism based on HTTP/2 and HTTP/3.

Points to remember

- WebAssembly is a binary instruction format that allows to run compiled applications inside browsers.

- Blazor is a technology that allows you to either compile .NET code into WebAssembly or build highly interactive Web pages.

- Blazor can be compiled into WebAssembly ahead of time, which makes the application faster and reduces the download file size.

- Blazor WebAssembly can be hosted inside a standard ASP.NET Core app.

- Blazor Server gets compiled into separate browser and server components that are tightly coupled with each other.

Multiple choice questions

1. **What is a Razor Component?**

    a. A keyword from Razor Pages

    b. An HTML helper from Razor Pages

    c. An individual module inside a Razor application

    d. All of the above

2. **What are the main benefits of AoT in Blazor?**

    a. Making download size smaller

    b. Making the application faster to run

    c. Making the application quicker to launch

    d. All of the above

3. **What are the disadvantages of using Blazor Server?**

    a. Cannot run the application when the client is offline

    b. Performance depends on network speed

    c. No serverless deployment possible

    d. All of the above

4. **What are the benefits of using Blazor Server?**

    a. Small download size

    b. Client and server can be developed independently

    c. Can work without a browser

    d. All of the above

Answers

    1. c

    2. b

    3. d

    4. a

Key terms

- **WebAssembly**: A set of binary instructions that allows execution of compiled code in the browser.

- **Blazor**: A technology that allows one to either compile .NET code into WebAssembly or create an interactive Web application.

- **Razor component**: An individual module in a Blazor application that inherits from **ComponentBase** class.

- **Blazor WebAssembly**: A Blazor project that compiles into WebAssembly.

- **Blazor Server**: A Blazor project that enables real-time interactivity between the browser and the server.

- **Ahead-of-time Compilation (AoT)**: Pre-compiling Blazor project into pure WebAssembly that does not rely on intermediate .NET code.

Join our book's Discord space

Join the book's Discord Workspace for Latest updates, Offers, Tech happenings around the world, New Release and Sessions with the Authors:

https://discord.bpbonline.com

CHAPTER 8
SignalR and Two-way Communication

Introduction

Real-time interactivity is a must in modern-day Web applications. When you visit a social media website, you expect to receive a notification as soon as you get a message or a post response. You are not expected to keep refreshing the page. The same applies to delivery tracking applications or any other application where the client (either the browser or a mobile app) is expected to receive updates from the server as soon as certain events take place.

Traditionally, building fully interactive applications where the client and the server can communicate with each other in real-time has been difficult as there were multiple options available. But none of them was easy to implement. As this functionality is expected to behave differently from how the standard request-response model of the internet has been designed to behave.

Normally, the client would send a request to the server, and the server would send a response back. But in an interactive app, you need to be able to send information either way on an ad-hoc basis. When you look at your delivery tracking app and watch the driver moving in real-time, it is the server that sends the information to the client and not the other way around.

Several techniques existed, but they were not necessarily easy to implement. One of such technique, long-polling, would work by submitting a request to the server and keeping the connection open until the response arrives. It was relatively easy to implement but was not efficient. There is also a WebSocket protocol that allows the client and the server to establish a persistent connection between themselves, which allows them to communicate both ways. But the implementation was not easy to write, as the protocol worked with raw bytes, so the code was not easy to follow.

But on ASP.NET Core, there is a library called SignalR that makes the process of building real-time applications easy. It still uses some complex communication mechanisms under the hood. But subtracts away the complexity, so it is easier to implement it in the code than using those communication mechanisms directly.

SignalR does not require any NuGet packages, as it is already included in ASP.NET Core, and the library has already received some noteworthy updates in the .NET 7 release. This is what we will talk about in this chapter.

Structure

In this chapter, we will discuss the latest features of SignalR on ASP.NET Core 7. We will cover the following topics:

- SignalR overview
- Creating SignalR hub on the server
- JavaScript client for SignalR
- .NET client for SignalR

Objectives

By the end of this chapter, you will have learned how to build interactive real-time Web applications by using SignalR. You will have learned how to use SignalR from both within the browser and inside any arbitrary client application.

Prerequisites

To follow this chapter, you will need the following:

- A machine running either Windows, MacOS, or Linux operating system
- .NET 7 SDK
- A suitable IDE or a code editor
- Being familiar with C# fundamentals

If you do not have any of the preceding listed dependencies installed already, you can use the setup instruction provided in *Chapter 1: Getting Familiar with .NET 7 Application Structure*, which also provides a recap of C# fundamentals.

SignalR overview

Since SignalR is a library that is inbuilt in ASP.NET Core, you do not need to install any NuGet packages to enable it. You can enable it by adding a few lines of code to the entry point of your program. But the functionality from the library will be available if you use any type of ASP.NET Core project template.

Although SignalR uses very intuitive language to get the client and server to communicate with each other, it does rely on some standard communication mechanisms internally. There are three mechanisms supported: WebSocket, server-sent events, and long-polling. But regardless of which of them is chosen, the client and the server code will remain the same. This code will be simpler compared to what it would have been if either of these mechanisms were implemented directly.

These mechanisms can be configured either on the client or the server. But the default fallback order is as follows:

- Use WebSocket if possible.

- If not possible to use WebSocket, use server-sent events.

- If neither WebSocket nor server-sent events are available, use long-polling.

In most cases, SignalR will just use WebSocket internally, as this is its default mechanism. But there are scenarios where the usage of WebSocket might not be possible due to network configuration. The same applies to server-sent events. Long-polling, however, is nothing more than a standard HTTP request. Therefore, anything that supports HTTP will support long-polling.

Let us now summarize what each of these transport mechanisms is.

WebSocket

WebSocket is a protocol that works alongside HTTP. But unlike pure HTTP, it opens a persistent duplex connection between the client and the server. Once established, the messages can flow each way.

This protocol is very efficient for two-way communication. The client-server handshake is only done once when the connection is being established. After this, there is only an occasional heartbeat message that flows through the network to check the connectivity status, which is only a couple of bytes in size.

Although the WebSocket protocol is efficient, there are some potential issues with it too. For example, there is a limit on concurrent connections. Plus, not every client type supports it. This is why it is not the only protocol supported by SignalR.

Server-sent events

Server-sent events allow the client to subscribe to the server and receive events from it. First, the client would make a normal HTTP request to the server with **Content-Type** set to **text/event-stream**. The request does not just expect a single response. It keeps a response channel open, so it can keep receiving messages from the server.

The main reason why server-sent events are not as efficient as WebSocket is that it only works one way. If the client needs to send a message to the server, it will need to re-submit an HTTP request. While doing so, it will need to go through the full handshake, so there is more overhead involved.

But not all types of clients may be able to subscribe to server-sent events. This is why SignalR has one more transport mechanism available.

Long-polling

Long-polling is the least efficient transport mechanism of those available in SignalR. But, it will work with any type of client that supports HTTP, as it is nothing more than a standard HTTP request that waits for the server to respond.

It is inefficient precisely because the client has to submit a new full HTTP request for every single message that it sends. On top of this, it will need to keep re-submitting a new request to listen to the next message from the server.

This completes the basic overview of SignalR. Now, we will create an ASP.NET Core application and will set up a server-side SignalR hub inside it.

Creating SignalR Hub on the server

In our example, we will use a Razor Pages ASP.NET Core application. However, SignalR can work with any other ASP.NET Core application type.

We will create an application project called **SignalRServer**. To do so from the CLI, we could execute the following command:

```
dotnet new webapp -o SignalRServer
```

Once the project has been created, we can create a SignalR hub. SignalR hub is a class that inherits from the **Hub** class of **Microsoft.AspNetCore.SignalR** namespace. This is where you define the endpoints that clients can call.

To create our own **Hub** implementation, we will create the **Hubs** folder inside our project and add the **MessageHub.cs** file to it with the following content:

```
using Microsoft.AspNetCore.SignalR;
using System.Runtime.CompilerServices;


namespace SignalRServer.Hubs;


public class MessageHub : Hub
{
}
```

This provides the basic structure of our SignalR hub. Now, we will populate it with various endpoint methods to demonstrate its capabilities. Each endpoint method must be public. It can also take an arbitrary number of parameters or any JSON-serializable types, such as primitive C# data types and data classes.

The first endpoint method will be called **BroadcastMessage**. It will take a single string parameter. When triggered by a client, it will broadcast this message to all other connected clients by calling the **SendAsync** method on all properties of the **Clients** property of the **Hub** base class:

```
public async Task BroadcastMessage(string message)
{
    await Clients.All.SendAsync("ReceiveMessage", message);
}
```

What this will do is trigger the **ReceiveMessage** event on the connected clients, which is the first parameter of the **SendAsync** call. The other parameters are the parameters that go into that event on the client side.

Then, we can add an endpoint that will re-route the message to the connected clients other than the original client that has triggered the endpoint. This is done by using the **Others** property of the **Clients**:

```
public async Task SendToOthers(string message)
{
    await Clients.Others.SendAsync("ReceiveMessage", message);
}
```

If you want to use the SignalR hub in a request-response manner and get it to only send a message back to yourself, this can be achieved via the **Caller** property, as the following code demonstrates:

```
public async Task SendToSelf(string message)
{
    await Clients.Caller.SendAsync("ReceiveMessage", message);
}
```

You can also send a message to a specific connected client. But to do so, you need to know its unique connection id, which is a GUID that gets auto-generated when a client connects. To obtain the connection id of the current client, you can access **Context.ConnectionId** property of the Hub base class. This is how it can be used to send a message to a specific client:

```
public async Task SendToSpecificClient(string message, string clientId)
{
    await Clients.Client(clientId).SendAsync("ReceiveMessage", message);
}
```

It is also possible to send a message to multiple clients. To do so, you can use **Clients.Clients** method and pass a collection of client ids as the parameter. But an easier way to do so is to add clients to a group and just send a message to the group. The following method demonstrates how it can be done:

```
public async Task SendToGroup(string message, string groupName)
{
    await Clients.Group(groupName).SendAsync("ReceiveMessage", message);
}
```

If the client that has triggered the endpoint happens to be in the group, we can use the **OthersInGroup** method to send the message to all other group members, excluding the calling client. The following method demonstrates how it can be done:

```
public async Task SendToOthersInGroup(string message, string groupName)
{
  await Clients.OthersInGroup(groupName).SendAsync("ReceiveMessage",
message);
}
```

So far, we have only covered singular messages. But, SignalR also supports streaming, both from the client to the server and vice versa. The following method, for example, demonstrates how we can read from a client stream. We just need to pass a collection of JSON-serializable objects that implements the **IAsyncEnumerable** interface. The code will be able to read from the stream until the stream gets closed by the client:

```
public async Task BroadcastStream(IAsyncEnumerable<string> stream)
{
    await foreach (var item in stream)
    {
        await Clients.Caller.SendAsync($"Server received {item}");
    }
}
```

With server-streaming, a client still needs to initiate the steam by sending a parametrized call to an appropriate endpoint. Then, we can just keep adding objects into the stream, as the following method demonstrates. These will be read from the stream by the client that triggered the endpoint.

```
public async IAsyncEnumerable<string> TriggerStream(
    int jobsToProcess,
    [EnumeratorCancellation]
        CancellationToken cancellationToken)
{
    for (var i = 0; i < jobsToProcess; i++)
    {
        cancellationToken.ThrowIfCancellationRequested();
        yield return $"Job {i} processed successfully.";
        await Task.Delay(1000, cancellationToken);
    }
}
```

SignalR hub also has some overridable methods that get triggered by events. For example, the **OnConnectedAsync** method gets triggered when a client connects. The following override example shows how the client can be added to a **ConnectedClients** group immediately after the connection:

```
public override async Task OnConnectedAsync()
{
    await Groups.AddToGroupAsync(Context.ConnectionId,
"ConnectedClients");
    await base.OnConnectedAsync();
}
```

Likewise, you can override the **OnDisconnectedAsync** method, which gets triggered when a client disconnects. In the following example, we are removing the client from the **ConnectedClients** group when this happens:

```
public override async Task OnDisconnectedAsync(Exception? exception)
{
    await Groups.RemoveFromGroupAsync(Context.ConnectionId,
"ConnectedClients");
    await base.OnDisconnectedAsync(exception);
}
```

Our initial implementation of a SignalR hub is complete. What we need to do now is register it and assign it to a URL path. To do so, we will first register all SignalR dependencies by placing this line of code into the **Program.cs** file before the app variable gets generated:

```
builder.Services.AddSignalR();
```

Then, you will need to register your hub class to a specific path by calling the **MapHub** method on the **app** variable. Before you do it, make sure you add the namespace of your **hub** class in a using statement at the beginning of the file content. In the following example, we are mapping our **MessageHub** class to the **/messageHub** URL path:

```
app.MapHub<MessageHub>("/messageHub");
```

Our hub is now ready. But we can make an improvement to it. As you may have noticed, the majority of our endpoint methods send messages to the **ReceiveMessage** event on the connected clients. We are using a string literal to specify the name of the event, but we do not have to. We can make our hub strongly typed, so client events will be accessible as methods.

Strongly-typed Hub

To implement a strongly-typed SignalR hub, we need to add an interface that represents the shape of our clients. In our example, we will add the **IMessageHubClient.cs** file into the **Hubs** folder and populate it with the following content:

```
namespace SignalRServer.Hubs;


public interface IMessageHubClient
{
    Task ReceiveMessage(string message);
}
```

Next, if we want to turn the **MessageHub** class into a strongly-typed SignalR hub, we will need to change its signature to the following:

```
MessageHub : Hub<IMessageHubClient>
```

Now, all the lines of code that called the **SendAsync** method will throw an error. You will just need to replace them with a call to the **ReceiveMessage** and remove the event name from its parameters, so your calls will be similar to the following:

```
await Clients.All.ReceiveMessage(message);
```

Next, we will have a look at how to inject dependencies into your SignalR hub.

Dependency injection in SignalR Hub

Just like MVC and Web API controllers, SignaLR hubs can have services injected into them. Those can be injected either into the constructor or individual endpoint methods.

For example, let us assume we have a class called **SomeService**. We can register a scoped instance inside the **Program.cs** file, as this line demonstrates:

```
builder.Services.AddScoped<SomeService>();
```

Then, we can define a private field inside the **MessageHub** class as follows:

```
private readonly SomeService _someService;
```

Furthermore, we can add the following constructor to this class, which will assign the value of this field to the instance it receives from dependency injection:

```
public MessageHub(SomeService someService)
{
    _someService = someService;
}
```

But, if all you need to do is use the service inside a single method, maybe injecting it into the constructor and setting a **class-wide** variable would be an overkill. So, you can also inject the service into individual endpoint methods by making it the last parameter of the method:

```
public async Task BroadcastMessage(string message, SomeService
someService)
```

You can also make it more explicit by adding the **[FromService]** attribute to it:

```
public async Task BroadcastMessage(string message,
  [FromServices] SomeService someService)
```

If you want to be able to only use the explicit version, you can set the **DisableImplicitFromServicesParameter**s to false while registering SignalR dependencies, as the following example demonstrates:

```
services.AddSignalR(options =>
{
    options.DisableImplicitFromServicesParameters = true;
});
```

Now, we will overview the message serialization formats that SignalR supports.

JSON versus MessagePack

By default, SignalR uses JSON to serialize messages when they get transferred between the client and the server. It also supports the **MessagePack** protocol. This protocol is similar to JSON, but it is binary. This means that the messages are not human-readable when they are serialized. But, at the same time, they are significantly smaller in size.

To enable **MessagePack** protocol on a SignalR server, you just need to download an additional NuGet package and apply some additional configuration. The name of the NuGet package you need to install is as follows:

```
Microsoft.AspNetCore.SignalR.Protocols.MessagePack
```

To enable **MessagePack**, you just need to call **AddMessagePackProtocol** method while registering SignalR dependencies in the **Program.cs** file:

```
services.AddSignalR().AddMessagePackProtocol();
```

This concludes the overview of SignalR server configuration. Next, we will have a look at SignalR clients. We will start with an in-browser JavaScript client.

JavaScript client for SignalR

To make a JavaScript client for SignalR work, we need to install a library for it. There are the following two primary ways of installing it:

1. Getting it from a **content delivery network (CDN)** or

2. Building one from the source.

Using CDN is the simplest way. There is already a JavaScript file available online. All you have to do is point at it. To do so, open the **_Layout.cshtml** file that is located in the **Shared** folder of the **Pages** folder. You will need to locate the script HTML element that references the **site.js** file and insert the following element before it:

```
<script src="https://cdnjs.cloudflare.com/ajax/libs/microsoft-
signalr/6.0.1/signalr.min.js"></script>
```

Even though a CDN link is very easy to set up, you are relying on a script that is hosted externally. This is why you have the option of building the library from the source and then just copying it directly into your project folder. Here are the steps you can follow to build the library by using **Node.js Package Manager** (**NPM**):

1. Install Node.js on your machine.

2. Execute **npm init -y** command in any folder.

3. Execute the following command to install the latest version of the SignalR library:

   npm install @microsoft/signalr

4. Now you should have a **node_modules** folder inside the folder where you have initiated the NPM project from. Inside this folder, you can navigate to the following path:

   @microsoft/signalr/dist/browser

This folder will contain **signalr.js** and **signalr.min.js** files. You can copy either of these files into an appropriate place inside the **wwwroot** folder of your ASP.NET Core project. These files are equivalent. The only difference between them is that signalr.js contains all the scripts in human-readable form, whereas **signalr.min.js** is minified, which means that all unnecessary characters (such as whitespaces) have been removed and all variable names have been shortened. This script is no longer human-readable but will occupy significantly less space.

Then, you just need to insert a reference to this file into the **_Layout.cshtml** file in the same place that you would insert the script element with the CDN link (assuming you have placed the signalr.js file into the **signalr** folder inside the **lib** folder):

```
<script src="~/lib/signalr/signalr.js"></script>
```

Our library is now ready. Now, we will need to build our client by adding appropriate HTML markup and JavaScript.

Adding HTML markup for SignalR client

To add the markup for our SignalR client, we will open the **Index.cshtml** file inside the **Pages** folder and replace the HTML markup inside the file with the following:

```
<div class="row" style="padding-top: 50px;">
<div class="col-md-4">

    </div>


    <div class="col-md-7">
        <p>SignalR Messages:</p>
```

```
        <pre id="signalr-message-panel"></pre>
    </div>
</div>
```

This markup provides an area where the messages received from the SignalR hub will be written into. It also has an empty section that we will populate with various text boxes and buttons to allow us to send SignalR messages. In our example, this section is represented by the "div" element with the **col-md-4** class. We will insert the following element into this section to allow us to broadcast a message to all connected clients:

```
<div class="control-group">
<div>
        <label for="broadcast">Message</label>
        <input type="text" id="broadcast" name="broadcast" />
</div>
    <button id="btn-broadcast">Broadcast</button>
</div>
```

Next, we will insert the following element to allow us to send a message to all clients other than the originator of the message:

```
<div class="control-group">
    <div>
        <label for="others">Message</label>
        <input type="text" id="others" name="others" />
    </div>
    <button id="btn-others">Send to Others</button>
</div>
```

Then, we will add this HTML to allow us to send a message back to ourselves:

```
<div class="control-group">
    <div>
        <label for="self">Message</label>
        <input type="text" id="self" name="self" />
    </div>
    <button id="btn-self">Send to Self</button>
</div>
```

Then, the following control will allow us to send a message to a specific SignalR client if we know its unique connection ID:

```
<div class="control-group">
    <div>
        <label for="individual">Message</label>
        <input type="text" id="individual" name="individual" />
    </div>
    <div>
        <label for="connection-id">User connection id:</label>
        <input type="text" id="connection-id" name="connection-id" />
    </div>
    <button id="btn-individual">Send to Specific User</button>
</div>
```

Next, we can add the following control to send a message to a specific group:

```
<div class="control-group">
    <div>
        <label for="group">Message</label>
        <input type="text" id="group" name="group" />
    </div>
    <div>
        <label for="group1">Group Name</label>
        <input type="text" id="group1" name="group1" />
    </div>
    <button id="btn-group">Send to Group</button>
</div>
```

This markup will allow us to send a message to all clients in the group, but it will exclude us if we happen to be a member of this group:

```
<div class="control-group">
    <div>
        <label for="others-in-group">Message</label>
        <input type="text" id="others-in-group" name="others-in-group"
/>
    </div>
    <div>
        <label for="group1">Group Name</label>
        <input type="text" id="group2" name="group2" />
    </div>
```

```
        <button id="btn-others-in-group">Send to Others in Group</button>
</div>
```

Then, we will add the following control that will allow us to send a stream of messages to the SignalR server:

```
<div class="control-group">
    <div>
        <label for="broadcast">Messages</label>
        <input type="text" id="broadcast-stream" name="broadcast-stream"
/>
    </div>
    <button id="btn-broadcast-stream">Broadcast Stream</button>
</div>
```

Finally, the following control will be inserted to trigger a stream from the server:

```
 <div class="control-group">
    <div>
        <label for="number-of-jobs">Number of Jobs</label>
        <input type="text" id="number-of-jobs" name="number-of-jobs" />
    </div>
    <button id="btn-trigger-stream">Trigger Server Stream</button>
</div>
```

Our HTML is completed. Now, we just need to apply some styling to it. To do so, we will insert the following CSS into the **site.css** file that is located in the **css** folder of **wwwroot**:

```
.body-content {
    padding-left: 15px;
    padding-right: 15px;
}

.control-group {
    padding-top: 50px;
}

label {
    width: 100px;
}
```

```
#signalr-message-panel {
    height: calc(100vh - 200px);
}
```

Now, we will start adding JavaScript to implement the JavaScript client.

Applying SignalR functionality in JavaScript

To apply JavaScript functionality, we will need to open the site.js file, which is located in the **js** folder of the **wwwroot**. We will start by adding the following script to it:

```
const connection = new signalR.HubConnectionBuilder()
    .withUrl("/messageHub")
    .configureLogging(signalR.LogLevel.Information)
    .build();

async function start() {
    try {
        await connection.start();
        console.log('connected');
    } catch (err) {
        console.log(err);
        setTimeout(() => start(), 5000);
    }
};

connection.onclose(async () => {
    await start();
});
```

What we are doing here is building a SignalR connection. We are making the connection to the **/messageHub** path of our application. This is the path that we have previously mapped our SignalR hub onto the server. We do not need to specify the base URL because we are running the client from the same Web application that hosts the hub. If we were running it from a stand-alone JavaScript application, we would have needed to specify the full URL.

Then, we have the start function, which starts the connection and automatically repairs it when a disconnection has been detected. This is also the function we call inside the **onclose** event, so we restart the connection if a connectivity error occurs and this event gets triggered.

Next, we will add an event to our connection that can get triggered from the SignalR server. If you recall, from our server-side hub setup, we expected the connected clients to have a **ReceiveMessage** event. This is what this event will look like in our JavaScript client:

```
connection.on("ReceiveMessage", (message) => {
    $('#signalr-message-panel').prepend($('<div />').text(message));
});
```

When the **hub** sends the message parameter to this event, the parameter gets prepended to the HTML element with the id of **signalr-message-panel**:

Next, we will add some onclick events to the HTML buttons we have added previously. Each of these will invoke an endpoint on the SignalR hub. The event handler for broadcasting the message will look like the following:

```
$('#btn-broadcast').click(function () {
    var message = $('#broadcast').val();
    connection.invoke("BroadcastMessage", message).catch(err => console.error(err.toString()));
});
```

So, on a JavaScript client, triggering a SignalR hub endpoint is done via the invoke method. The first parameter of this method is the name of the SignalR hub method that you want to invoke. The rest are the input parameters for this method. It is very similar to how client-side events are called from the server-side hub, but the other way around.

We can now add event handlers to all other buttons that send singular messages to the hub:

```
$('#btn-others').click(function () {
    var message = $('#others').val();
    connection.invoke("SendToOthers", message).catch(err => console.error(err.toString()));
});


$('#btn-self').click(function () {
    var message = $('#self').val();
    connection.invoke("SendToSelf", message).catch(err => console.error(err.toString()));
```

```
});


$('#btn-individual').click(function () {
    var message = $('#individual').val();
    var connectionId = $('#connection-id').val();
    connection.invoke("SendToSpecificClient", message, connectionId).
catch(err => console.error(err.toString()));
});


$('#btn-group').click(function () {
    var message = $('#group').val();
    var group = $('#group1').val();
    connection.invoke("SendToGroup", message, group).catch(err =>
console.error(err.toString()));
});


$('#btn-others-in-group-group').click(function () {
    var message = $('#others-in-group').val();
    var group = $('#group2').val();
    connection.invoke("SendToOthersInGroup", message, group).catch(err
=> console.error(err.toString()));
});
```

Next, we will add some functionality to deal with message streams. We will first add the following code that will send a stream of messages to the server:

```
$('#btn-broadcast-stream').click(function () {
    var message = $('#broadcast-stream').val();
    var messages = message.split(';');
    var subject = new signalR.Subject();


    connection.send("BroadcastStream", subject).catch(err => console.
error(err.toString()));
    for (var i = 0; i < messages.length; i++) {
        subject.next(messages[i]);
    }


    subject.complete();
});
```

This code will split a string into multiple messages by semicolon. Then, it will create a SignalR subject, which will represent our client-side stream. Then, by calling the send method on the connection object, we are getting a specific endpoint in the SignalR server hub to listen to the stream from the client. Thereafter, we put individual messages into the stream by calling the next method on the subject. And finally, once we are finished sending messages, we call the complete method on the subject to close the stream.

Next, we will insert the following code to trigger a stream from the server:

```
$('#btn-trigger-stream').click(function () {
    var numberOfJobs = parseInt($('#number-of-jobs').val(), 10);

    connection.stream("TriggerStream", numberOfJobs)
        .subscribe({
            next: (message) => $('#signalr-message-panel').
prepend($('<div />').text(message))
        });
});
```

In this code, we are triggering a server-streaming endpoint on the SignalR hub by calling the stream method on the connection object. Then, we are calling the **subscribe** method to subscribe to the stream.

Once we have configured our SignalR connection and have added all appropriate event handlers, we can start our connection. In our case, we can just call the start function that we have created earlier:

```
start();
```

So, we have completed the overview of a JavaScript SignalR client. Next, we will build a .NET-based client.

.NET client for SignalR

To demonstrate .NET SignalR client functionality, we will build a .NET console application. But the same principles can be applied to any other application type, even including Blazor WebAssembly.

We will create a console application project, which can be done by executing the following command in the CLI:

dotnet new console -o SignalRClient

Next, we will need to add a NuGet package to the project to enable the SignalR client functionality. This is the name of the package we need to install:

```
Microsoft.AspNetCore.SignalR.Client
```

It will be the same package regardless of what type of .NET application you want to add SignalR client functionality to.

Next, we will add the following code to the **Program.cs** file:

```
using Microsoft.AspNetCore.SignalR.Client;
using System.Threading.Channels;


var url = args[0];


var hubConnection = new HubConnectionBuilder()
                        .WithUrl(url)
                        .Build();


hubConnection.On<string>("ReceiveMessage",
    message => Console.WriteLine($"Message received from the server:
{message}"));


await hubConnection.StartAsync();
```

In the preceding code, we are building a SignalR connection from the URL we have provided as the **application** parameter. It needs to be the full URL to the Web application that hosts the SignalR hub, including the path that is mapped to the hub.

Next, we will insert the following code that will allow us to interact with the console app and trigger various actions on the SignalR server:

```
var running = true;


while (running)
{
    var message = string.Empty;
    var groupName = string.Empty;

    Console.WriteLine("Please specify the action:");
    Console.WriteLine("0 - Broadcast a message to all");
    Console.WriteLine("1 - Send a message to others");
    Console.WriteLine("2 - Send a message to self");
    Console.WriteLine("3 - Send a message to a specific client");
    Console.WriteLine("4 - Send a to a group");
    Console.WriteLine("5 - Send a message to others in the group");
```

```
    Console.WriteLine("6 - Broadcast messages from client");
    Console.WriteLine("7 - Trigger a stream from the server");
    Console.WriteLine("exit - Terminate the program");

    var action = Console.ReadLine();

    if (action != "7")
    {
        Console.WriteLine("Please specify the message:");
        message = Console.ReadLine();
    }

    if (action == "4")
    {
        Console.WriteLine("Please specify the group name:");
        groupName = Console.ReadLine();
    }

    switch (action)
    {
    }
}
```

Now, we will just need to insert the cases into the **switch** block. First, we will insert the cases that will handle singular messages:

```
case "0":
    await hubConnection.SendAsync("BroadcastMessage", message);
    break;
case "1":
    await hubConnection.SendAsync("SendToOthers", message);
    break;
case "2":
    await hubConnection.SendAsync("SendToCaller", message);
    break;
case "3":
    Console.WriteLine("Please specify the connection id:");
    var connectionId = Console.ReadLine();
await hubConnection
.SendAsync("SendToSpecificClient", message, connectionId);
```

```
        break;
case "4":
    await hubConnection.SendAsync("SendToGroup", message, groupName);
    break;
case "5":
    await hubConnection.SendAsync("SendToOthersInGroup", message,
groupName);
break;
```

The principle is the same and is similar to what we have used in the JavaScript client. We are calling the **SendAsync** method on the SignalR connection object. The first parameter is the name on the server-side SignalR hub. And the remaining parameters are the parameters that this method accepts.

Then, we will insert the following case to handle client streaming:

```
case "6":
    var channel = Channel.CreateBounded<string>(10);
    await hubConnection.SendAsync("BroadcastStream", channel.Reader);

    foreach (var item in message.Split(';'))
    {
        await channel.Writer.WriteAsync(item);
    }

    channel.Writer.Complete();
break;
```

Here, we create a channel. Then, we call the **SendAsync** method, and we pass the reader from the channel as one of its parameters. Then, we write messages into the channel by using its writer. Once we are done with it, we close the channel writer.

After this, we will add the following case to handle server-streaming functionality:

```
case "7":
    Console.WriteLine("How many jobs to run?");
    var numberOfJobs = int.Parse(Console.ReadLine() ?? "0");
    var cancellationTokenSource = new CancellationTokenSource();
    var stream = hubConnection.StreamAsync<string>(
        "TriggerStream", numberOfJobs, cancellationTokenSource.Token);

    await foreach (var reply in stream)
    {
```

```
        Console.WriteLine(reply);
    }
break;
```

In here, we create a stream by calling the **StreamAsync** method on the **hubConnection** object. And then, we read from this stream.

We can complete our **switch** block by adding the following cases to it:

```
case "exit":
    running = false;
    break;
default:
    Console.WriteLine("Unknown action. Please try again.");
    break;
```

Now, we can test our SignalR client functionality by first launching our ASP.NET Core application that hosts the SignalR hub and then executing the following command to launch the newly added console application, replacing the base URL placeholder with the actual base URL of the Web application:

dotnet run -- {base URL}/messageHub

This concludes the overview of SignalR on .NET 7. Let us summarize what we have learned.

Conclusion

In this chapter, we had a look at how to build interactive Web applications by using SignalR on ASP.NET Core. We have learned how to enable it on the server-side in an ASP.NET Core app and what dependencies we need to install to enable it on the clients.

We have also learned that SignalR uses either of three mechanisms for communication, which can be configured. But regardless of the mechanism selected, the application code that uses SignalR will remain the same as the library abstracts away the specific implementations of its transport mechanisms.

We have also learned that any type of SignalR client is supported. There are some JavaScript libraries that will help you to build a SignalR client inside either a Web page or in a stand-alone Node.js application. But there are also .NET NuGet packages that can turn any .NET app into a SignalR client, including an in-browser Blazor WebAssembly app.

In the upcoming chapter, we will have a look at gRPC implementation on .NET, which is a framework for very efficient communication between services over the network.

Points to remember

- SignalR is designed for enabling a persistent connection between the client and the server that allows both of them to exchange ad-hoc messages with each other in real-time.

- The server components of SignalR are included in ASP.NET Core, but client components need to be installed.

- SignalR uses either of the three communication mechanisms internally: WebSocket, Server-sent Events, and long-polling.

- SignalR works with any type of client, both in-browser and stand-alone.

- SignalR uses JSON payload, but it can also use MessagePack, which is a binary version of JSON and, as such, takes up less space.

Multiple choice questions

1. **What communication mechanism is not supported by SignalR on ASP. NET Core?**

    a. Long-polling

    b. Server-sent events

    c. ForeverFrame

    d. WebSocket

2. **What is the fallback order on communication mechanisms in SignalR?**

    a. WebSocket, long-polling, server-sent events

    b. WebSocket, server-sent events, long-polling

    c. ForeverFrame, WebSocket, long-polling

    d. Server-sent events, long-polling, WebSocket

3. **What SignalR client types are officially supported by Microsoft?**

    a. JavaScript

    b. Blazor WebAssembly

    c. Generic .NET client

    d. All of the above

4. **What NuGet package do you need to install to enable SignalR client functionality in a .NET app?**

   a. Microsoft.AspNetCore.SignalR.Client

   b. Microsoft.AspNet.SignalR.JS

   c. Microsoft.AspNet.SignalR

   d. Any of the above

Answers

1. c
2. b
3. d
4. a

Key terms

- **SignalR**: A library inbuilt in ASP.NET Core that enables two-way real-time communication between the client and the server.

- **WebSocket**: An internet communication protocol that allows the client to establish a persistent connection to the server to enable two-way communication between the two machines.

- **Server-sent events**: A server push technology that allows sending messages to the subscribed clients.

- **Long-polling**: HTTP requests that keep the connection open for potentially a long time until the server responds.

Join our book's Discord space

Join the book's Discord Workspace for Latest updates, Offers, Tech happenings around the world, New Release and Sessions with the Authors:

https://discord.bpbonline.com

CHAPTER 9
gRPC on ASP.NET Core

Introduction

There are many ways for your services to communicate over the network. There is a REST protocol that allows you to submit HTTP requests against a Web API endpoint, as we have covered in *Chapter 6: Web Application Types on .NET*. You can also define a more strongly typed message schema by using SOAP. You can use GraphQL and add some advanced querying capabilities.

Although all these communication mechanisms are good for the purposes they have been designed for, they have a major disadvantage. They operate over HTTP/1.1. This means that the new capabilities of HTTP/2 and HTTP/3 are not available to them. For example, none of these mechanisms can have the same level or performance as a mechanism that relies on a more recent version of the HTTP protocol.

But there is a communication framework that takes advantage of the latest HTTP/2 and HTTP/3 features while abstracting away their implementation complexity, called gRPC. It is widely used by software developers across most languages and platforms. Since 2019, it has been a first-class citizen of ASP.NET Core, meaning that it is available as an official extension to ASP.NET Core.

The *RPC* part of *gRPC* stands for *remote procedure calls*. And this sufficiently explains what the technology does. Even though different pieces of software (the client and the server) exchange messages across the network, the code that you write looks like you are simply calling some procedure inside a single application. And as we will go through the examples in this chapter, you will see how this works.

Structure

In this chapter, we will go through the usage of gRPC on ASP.NET Core 7. We will cover the following topics:

- gRPC overview
- Setting up gRPC server
- Setting up gRPC client
- Overview of gRPC data types

Objectives

By the end of this chapter, you will have learned how to enable the gRPC communication framework on both the client and the server. You will have also learned the fundamentals of Protobuf, which is the message serialization protocol that gRPC uses.

Prerequisites

To follow this chapter, you will need the following:

- A machine running either Windows, MacOS, or Linux OS
- .NET 7 SDK
- A suitable IDE or a code editor
- Being familiar with C# fundamentals

If you do not have any of the preceding listed dependencies installed already, you can use the setup instruction provided in *Chapter 1: Getting Familiar with .NET 7 Application Structure*, which also provides a recap of C# fundamentals.

gRPC overview

gRPC was initially created by Google and used as one of its internal transport mechanisms. But, in 2016, it was released as an open-source communication framework. Since then, it has been adopted by a variety of programming languages and software platforms making it highly standardized. Therefore, almost any popular programming language has its implementation.

Behind the scenes, gRPC relies on the latest features of the HTTP/2 protocol. This is what makes it very efficient in comparison to other communication mechanisms. For example, the HTTP/2 feature, also known as multiplexing, allows gRPC to perform multiple concurrent communications on the same connection. This makes gRPC efficient in terms of using the network bandwidth and in terms of not having to open many separate connections.

The new HTTP/2 features are not necessarily easy to write code against. But gRPC hides all this implementation complexity from developers. This is why it is often referred to as a wrapper protocol. The core gRPC functionality performs some complex connection management logic. But all that developers are exposed to are very user-friendly APIs. From the developer's perspective, making gRPC calls over the network is in no way different from calling a method inside the same application. This is made easy by the structure of gRPC's message serialization protocol, which is known as Protocol buffers or simply Protobuf.

Protobuf as the main message serialization protocol

Protobuf has two purposes:

1. Making it easy to generate abstractions in the code.

2. Making it easy to generate messages that can be efficiently transferred over the network.

The former is the reason why gRPC is so easy to implement in the code. Protobuf relies on service definition files. These files, which come with a proto extension, define the structure of the gRPC services, the callable procedures, and the request and response messages. But all of this has been structured in such a way that it can easily translate into structures that are commonly supported by programming languages, such as classes, objects, and so on.

The latter is achieved by serializing messages into a binary form and only keeping as much information as needed. For example, here, Protobuf data types have default values, and if a value of a particular field is the same as its default value, it is not necessary to transmit this field over the network. Likewise, even though field names are used by Protobuf for readability, these are not transferred over the network. Each field has an integer sequence number, which occupies much less space than an arbitrary name. This is what the receiver of the message can accurately identify the fields from.

We will have a look at the structure of Protobuf messages. To do so, will now set up a basic gRPC Service application that will act as a server for our incoming messages.

Setting up gRPC server

.NET SDK already has an ASP.NET Core project template with all the required gRPC service dependencies along with some basic code samples. Let us now use this template to create a project and call it **GrpcServiceApp**. If you are using an IDE, you can use the **ASP.NET Core gRPC Service** template to create the project from. Otherwise, you can create the project by executing the following command in a terminal:

```
dotnet new grpc -o GrpcServiceApp
```

Once the project is created, we can have a look at its structure.

ASP.NET Core gRPC project structure

The project that gets created resembles a basic ASP.NET Core application. However, it has some additional components. One of them is the **Protos** folder, which contains files with the **.proto** extension. The other one is the **Services** folder, which contains the classes that implement the service definitions from the **proto** files. The structure of the project is demonstrated in *figure 9.1*:

```
▲ 🗊 GrpcServiceApp
    ▷  ⊕ Connected Services
    ▷  🖴 Dependencies
    ▲  🗔 Properties
            🗋 launchSettings.json
    ▲  🗀 Protos
            ⊷ greet.proto
    ▲  🗀 Services
        ▷  c# GreeterService.cs
    ▷  🗋 appsettings.json
        c# Program.cs
```

Figure 9.1: gRPC Service project structure

Here is our opportunity to have a closer look at the structure of a typical **proto** file. If we open the **greet.proto** file in the **Protos** folder, we can see that it starts with the following statement:

```
syntax = "proto3";
```

This indicates that we are using version 3 of Protobuf, which, at the time of writing, is the most recent protocol version. Then, there is the following statement:

```
option csharp_namespace = "GrpcServiceApp";
```

The option keyword indicates that we are dealing with a custom configurable option. In this specific case, we have the **csharp_namespace** option. This option is only applicable for C# applications and will override the namespace for the auto-generated code files.

The next statement is as follows:

```
package greet;
```

This is the gRPC package name. It is analogous to a C# namespace. If we did not have the **csharp_namespace** option mentioned previously, the C# namespace would be the Pascal-case version of this package name.

Next, we have the following service definition:

```
service Greeter {
  rpc SayHello(HelloRequest) returns (HelloReply);
}
```

This is the signature of a gRPC service. In our example, the service is called **Greeter**. It has one RPC called **SayHello.** This RPC accepts a **HelloRequest** message as its request and a **HelloRequest** as its response. Each RPC definition must have both the request and the response type. However, it is permitted for either of these types to have no fields.

The definition of the **HelloRequest** message is as follows:

```
message HelloRequest {
  string name = 1;
}
```

Here, we have a single field of the type string. The number 1 next to it is its sequence number. Each field in a message definition must have a sequence number associated with it. And each sequence number must be unique.

The definition of our **HelloReply** message is as follows:

```
message HelloReply {
  string message = 1;
}
```

When we translate this Protobuf definition into code, each message and service will be represented by a class. The class representing service will be abstract, as we will want to apply custom logic to its methods by overriding them. Each RPC definition within the service will be represented by a method. We can see how this gets translated into the C# code by opening the **GreeterService** class that can be found inside the **Services** folder. The signature of the class will look like the following, as we are overriding a class that has been automatically generated from the proto file:

```
public class GreeterService : Greeter.GreeterBase
```

Here is the implementation of the **SayHello** RPC. The additional **ServerCall Context** parameter is used for storing session-specific metadata:

```
public override Task<HelloReply> SayHello(
  HelloRequest request, ServerCallContext context)
```

To enable the gRPC functionality in our ASP.NET Core application, we need to have the following NuGet package installed:

```
Grpc.AspNetCore
```

Also, our **CSPROJ** file must have a **Protobuf** XML pointing at each proto file we want to use. We have it defined as follows inside the **GrpcServiceApp** file:

```
<ItemGroup>
  <Protobuf Include="Protos\greet.proto" GrpcServices="Server" />
</ItemGroup>
```

Please note that the **GrpcServices** parameter is set to Server. This will limit the code generator to only produce server-related gRPC components for the proto file specified. We can also set the value of this attribute to the **Client**. If we do not set it at all, the code generator will produce both the client and the server components.

There are a few more things we need to do before we can start using gRPC inside our application. If we open the **Program.cs** file, we can locate the following line:

```
builder.Services.AddGrpc();
```

This statement will add all the required gRPC dependencies to our application. Then we also need to register every gRPC service implementation that we intend to use. This is done by calling the **MapGrpcService** method on the app variable with the service implementation specified as its type. We have the following example in our code:

```
app.MapGrpcService<GreeterService>();
```

This concludes the overview of the basic gRPC service setup. Next, we will have a look at call types and data types supported by gRPC.

gRPC call types and data types

So far, we have only had a look at a single type of RPC, known as a unary call. This call type accepts a single request and returns a single response. However, gRPC also supports the following call types:

- Server-streaming
- Client-streaming
- Bi-directional streaming

To demonstrate them all, we will modify the definition of the **Greeter** service in the **greet.proto** file as follows:

```
service Greeter {
  rpc SayHello (HelloRequest) returns (HelloReply);
  rpc RequestManyReplies (HelloRequest) returns (stream HelloReply);
  rpc SendManyRequests (stream HelloRequest) returns (HelloReply);
  rpc InitiateBidirectionalStreaming (stream HelloRequest) returns
(stream HelloReply);
}
```

So, to define any streaming calls, you just need to place the stream keyword either before the input type, the output type, or both. In this example, The **RequestManyReplies** RPC is a server-streaming call, the **SendManyRequests** RPC is a client-streaming call, and the **InitiateBidirectionalStreaming** RPC is a bi-directional streaming call.

We will also have a look at some inbuilt data types. For this, we will modify the definition of the **HelloReply** message, so it will become the following:

```
message HelloReply {
  string message = 1;
  int32 message_id = 2;
  bytes content_in_bytes = 3;
  float message_size_in_kilobytes = 4;
  bool reply_processed = 5;
}
```

We will have a more detailed look at the inbuilt Protobuf data types later. But in this example, we have the following:

- **int32**, which is a 32-bit integer that gets translated into the standard int type in C#

- **bytes**, which acts like a byte array and is represented by the **ByteString** data type from **Google.Protobuf** namespace in C#

- **float**, which is a direct equivalent to the float type in C#

- **bool**, which is a direct equivalent to the bool type in C#

Now, we will make some modifications to the **GreeterService** class to see how these data types work. The first thing we will need to do is add the following **using** statement to it:

```
using Google.Protobuf;
```

Then, we will add the following private method that all our RPC implementations will use to generate the response:

```
private HelloReply GenerateReplyMessage(HelloRequest request)
{
    var message = "Hello " + request.Name;

    return new HelloReply
    {
        Message = message,
        MessageId = 1,
        ContentInBytes = ByteString
.CopyFrom(Encoding.ASCII.GetBytes(message)),
        MessageSizeInKilobytes = (float)ByteString.CopyFrom(Encoding.
ASCII.GetBytes(message)).Length / 1024,
        ReplyProcessed = false
    };
}
```

As we can see, there are some data types that we can apply directly. There is also the **ByteString** type that we can populate from a standard byte string by calling the **CopyFrom** method. Then our original **SayHello** method will become this:

```
public override Task<HelloReply> SayHello(HelloRequest request,
ServerCallContext context)
{
    return Task.FromResult(GenerateReplyMessage(request));
}
```

The implementation of the server-streaming **RequestManyReplies** method will be this:

```
public override async Task RequestManyReplies(
  HelloRequest request,
  IServerStreamWriter<HelloReply> responseStream,
  ServerCallContext context)
{
    var i = 3;

    while (i > 0)
    {
        await responseStream.WriteAsync(GenerateReplyMessage(request));
        i--;
    }
}
```

Here, we put three messages onto the response stream. The method does not have a return type, as the stream gets populated before we return from the method. The client will be able to read the data from the stream as it is populated.

We will add the following implementation for our **SendManyRequests** method:

```
public override async Task<HelloReply> SendManyRequests(
  IAsyncStreamReader<HelloRequest> requestStream,
  ServerCallContext context)
{
    var reply = new HelloReply();

    await foreach (var request in requestStream.ReadAllAsync())
    {
        reply = GenerateReplyMessage(request);
    }

    return reply;
}
```

In this method, we read from the client stream. We will keep doing it until the client closes its stream.

Finally, the bi-directional streaming method will look as follows:

```
public override async Task InitiateBidirectionalStreaming(
  IAsyncStreamReader<HelloRequest> requestStream,
```

```
    IServerStreamWriter<HelloReply> responseStream,

    ServerCallContext context)

{

    await foreach(var request in requestStream.ReadAllAsync())

    {

        await responseStream.WriteAsync(GenerateReplyMessage(request));

    }

}
```

In this type of call, we do not return a response. Instead, we have two streams as the input parameters: client stream and server stream. We can read from the client stream and write into the server stream.

We will shortly have a look at how to set up a gRPC client in .NET. But before we do so, we will have a look at the feature that has been added to gRPC in ASP.NET Core 7 called JSON transcoding.

gRPC JSON transcoding

JSON transcoding allows developers to connect to gRPC servers via the standard REST protocol. It works by converting Protobuf messages into JSON objects.

There are limits to JSON transcoding. First, it still operates under the standard HTTP/1.1 protocol, so the advantages of HTTP/2 are lost. Second, it does not support client streaming. However, it is still useful because the developers will no longer have to write separate gRPC and REST implementations.

We can even use Swagger with it. To do so, we will need to install the following NuGet package:

```
Microsoft.AspNetCore.Grpc.Swagger
```

Then, we will need to open the **Program.cs** file and amend the **AddGrpc** call to look as follows:

```
builder.Services.AddGrpc().AddJsonTranscoding();
```

Then, we can add the standard Swagger dependencies:

```
builder.Services.AddGrpcSwagger();

builder.Services.AddSwaggerGen(c =>

{

    c.SwaggerDoc("v1",

        new OpenApiInfo { Title = "REST API to gRPC", Version = "v1" });

});
```

Once we have all dependencies added, we can register the Swagger middleware by adding the following code:

```
app.UseSwagger();
app.UseSwaggerUI(c =>
{
    c.SwaggerEndpoint("/swagger/v1/swagger.json", "My API V1");
});
```

Now, to make the JSON transcoding work, we will need to copy some Protobuf files into our project folder. First, we will have to create a folder called **google** in the root of our project. Then, we will create **api** folder inside this folder. Thereafter, we will add an **http.proto** file to this folder with the following content:

```
syntax = "proto3";

package google.api;

option cc_enable_arenas = true;
option go_package = "google.golang.org/genproto/googleapis/api/
annotations;annotations";
option java_multiple_files = true;
option java_outer_classname = "HttpProto";
option java_package = "com.google.api";
option objc_class_prefix = "GAPI";

message Http {
  repeated HttpRule rules = 1;
  bool fully_decode_reserved_expansion = 2;
}

message HttpRule {
  string selector = 1;

  oneof pattern {
    string get = 2;
    string put = 3;
    string post = 4;
    string delete = 5;
```

```
    string patch = 6;
    CustomHttpPattern custom = 8;
  }
  string body = 7;
  string response_body = 12;
  repeated HttpRule additional_bindings = 11;
}

message CustomHttpPattern {
  string kind = 1;
  string path = 2;
}
```

Then, we will create an **annotations.proto** file in the same folder and populate it with the following content:

```
syntax = "proto3";

package google.api;

import "google/api/http.proto";
import "google/protobuf/descriptor.proto";

option go_package = "google.golang.org/genproto/googleapis/api/
annotations;annotations";
option java_multiple_files = true;
option java_outer_classname = "AnnotationsProto";
option java_package = "com.google.api";
option objc_class_prefix = "GAPI";

extend google.protobuf.MethodOptions {
  HttpRule http = 72295728;
}
```

Now, we will open our original **greet.proto** file and add the following statement to it just before the package definition:

```
import "google/api/annotations.proto";
```

Next, we will modify our **SayHello** and **RequestManyReplies** RPCs by making them look like the following:

```
rpc SayHello (HelloRequest) returns (HelloReply) {
  option (google.api.http) = {
    get: "/v1/greeter/{name}"
  };
}
rpc RequestManyReplies (HelloRequest) returns (stream HelloReply) {
  option (google.api.http) = {
    get: "/v1/greeter/{name}/stream"
  };
}
```

This will now link these RPCs with RESP API paths. We can test these paths by launching our application and navigating to its **Swagger** page, which is available on the **/swagger** path by default. As we can see in *figure 9.2*, we can now have these paths available:

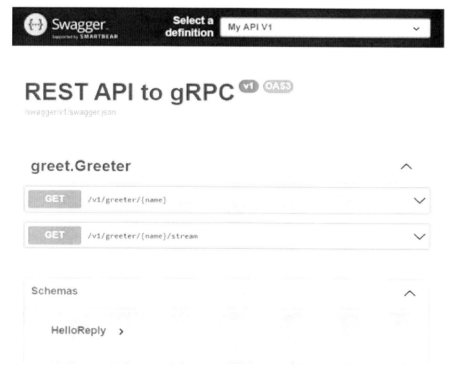

Figure 9.2: Swagger page with REST endpoints that map to gRPC methods

When we use JSON transcoding, unary gRPC calls are translated into standard request-response endpoints, and server-streaming calls return JSON collections.

This concludes our gRPC server setup. Let us now set up our client.

Setting up gRPC client

gRPC client functionality can be added to any .NET application type, including the most basic console application. Therefore, to demonstrate the client functionality, we will create a console application called **BasicGrpcClient**. We can do so via the CLI by executing the following command:

```
dotnet new console -o BasicGrpcClient
```

We need to install the following three NuGet packages to enable the client functionality:

Google.Protobuf

- **Grpc.Net.Client**
- **Grpc.Tools**

Next, since we will be using the same Protobuf definition as our server uses, we will need to copy the **Protos** folder from the **GrpcServiceApp** project into the **BasicGrpcClient** project. This time, however, we do not need the JSON transcoding functionality. Therefore, our **greet.proto** file in the **BasicGrpcClient** project should look like the following after we remove all the redundant references from it:

```
syntax = "proto3";


option csharp_namespace = "GrpcServiceApp";


package greet;


service Greeter {
  rpc SayHello (HelloRequest) returns (HelloReply);
  rpc RequestManyReplies (HelloRequest) returns (stream HelloReply);
  rpc SendManyRequests (stream HelloRequest) returns (HelloReply);
  rpc InitiateBidirectionalStreaming (stream HelloRequest) returns
(stream HelloReply);
}


message HelloRequest {
  string name = 1;
```

```
}

message HelloReply {
  string message = 1;
  int32 message_id = 2;
  bytes content_in_bytes = 3;
  float message_size_in_kilobytes = 4;
  bool reply_processed = 5;
}
```

Next, we will need to register this proto file in the **BasicGrpcClient.csproj** file by adding the following markup to it:

```
<ItemGroup>
  <Protobuf Include="Protos\greet.proto" GrpcServices="Client" />
</ItemGroup>
```

This time, the **GrpcServices** attribute is set to Client, as we are only interested in importing the client functionality.

Next, we will replace the content of the **Program.cs** file with the following:

```
using Grpc.Core;
using Grpc.Net.Client;
using GrpcServiceApp;


using var channel = GrpcChannel.ForAddress("https://localhost:7222");
```

We are adding the required namespaces. Then, we are creating a disposable instance of a **GrpcChannel** type. Inside the **ForAddress** call, we are specifying the address of our gRPC server application, which can be found in the **launchSetting.json** file in the **Properties** folder. In this example, the address is **https://localhost:7222**. But it will probably be different in your instance.

It is important to note that gRPC uses the secure HTTPS protocol by default. This is because the unsecure HTTP URL is mapped to HTTP/1.1 protocol by default, which does not support gRPC. But we can make some changes to our server code to enable unsecure access to HTTP/2, which may be done if you do not want to use a development TLS certificate. If you are using Mac, we must do it because macOS does not support TLS mapping to HTTP/2 on the OS level. To do so, we will need to insert the following code into the **Program.cs** file of our gRPC server application, where we replace the **{port number}** with the actual port number we want to map:

```
builder.WebHost.ConfigureKestrel(options =>
{
    options.ListenLocalhost({port number}, o => o.Protocols =
        HttpProtocols.Http2);
});
```

Let us now continue setting up our client functionality. We already have our gRPC channel opened. Now, we need to add some console prompt and create an instance of a **HelloRequest** class based on the user's console input. Then, we can create an instance of a client:

```
Console.WriteLine("What is your name?");
var name = Console.ReadLine();

var request = new HelloRequest()
{
    Name = name
};


var client = new Greeter.GreeterClient(channel);
```

Now, we can use the instance of a client to make a unary call:

```
var reply = await client.SayHelloAsync(request);
Console.WriteLine("Message received from a unary call: " + reply.
Message);
```

Please note that the name of the client-side method that represents a unary gRPC call has the **Async** suffix. This is because we are using an asynchronous version of it. But there is also a synchronous version of the method that does not have this suffix.

Then, we can make a server-streaming call. This is done by opening a disposable stream and reading from it:

```
using var serverStreamingCall = client.RequestManyReplies(request);
while (await serverStreamingCall
    .ResponseStream.MoveNext(CancellationToken.None))
{
    Console.WriteLine("Message received from a server streaming call: "
+
        serverStreamingCall.ResponseStream.Current.Message);
}
```

Next, we will create a client-streaming call. Here, we will open a stream, write some messages into it, close the stream, and wait for the response:

```
using var clientStreamingCall = client.SendManyRequests();

for (var i = 0; i < 3; i++)
{
    await clientStreamingCall.RequestStream.WriteAsync(request);
}
await clientStreamingCall.RequestStream.CompleteAsync();
var response = await clientStreamingCall;
Console.WriteLine("Message received from a client streaming call: " +
        response.Message);
```

After this, we will add a bi-directional streaming call. Here, we will create a disposable object that represents both the client and the server streams. We write into the client stream and read from the server stream by creating via an asynchronous task. Then, we close the client stream and wait for this task to complete:

```
using var bidirectionalCall = client.InitiateBidirectionalStreaming();
var readTask = Task.Run(async () =>
{
    await foreach (var response in bidirectionalCall.ResponseStream.
ReadAllAsync())
    {
        Console.WriteLine("Message received from a bidirectional call: "
            + response.Message);
    }
});
await bidirectionalCall.RequestStream.WriteAsync(request);
await bidirectionalCall.RequestStream.CompleteAsync();
await readTask;
```

Finally, we might want to add the following lines to make sure the terminal does not get closed once the application executes its logic:

```
Console.WriteLine("Press any key to exit...");
Console.ReadKey();
```

This completes the overview of basic gRPC client functionality. In real life, however, a gRPC client is often another Web application or a hosted Web service. The good news is that ASP.NET core supports dependency injection of gRPC client components. This is what we will have a look at next.

Using gRPC client factory and dependency injection

We will now create an ASP.NET Core MVC application called **GrpcMvcClient**. This can be done by executing the following command from the CLI:

```
dotnet new mvc -o GrpcMvcClient
```

All the client functionality, including dependency injection, can then be added by installing the following NuGet package:

Grpc.AspNetCore.Server.ClientFactory

If you want to potentially use your application as both a gRPC client and a gRPC server, you can just install the **Grpc.AspNetCore** package instead. It will contain all the necessary client packages, including the preceding one.

We then need to copy the Protos folder from the **BasicGrpcClient** project folder we have created earlier into the **GrpcMvcClient** one. Then, we need to register the proto file inside the **GrpcMvcClient.csproj** file. We can either use the same markup that we have used inside the **BasicGrpcClient.csproj** or we can apply this alternative markup instead:

```
<ItemGroup>
  <None Update="Protos\greet.proto">
    <GrpcServices>Client</GrpcServices>
  </None>
</ItemGroup>
```

Next, we will register our gRPC client for dependency injection. To do this, we will first add the following statement to the top of the **Program.cs** file:

```
using GrpcServiceApp;
```

Then, we will add the following anywhere before the **app** variable is created:

```
builder.Services.AddGrpcClient<Greeter.GreeterClient>(o =>
{
    o.Address = new Uri("https://localhost:7222");
});
```

Please note that the input into the constructor of the Uri class is the URL of the gRPC server application. The port number in your instance will probably be different.

Now, we will put the **ResponseModel.cs** file into the **Models** folder and will populate it with the following content:

```
namespace GrpcMvcClient.Models;


public class ResponseModel
{
    public string Message {  get; set; }
}
```

Next, we will add the following statement to the **HomeController.cs** file, which can be found inside the **Controllers** folder:

```
using GrpcServiceApp;
```

Then, we will add the following private field into the **HomeController** class:

```
private readonly Greeter.GreeterClient _client;
```

After this, we will replace the class constructor with the following:

```
public HomeController(
    ILogger<HomeController> logger,
    Greeter.GreeterClient client)
{
    _logger = logger;
    _client = client;
}
```

Here, we are injecting an instance of a gRPC client that we have previously registered inside the **Program.cs** file. Now, we can use this client instance. To do so, we will replace the **Index** method with the following:

```
public async Task<IActionResult> Index()
{
    var reply = await _client.SayHelloAsync(
        new HelloRequest
        {
            Name = "User"
        });

    var response = new ResponseModel
```

```
    {
        Message = reply.Message
    };


    return View(response);
}
```

Here, we are making a unary gRPC call. Then we extract the message received from the gRPC server and put it into the view model. To display its value, we will need to locate **Index.cshtml** file that is located in the **Home** folder under the **Views** folder. We will replace its content with the following:

```
@model ResponseModel


@{
    ViewData["Title"] = "Home Page";
}


<div class="text-center">
    <h1 class="display-4">@Model.Message</h1>
</div>
```

When we launch this application and open its homepage in the browser, we will see the message that we have retrieved from the gRPC server application, as long as it is also running and we have configured our connection correctly.

This concludes the overview of setting up a gRPC server on .NET. Let us now go through the data types supported by gRPC.

Overview of gRPC data types

The primitive data types in gRPC, which are also known as scalar value types, are not nullable. Instead, each of these types has a default value. For example, the default value for any numeric data type is 0, whereas it is **false** for the **bool** type. This is very similar to how the equivalent data types work in C#.

Unlike C#, however, Protobuf has different types of integers. This allows for more flexibility and efficiency while transferring messages via the network. All inbuilt data types supported by Protobuf are listed in *table 9.1*:

Type	Description	Default value	C# Equivalent
int32	An integer that occupies up to 32 bits but can occupy less if the value is small. Supports both the positive and the negative values.	0	int
int64	An integer that occupies up to 64 bits but can occupy less if the value is small. Supports both the positive and the negative values.	0	long
uint32	An integer that occupies up to 32 bits but can occupy less if the value is small. Supports only the positive values.	0	uint
uint64	An integer that occupies up to 64 bits but can occupy less if the value is small. Supports only the positive values.		ulong
sint32	An integer that occupies up to 32 bits but can occupy less if the value is small. Supports both the positive and the negative values, but it is especially efficient for encoding negative values.	0	int
sint64	An integer that occupies up to 64 bits but can occupy less if the value is small. Supports both the positive and the negative values, but it is especially efficient for encoding negative values.	0	int
fixed32	An integer that always occupies exactly 32 bits and is especially efficient for encoding large numbers. Supports only the positive values.	0	uint
fixed64	An integer that always occupies exactly 64 bits and is especially efficient for encoding large numbers. Supports only the positive values.	0	ulong
sfixed32	An integer that always occupies exactly 32 bits and is especially efficient for encoding large numbers. Supports both the positive and the negative values.	0	int
sfixed64	An integer that always occupies exactly 64 bits and is especially efficient for encoding large numbers. Supports both the positive and the negative values.	0	long

Type	Description	Default value	C# Equivalent
float	A numeric data type that supports a decimal point.	0	float
double	A numeric data type that supports a decimal point and has a double precision.	0	double
string	Free text	""	string
bytes	A collection of bytes	Empty byte array	Google.Protobuf.ByteString
bool	Either true or false	false	bool

Table 9.1: Protobuf data types

In addition to these, Protobuf supports enums, repeated fields, map fields and one of the keyword. Let us have a brief overview of these.

Protobuf enums

Enums in Protobuf are similar to enums in C#. Even the syntax is similar. But there are a few points to remember. For example, since each inbuilt data type in Protobuf has a default value, enums do too. For any **enum** type, the value is 0. Therefore, each **enum** type must have a value that maps to 0. Also, Enums in Protobuf must have a numeric value specified next to each key. This is what an **enum** definition may look the following:

```
enum DemoEnum {
    VALUE_ONE = 0;
    VALUE_TWO = 1;
    VALUE_THREE = 2;
}
```

Next, we will have a look at the repeated keyword, which is used for representing Protobuf collections.

Enabling collections with a repeated keyword

If we want to have any of the message fields as a collection, all we need to do is place the **repeated** keyword before the field definition. This way, instead of having a single value of a specific data type, we will have a collection of values of this data type.

You can also have dictionary-like functionality in Protobuf. This is enabled by the **map** keyword that we will have a look at next.

Dictionary-like Protobuf functionality

In Protobuf, the **map** keyword allows us to have a dictionary-like functionality. When applied, the field becomes a storage for key-value pairs where each key must be unique. The following is an example of this keyword. In this example, we have a 32-bit integer as the key and a string as the value:

```
map<int32, string> map_example = 1;
```

Next, we will have a look at the **oneof** keyword that does not have a C# equivalent.

Using the oneof keyword in Protobuf

When you use the **oneof** keyword in a Protobuf message, we can have a collection of fields where only one field can be populated at a time. When we set the value for any of the fields, any field that was set previously is automatically unset.

We have an example of the **oneof** keyword in the **http.proto** file that we have inside the **google/api** folder of the **GrpcServiceApp** project. We have the following block in the **HttpRule** message definition:

```
oneof pattern {
string get = 2;
  string put = 3;
  string post = 4;
  string delete = 5;
  string patch = 6;
CustomHttpPattern custom = 8;
}
```

This concludes the overview of the inbuilt data types and keywords that Protobuf supports. The good news is that we are not stuck with these types. We can create our own custom message types and add any functionality that we need. Luckily, some of these types are already provided to us by the core Google library. They are referred to as the so-called **well-known types**.

Well-known data types

To demonstrate how well-known types work, we will add a **nullable_greet.proto** file to the **Protos** folder of the **GrpcServiceApp** project. We will then populate this file with the following content:

```
syntax = "proto3";

option csharp_namespace = "GrpcServiceApp";

import "google/protobuf/wrappers.proto";

package greet;

service NullableGreeter {
  rpc SayHello (NullableHelloRequest) returns (NullableHelloReply);
  rpc RequestManyReplies (NullableHelloRequest) returns (stream
NullableHelloReply);
  rpc SendManyRequests (stream NullableHelloRequest) returns
(NullableHelloReply);
  rpc InitiateBidirectionalStreaming (stream NullableHelloRequest)
returns (stream NullableHelloReply);
}

message NullableHelloRequest {
  google.protobuf.StringValue name = 1;
}

message NullableHelloReply {
  google.protobuf.StringValue message = 1;
  google.protobuf.Int32Value message_id = 2;
  google.protobuf.BytesValue content_in_bytes = 3;
  google.protobuf.FloatValue message_size_in_kilobytes = 4;
  google.protobuf.BoolValue reply_processed = 5;
}
```

This file is equivalent to the **greet.proto** we worked with previously. But this time, all fields are nullable. This is because we have imported the **google/ protobuf/wrappers.proto** package, which contains all the nullable types, such as **StringValue**, **Int32Value**, and so on. But this is not the only inbuilt package we can import, and well-known types are not only limited to nullable types. *Table 9.2* lists the main well-known types:

Data type	Package name	Description
Any	`google/protobuf/any.proto`	A type that can store any data type. Equivalent to dynamic in C#.
BoolValue	`google/protobuf/wrappers.proto`	Nullable bool
StringValue	`google/protobuf/wrappers.proto`	Nullable string
BytesValue	`google/protobuf/wrappers.proto`	Nullable bytes
FloatValue	`google/protobuf/wrappers.proto`	Nullable float
DoubleValue	`google/protobuf/wrappers.proto`	Nullable double
Int32Value	`google/protobuf/wrappers.proto`	Nullable int32
Int64Value	`google/protobuf/wrappers.proto`	Nullable int64
UInt32Value	`google/protobuf/wrappers.proto`	Nullable uint32
UInt64Value	`google/protobuf/wrappers.proto`	Nullable uint64
Duration	`google/protobuf/duration.proto`	Equivalent to TimeSpan in C#
Timestamp	`google/protobuf/timestamp.proto`	Equivalent to DateTime in C#
Empty	`google/protobuf/empty.proto`	A filler for empty requests and responses

Table 9.2: Well-known types from the Protobuf Google library

There are some more data types that can be imported from the Google libraries. But these are the main ones that will be more than sufficient for many use cases.

Now, we have concluded the overview of gRPC on ASP.NET Core. Let us summarize what we have learned.

Conclusion

In this chapter, we have covered gRPC and the .NET implementation. We should now be familiar with how to use gRPC Service project templates with all the pre-installed dependencies and how to retrofit gRPC dependencies in existing ASP.NET Core applications. We have covered its setup on both the client and the server.

We saw how easy gRPC is to implement and how writing calls between the client and the server is almost as easy as calling a method inside a single application. Although gRPC uses some advanced HTTP/2 and HTTP/3 features internally, we never see it as the consumer of gRPC libraries. It has all been abstracted away. And that significantly simplifies the process of writing code.

We have also gone through Protobuf, which is the primary message serialization protocol used by gRPC. We have learned its syntax, its fundamental structure, and its data types. We have also learned how to extend it by referencing external packages. For example, this is how we could add the so-called *well-known types* to our message definitions.

In the upcoming chapter, we will have a look at ML.NET, which is a .NET-based framework for building machine learning models.

Points to remember

- gRPC is a strongly-typed communication framework that was specifically designed for utilizing the latest features of the HTTP/2 protocol.

- gRPC uses Protobuf as its primary message serialization protocol

- There are four types of calls in gRPC: unary, client-streaming, server-streaming, and bi-directional streaming

- The unary call expects a single request and returns a single response

- Client-streaming call expects a stream of messages from the server and returns a single response

- Server-streaming call expects a single request and returns a stream of messages

- The bi-directional streaming call uses stream both from the client to the server and vice versa

- The default data types in Protobuf are not nullable

- Each RPC in gRPC needs to have both a request message type and a response message type, although either of them can be placed in a stream

Multiple choice questions

1. **What is fixed 32 data type in Protobuf?**

    a. Fixed-size 32-bit integer that can store negative values

    b. Fixed-size 32-bit integer that can store only negative values

    c. Fixed-side 32 floating point number

    d. Fixed-size 32-bit integer that can only store positive numbers

2. **What is a unary call in gRPC?**

    a. A call that accepts a single request message and returns a single response message

b. A call that accepts a single request message and can return either a single response message or a stream

c. A call that accepts either a single request message or a request stream but always returns a single response

d. A call where streaming can be done both ways

3. **Which of the following is an example of a well-known type?**

a. Int32

b. double

c. StringValue

d. All of the above

4. **Which NuGet packages do you need to install to enable gRPC client functionality?**

a. Grpc.Net.Client

b. Google.Protobuf

c. Grpc.Tools

d. All of the above

Answers

1. d
2. a
3. c
4. d

Key terms

- **gRPC:** A communication framework originally developed by Google that was designed for efficient communication between services.

- **Protobuf:** The primary message serialization protocol used by gRPC.

- **gRPC service:** A Protobuf structure that provides the signatures of the endpoints that clients can call and servers can implement.

- **gRPC message:** A Protobuf structure that holds data that gets exchanged between the server and the client.

- **Unary gRPC call:** An RPC call that accepts a single request and returns a single response.

- **Client-streaming gRPC call:** An RPC call that accepts a stream of messages from the client and returns a single response message.

- **Server-streaming gRPC call:** An RPC call that accepts a single request message from the client and returns a stream of response messages.

- **Bi-directional streaming gRPC call:** An RPC call that accepts a message stream from the client and returns a message stream from the server.

- **Well-known types:** Protobuf data types that exist in all popular programming languages but have to be added to Protobuf via external package references.

- have to be added to Protobuf via external package references.

Join our book's Discord space

Join the book's Discord Workspace for Latest updates, Offers, Tech happenings around the world, New Release and Sessions with the Authors:

https://discord.bpbonline.com

CHAPTER 10
Machine Learning with ML.NET

Introduction

Historically, **artificial intelligence (AI)** and **machine learning (ML)** were the domains of those who were experts in statistics and advanced Math, such as calculus. Also, Python and R were de facto the only programming languages used by data scientists to write ML models. However, ML.NET has changed all of this. With this tool, any .NET developer can take the role of a data scientist. They no longer need to learn R and Python. Although knowing the actual mathematical formulae for various specific algorithms is still useful, it is no longer necessary.

ML.NET is a tool that helps developers build ML models by just supplying a combination of simple and intuitive parameters. All we need to do is execute a simple command, telling the tool which task we want to perform. The tool will then take the input data, try to figure out how to work with this data based on some parameters we have supplied, and generate the code that we can then re-use in our applications whenever we need to perform a task of a similar nature. For example, we can determine whether a record with specific properties represents a person who is younger than 24, predict a house price based on some information about the house, and so on.

The ML models require some complex code if we were to build them from scratch. And they cannot be built unless you know what algorithm works best with which type of task and what formula the algorithm uses. But with ML.NET, neither of these is necessary. It will not only generate the code but also attempt to use different algorithms to accomplish a certain task, so the most suitable one can be determined. Of course, the auto-generated code can be optimized further by someone who has knowledge about ML. But it is still a lot easier to optimize the existing model than write one from scratch.

To make it even more user-friendly, ML.NET can use a visual low-code editor to build models with. Instead of writing a command to build a model with, all the required parameters can be defined on an input form. Then, various components can just be added to the model by dragging and dropping them.

Structure

In this chapter, we will go through the steps of installing and running ML.NET on all supported operating systems. We will cover the following topics:

- ML.NET fundamentals
- Choosing a problem for ML
- Training and evaluating your model
- Using a low-code model builder

Objectives

By the end of this chapter, you will have known the fundamentals of ML. You will also know how to use ML.NET and build models with it, both from the command line and a low-code visual editor.

Prerequisites

To follow this chapter, you will need the following:

- A 64-bit machine running either Windows, MacOS, or Linux OS
- .NET 7 SDK
- A suitable IDE or a code editor
- Being familiar with C# fundamentals

If you do not have any of the preceding listed dependencies installed already, you can use the setup instruction provided in *Chapter 1: Getting Familiar with .NET 7 Application Structure*, which also provides a recap of C# fundamentals.

ML.NET fundamentals

Before we can start talking about the fundamentals of ML.NET, we need to cover the fundamentals of ML. Even though you do not necessarily need to be a data science expert or have a good knowledge of Math in order to be able to use ML.NET, you will still need to understand some basic ML concepts.

At its most basic level, ML is when software is written to automatically adjust its decision-making logic based on the data provided. It is the opposite of the traditional way of enabling software to make decisions, where such functionality is simply hard-coded as conditions by using **if** and **switch** keywords. ML is especially useful for dealing with complex real-world problems where the decision-making logic may need to be adjusted based on ever-evolving sets of data or where such logic is simply too complex to be hard-coded as a bunch of **if** statements.

There are different ML algorithms that have different formulae and internal logic. But all of them share some common characteristics. At the most basic level, the ML model gets initialized with some random numeric parameters internally. These are the parameters that enable the model to produce specific results. Then the process of learning happens by running a specific set of input data against the model in multiple iterations. In each iteration, the formula inside the model is used to adjust the values of those internal parameters based on how different the output results were from the expected result. In the case of unsupervised learning, these parameters are readjusted to improve the way the data items are classified.

What happens inside the model when it adjusts itself to produce better results is known as learning. The process of configuring the learning process is known as training. The accuracy of the final model will then depend on the following factors:

- The volume of the data used for training

- The diversity of the data points provided

- The number of learning iterations

- The choice of the learning algorithm

- The choice of configuration specific to the algorithm

There are also some trade-offs that need to be made. We cannot apply an infinite set of iterations and use billions of data points to train our model with. There is a limit to how much storage space, CPU, and memory we have. Therefore, our goal should be to make our model accurate enough for the purpose we are building it and not to make it completely flawless.

The accuracy of the model can always be determined during the learning process based on how many of the model's outputs were either correct or close to the expected value. Then, we keep training the model until either the accuracy becomes acceptable or until the training algorithm has reached its limits by not being able to improve the accuracy in further iterations.

Once the model has been trained, we can run it against records that it has never seen before. Then, depending on the task that we have built the model for, our model should assign a specific category to this record, make some predictions, and so on.

Types of machine learning

Overall, there are three types of machine learning: supervised learning, unsupervised learning, and reinforcement learning. Let us have a look at each category.

Supervised learning

This type of learning uses input data together with expected values. For example, if we have a record with various fields, such as job title, income level, and the type of property the person owns (if any), we can place the person's age as the expected output value. Then, as the model goes through many of such records, it will keep adjusting its internal parameters until it comes as close to the expected results for as many of the training values as possible.

Supervised learning is used for tasks that involve classification and prediction. A good example of it is image classification. This is where an ML model is given image data and is told which category the image should be placed under. Then the model keeps adjusting itself until it can associate a particular pattern of pixels and color as a particular category.

Unsupervised learning

Unsupervised learning does not come with expected values. Instead, it looks at the data and performance in its own classification of it. This might be done to either cluster data points with common characteristics together or to detect anomalies in the data.

Reinforcement learning

Reinforcement learning is the most complex of all learning types. This is when the ML model is given a score for performing a particular type of action. The more desirable the action is—the higher the score. Therefore, this learning method uses a combination of rewards and punishments. The real-life usages of reinforcement learning include natural language processing, self-driving cars, training AI to play a video game, and so on.

Reinforcement learning is not supported by ML.NET out of the box. However, such functionality can be added to ML.NET by either adding your own algorithms to it, applying new extension methods to the existing classes, or modifying the code of the model that has been generated for one other type of tasks.

Now, we will go through the process of setting up the ML.NET tools on our environment and using the tools to build our first ML model. This process will slightly differ depending on which OS you are using.

Getting started with ML.NET

Before we can start building our ML models by using ML.NET, we need to install the right set of tools for our environment.

Installing ML.NET tools

The command to install ML.NET CLI tools will be slightly different depending on what operating system and CPU architecture you are using on your development machine. We will have a look at all supported scenarios as follows.

Installing ML.NET on Windows

On a Windows machine that uses Intel/AMD CPU, we can execute the following command to install the ML.NET tools:

```
dotnet tool install -g mlnet-win-x64
```

If our machine uses ARM CPU architecture, then the command will be as follows:

dotnet tool install -g mlnet-win-arm64

In addition to this, Visual Studio IDE on Windows allows us to install the tools via GUI. To do so, we will need to open the Visual Studio Installer, select the **.NET desktop**

development, check the **ML.NET Model Builder** option, and click the **Install** button, as shown in *figure 10.1*:

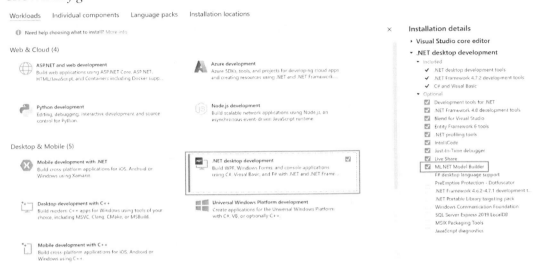

Figure 10.1: *Selecting the ML.NET Model Builder option in Visual Studio Installer*

Visual Studio does not only allow us to install ML.NET tools in a low-code manner but also allows us to setup ML models by using GUI. We will cover this process later in the chapter.

Installing ML.NET on Linux

Linux machines running on Intel/AMD (×64) CPU will have the following installation command:

```
dotnet tool install -g mlnet-linux-x64
```

For ARM-based machines, the installation command will be as follows:

```
dotnet tool install -g mlnet-linux-arm64
```

Installing ML.NET on MacOS

On a Mac running on ×64 CPU architecture, the installation command will be as follows:

```
dotnet tool install -g mlnet-osx-x64
```

If the Mac device has ARM64 CPU architecture, then the following command should be used:

```
dotnet tool install -g mlnet-osx-arm64
```

Now, once the ML.NET tools are installed, we can start using them to build an ML model.

Using ML.NET to create your first ML model

We will start by creating a folder for our ML model. Then, we will download a training dataset from which we can build our model off. We will use a well-known dataset that is frequently used for such purposes. It can be obtained via the following URL:

https://archive.ics.uci.edu/ml/machine-learning-databases/00331/sentiment%20 labelled%20sentences.zip

Then, once the zip file is downloaded, we can copy the **yelp_labelled.txt** file from the archive into the folder that we have just created. This text file contains tab-separated data where the first column contains input, and the second column contains the so-called label. In machine learning, the label is the value that the model produces based on the input data. In this case, we have two integer values representing the sentiment of the sentence. Here, 1 represents positive sentiment, whereas 0 represents negative sentiment.

Once we have copied the file into the folder, we can run the following command from inside the folder:

```
mlnet classification --dataset "yelp_labelled.txt" --label-col 1 --has-
header false --train-time 60
```

We are choosing classification as our task, and the file that we have just copied as the training dataset. We are saying that the second column (the column with an index of 1) is our label column. We are telling the model that the data has no header and that the first row should be treated as data. We are setting the training time to 60 seconds. The more time we give it—the more accurate our model will be.

While the training process is running, the console will show us what training algorithms are evaluated, how long it has spent evaluating each algorithm and what the accuracy of each algorithm is. The accuracy is based on how many sentences the model has correctly categorized as either 1 or 0 after seeing the initial data. The output of the training will look similar to what is *figure 10.2*:

	Trainer	MicroAccuracy	MacroAccuracy	Duration	#Iteration
0	SdcaMaximumEntropyMulti	0.4838	0.5000	2.7	0
1	SdcaMaximumEntropyMulti	0.4838	0.5000	1.4	1
2	FastForestOva	0.7184	0.7185	6.7	2
3	FastTreeOva	0.6488	0.6473	3.3	3
4	SdcaLogisticRegressionOva	0.4838	0.5000	2.4	4
5	LightGbmMulti	0.6889	0.6855	2.9	5
6	LbfgsMaximumEntropyMulti	0.8060	0.8071	2.4	6
7	LbfgsLogisticRegressionOva	0.8047	0.8057	2.8	7
8	FastForestOva	0.7545	0.7548	14.0	8
9	SdcaMaximumEntropyMulti	0.6915	0.6937	1.4	9
10	LightGbmMulti	0.7142	0.7149	2.7	10
11	LbfgsMaximumEntropyMulti	0.7905	0.7914	4.6	11
12	FastTreeOva	0.7485	0.7489	6.3	12
13	SdcaLogisticRegressionOva	0.7292	0.7294	2.4	13

Figure 10.2: Output of the ML training process

Once the training process is completed, a new folder is generated inside the folder in which we have executed our training. By default, this folder is called **SampleClassification**, which is the same as our model's name. But we can change its name to anything we want by adding the **--name** parameter to the **mlnel classification** command mentioned previously. The content of the folder is a console application that has an auto-generated code for our model.

Program.cs file inside the folder is the entrypoint into the application. It can be executed to run the model. The **{modle name}.consumption.cs** file contains the inputs and outputs of the model. It also contains the **Predict** method that is used for model consumption. The **{model name}.mbconfig** file contains detailed model configuration and results from the training. The **{model name}.training.cs** file contains the code for the data transformation pipeline that is used during training. Finally, **{model name}.zip** folder contains the actual ML model that is used by this code.

Internally, the code in the C files has been structured in such a way that it can be as intuitive as possible to experienced .NET developers, even when they do not have any prior machine learning experience. For example, the class that represents the model input will look similar to the following, which is also similar to a typical database model abstraction in frameworks like MVC and Entity Framework:

```
public class ModelInput
{
    [ColumnName(@"col0")]
    public string Col0 { get; set; }

    [ColumnName(@"col1")]
```

```
    public float Col1 { get; set; }
```

```
}
```

The bulk of ML-related functionality is accessed by the **MLContext** class, which is conceptually similar to a **DbContext** class used by Entity Framework. The transformation pipeline used during training is conceptually similar to the request processing pipeline of ASP.NET Core.

Our training data is represented by an implementation of the **IDataView** interface, which is passed into the **RetrainPipeline** method. The training pipeline, with its multiple transformation steps, implements the **IEstimator<ITransformer>** interface. We need multiple transformation steps on the input data because each training algorithm can only work with data in a specific shape, so we cannot just use the raw data. Once we have built our pipeline, we can build our model from it by calling the **Fit** method on the pipeline object by passing our **IDataView** implementation into it. So, our **RetrainPipeline** method will look similar to the following:

```
public static ITransformer RetrainPipeline(MLContext mlContext,
IDataView trainData)
{
    var pipeline = BuildPipeline(mlContext);
    var model = pipeline.Fit(trainData);


    return model;
}
```

We have now built our first simple ML model. Let us have a look at what else we can do with ML.NET.

Choosing a problem for ML

Here is the complete list of the tasks that ML.NET is capable of dealing with. For each of these, we will go through its basic overview, have a look at how we can construct a command for it, and look at internal trainer algorithms that this type of task can use.

Binary classification

Binary classification is the process of determining whether a particular record in the data set belongs in either of two categories. This is the simplest type of classification that ML can do, as the categories can either be defined by binary values (1 and 0) or as a Boolean (true or false).

This algorithm can be used to determine whether a person is employed or unemployed, whether the person is a homeowner or not, and for many other situations where either-or decision or prediction is required. Binary classification is a type of supervised learning.

The classification task that we performed previously when we ran the `mlnet` `classification` command is a binary classification problem because we only have two sentiment categories: 1 and 0.

A binary classification model can be generated by running the following command with appropriate parameters:

`mlnet classification`

Here is the list of the parameters supported by the following command:

```
--dataset <dataset> (REQUIRED)
```
File path to single dataset or training dataset for train/test approaches.


```
--label-col <label-col> (REQUIRED)
```
Name or zero-based index of label (target) column to predict.


```
--cache <Auto|Off|On>
```
Specify [On|Off|Auto] for cache to be turned on, off, or auto-determined (default). [default: Auto]


```
--has-header
```
Specify [true|false] depending on if dataset file(s) have header row. Use auto-detect if this flag is not set.


```
--ignore-cols <ignore-cols>
```
pecify columns to be ignored in given dataset. Use space-seperated column names or zero-based indexes.


```
--log-file-path <log-file-path>
```
Path to log file.


```
--name <name>
```

Name for output project or solution to create. Default is
SampleClassification. [default: SampleClassification]

-o, --output <output>
Location folder for generated output. Default is current directory.

--test-dataset <test-dataset>
File path for test dataset in train/test approaches.

--train-time <train-time>
Maximum time in seconds for exploring models with best configuration.
Default time is 100 sec. [default: 100]

-v, --verbosity <verbosity>
Output verbosity choices: q[uiet], m[inimal] (default) and diag[nostic].
[default: m]

The list of algorithms suitable for binary classification is as follows:

AveragedPerceptronTrainer

SdcaLogisticRegressionBinaryTrainer

SdcaNonCalibratedBinaryTrainer

SymbolicSgdLogisticRegressionBinaryTrainer

LbfgsLogisticRegressionBinaryTrainer

LightGbmBinaryTrainer

FastTreeBinaryTrainer

FastForestBinaryTrainer

GamBinaryTrainer

FieldAwareFactorizationMachineTrainer

PriorTrainer

LinearSvmTrainer

Multiclass classification

Multiclass classification is conceptually similar to binary classification. However, it typically deals with situations where there are more than two categories. It makes this type of problem significantly more complicated than a binary classification problem, as our categories can no longer be represented by either binary or Boolean values.

The usages of this algorithm include anything that requires to determine if a given record belongs in a given category. For example, we may use it to determine which age group a particular person belongs to based on their interests, income, job title, and home ownership status. As multiclass classification is conceptually similar to binary classification, it belongs in the supervised learning category.

A multiclass classification model can also be created by executing the **mlnet classification** command.

The algorithms supported by this task are as follows:

```
LightGbmMulticlassTrainer

SdcaMaximumEntropyMulticlassTrainer

SdcaNonCalibratedMulticlassTrainer

LbfgsMaximumEntropyMulticlassTrainer

NaiveBayesMulticlassTrainer

OneVersusAllTrainer

PairwiseCouplingTrainer
```

Regression

Regression is an attempt to predict how a particular feature will change based on the changes in related features. When we use a regression algorithm to train our model, we try to make it come up with a mathematical function that will produce a reasonably accurate result when the values of the features change.

Regression can be used to predict how house prices will change in the future based on house attributes and historic market data. It can also be used to predict changes in stock prices. Regression is a type of supervised learning.

A regression model can be created by executing the following command:

```
mlnet regression
```

The supported arguments are as follows:

```
--dataset <dataset> (REQUIRED)
File path to single dataset or training dataset for train/test
approaches.

  --label-col <label-col> (REQUIRED)  Name or zero-based index of label
(target) column to predict.


--cache <Auto|Off|On>
Specify [On|Off|Auto] for cache to be turned on, off, or auto-determined
(default). [default: Auto]
```

```
--has-header
```

Specify [true|false] depending on if dataset file(s) have header row. Use auto-detect if this flag is not set.

```
--ignore-cols <ignore-cols>
```

Specify columns to be ignored in given dataset. Use space-seperated column names or zero-based indexes.

```
--log-file-path <log-file-path>
```

Path to log file.

```
--name <name>
```

Name for output project or solution to create. Default is SampleRegression.

```
-o, --output <output>
```

Location folder for generated output. Default is current directory.

```
--test-dataset <test-dataset>
```

File path for test dataset in train/test approaches.

```
--train-time <train-time>
```

Maximum time in seconds for exploring models with best configuration. Default time is 100 sec. [default: 100]

```
-v, --verbosity <verbosity>
```

Output verbosity choices: q[uiet], m[inimal] (default) and diag[nostic]. [default: m]

The regression task supports the following algorithms:

LbfgsPoissonRegressionTrainer

LightGbmRegressionTrainer

SdcaRegressionTrainer

OlsTrainer

OnlineGradientDescentTrainer

FastTreeRegressionTrainer

```
FastTreeTweedieTrainer
FastForestRegressionTrainer
GamRegressionTrainer
```

Recommendations

The goal of this task is to come up with a list of recommended items based on historic data. For example, we can use it to offer product recommendations to a user based on which products the user bought in the past.

This type of task belongs under the unsupervised learning category, as we cannot have a definite answer to train the model against. Instead, it is up to the algorithm to establish the relationships in the data.

The recommendation ML model can be created by executing the following command:

```
mlnet recommendation
```

The following parameters are supported:

```
--dataset <dataset> (REQUIRED)
File path to single dataset or training dataset for train/test
approaches.
```

```
--item-col <item-col> (REQUIRED)
Name or zero-based index of item column. Items are recommended to users.
```

```
--rating-col <rating-col> (REQUIRED)
Name or zero-based index of ratings (target) column to predict.
```

```
--user-col <user-col> (REQUIRED)
Name or zero-based index of user column. Users receive recommended items.
```

```
--cache <Auto|Off|On>
Specify [On|Off|Auto] for cache to be turned on, off, or auto-determined (default). [default: Auto]
```

```
--has-header
Specify [true|false] depending if dataset file(s) have header row. Use auto-detect if this flag is not set.
```

```
--log-file-path <log-file-path>
```
Path to log file.

```
--name <name>
```
Name for output project or solution to create. Default is SampleRecommendation.

```
-o, --output <output>
```
Location folder for generated output. Default is current directory.

```
--test-dataset <test-dataset>
```
File path for test dataset in train/test approaches.

```
--train-time <train-time>
```
Maximum time in seconds for exploring models with best configuration. Default time is 100 sec. [default: 100]

```
-v, --verbosity <verbosity>
```
Output verbosity choices: q[uiet], m[inimal] (default) and diag[nostic]. [default: m]

The task supports the following algorithm:

```
MatrixFactorizationTrainer
```

Forecasting

Forecasting can be used to predict future events based on some past data, such as weather and stock market prices, or determine when a particular action would be required, such as a car maintenance task.

Supervised learning tasks, such as classification and regression, can be used for forecasting. However, it also comes with algorithms that are specific to forecasting. Also, depending on the type of forecasting that is done, it can fall under the unsupervised learning category. In this case, forecasting will be done by the pattern found in the historic data.

The following command can be used to train a forecasting model:

```
mlnet forecasting
```

The command supports the following parameters:

`--dataset <dataset> (REQUIRED)`

File path to single dataset or training dataset for train/test approaches.

`--horizon <horizon> (REQUIRED)`

Defines how many periods forward you would like to forecast. The horizon is in units of the time series frequency. Units are based on the time interval of your training data, for example, monthly, weekly that the forecaster should predict out.

`--label-col <label-col> (REQUIRED)`

Name or zero-based index of label (target) column to predict.

`--time-col <time-col> (REQUIRED)`

Used to specify the datetime column in the input data used for building the time series and inferring its frequency.

`--cache <Auto|Off|On>`

Specify [On|Off|Auto] for cache to be turned on, off, or auto-determined (default). [default: Auto]

`--has-header`

Specify [true|false] depending on if dataset file(s) have header row. Use auto-detect if this flag is not set.

`--log-file-path <log-file-path>`

Path to log file.

`--name <name>`

Name for output project or solution to create. Default is SampleClassification. [default: SampleClassification]

`-o, --output <output>`

Location folder for generated output. Default is current directory.

`--test-dataset <test-dataset>`

File path for test dataset in train/test approaches.

```
--train-time <train-time>
```

Maximum time in seconds for exploring models with best configuration. Default time is 100 sec. [default: 100]

```
-v, --verbosity <verbosity>
```

Output verbosity choices: q[uiet], m[inimal] (default) and diag[nostic]. [default: m]

Forecasting can use the following algorithm:

```
ForecastBySsa
```

Image classification

Image classification is a type of multiclass classification but is specific to images. A complex algorithm that usually involves multi-level processing, such as a neural network, is used to determine what patterns of colors and pixels are common to a specific category. Then, it will attempt to place a newly seen image into one of the known categories. Since image classification is a type of multiclass classification, it is an example of supervised learning.

An image classification model can be trained by using the following command:

```
mlnet image-classification
```

This command uses the following parameters:

```
--dataset <dataset> (REQUIRED)
```

Path to local folder which contains labelled sub-folders of all images.

```
--cache <Auto|Off|On>
```

Specify [On|Off|Auto] for cache to be turned on, off, or auto-determined (default). [default: Auto]

```
--log-file-path <log-file-path>
```

Path to log file.

```
--name <name>
```

Name for output project or solution to create. Default is SampleImageClassification.

```
-o, --output <output>
```

Location folder for generated output. Default is current directory.

`--test-dataset <test-dataset>`

File path to parent folder that contains test dataset in train/test approaches.

`-v, --verbosity <verbosity>`

Output verbosity choices: q[uiet], m[inimal] (default) and diag[nostic]. [default: m]

Image classification can use the following training algorithm:

`ImageClassificationTrainer`

Clustering

Clustering is the process of grouping records together in clusters based on some shared features. It can be used to establish relationships between different records based on their similarities. Clustering is especially useful in marketing for the purpose of understanding the target audience. It is an example of unsupervised learning.

Clustering does not use its own dedicated command. An ML model dedicated to a clustering task can be created by creating the following generic command:

`mlnet train`

The parameters of the command are as follows:

`--training-config <training-config> (REQUIRED)`

path to training config file

`--log-file-path <log-file-path>`

Path to log file.

`-v, --verbosity <verbosity>`

Output verbosity choices: q[uiet], m[inimal] (default) and diag[nostic]. [default: m]

The task selection and other configurations are performed inside a file with the **mbconbfig** extension, such as the one that we have generated earlier. The path to this file is added to the **--training-config** parameter.

The clustering ML model can use the following training algorithm:

`KMeansTrainer`

Anomaly detection

Anomaly detection is the process of identifying data points that look out of place in the set of data. For example, it can be used to determine if the Web traffic is behaving abnormally to detect potential attacks on the server.

Anomaly detection is a task that can fall either under the supervised or unsupervised learning category. With supervised learning, each item in training data can be given a binary label to identify it either as an anomaly or not, which makes it similar to binary classification. On the other hand, an activity similar to clustering can be used to separate abnormal data from the rest of the data, as anomalies will have distinctive characteristics.

Anomaly detection does not have its own dedicated command. Instead, the generic **mlnet train** command is used, and the configuration is added to the **mbconfig** file. The training algorithm that an anomaly detection task can use is as follows:

```
RandomizedPcaTrainer
```

Ranking

This type of ML task has a numeric rank next to each record. Then the job of the model is to figure out how the combination of features in the data determines the rank.

This is a type of supervised learning that is conceptually similar to multiclass classification. However, there is also a major difference. While categories in multiclass classification are distinct, each rank value represents whether a particular record is "better" or "worse" than other records. This is why a model built for this specific problem can be used as a base for a reinforcement learning task.

The ranking does not have its own dedicated command. Instead, the generic **mlnet train** command is used, and the configuration is added to the **mbconfig** file. The training algorithms that a ranking task can use are as follows:

```
LightGbmRankingTrainer
FastTreeRankingTrainer
```

Training and evaluating your model

When we are training an ML model, the algorithms that are involved in the process will try to figure out the relationship between the input data (features) and output data (labels). Then a subset of the training data will be used to evaluate the accuracy of the model by passing input values into it and checking what output value is produced. The learning process will then adjust some internal variables of the model to improve the accuracy on the next run.

Training models for longer usually improve their accuracy. But it is rare for a model git to be 100% accuracy against complex real-world data. Therefore, there is a risk that if we run the model for too long, we will just be wasting time and resources. There is also a risk of overfitting the model to the sample data. This is where the model fits the data from the particular dataset reasonably well, but its configuration is not generic enough. When this happens, the model will make accurate predictions against the input data from the training dataset but will perform poorly against data that it has never seen before. This is why we need to strive for a tolerable degree of accuracy rather than 100% accuracy. This is also why we need to check other metrics and not just accuracy.

The metrics that we can evaluate are displayed while the model is being trained and when the training is completed. The exact metrics available to us will depend on the task that we are training our model to perform. Let us go through them.

Binary classification metrics

The following metrics are displayed when binary classification training is performed:

- **Accuracy**: Indicates how often the model comes up with the right answer. The number can range from 0 to 1. The closer the number to 1—the better the accuracy. But if the number is exactly 1, it indicates a potential issue with overfitting.

- **Area Under Curve (AUC)**: A curve is generated by sweeping the true positive rate versus the false positive rate. The value should be as close to 1 as possible but should be greater than 0.5. If the value is less than 0.5, the model is not useful.

- **Area Under curve for Precision-Recall (AUCPR)**: The value closer to 1 indicates that the model returns accurate results and returns the majority of positive results. This measure is especially useful in highly imbalanced data sets.

- **F1-score**: The score ranges from 0 to 1 and tells us how precise our classifier is. The closer to 1 the score is—the better our classifier is.

Multiclass classification metrics

Multiclass classification has its own metrics that are different from those used by binary classification.

- **Micro-accuracy**: The value ranges from 0 to 1. The closer the value to 1—the better. This metric is preferable over macro-accuracy

- **Macro-accuracy**: The value ranges from 0 to 1. The closer the value to 1—the better.

- **Log-Loss**: The value ranges from 1 to 0. The closer the value is to 0—the better.

Log-Loss reduction

The value can range from negative infinity to 1. A value of less than 0 indicates that the model performs worse than a random guess. The closer the value to 1—the better.

Image classification

Image classification has the following metrics:

- **Log-Loss**: The value ranges from 1 to 0. The closer the value is to 0 - the better.

- **Per-class Log Loss**: A range of log-loss values is calculated per each image category. This helps us to determine how good the model is at identifying specific image types.

Forecasting

Forecasting has the following metrics:

- **Mean Absolute Error**: The number represents the average difference between the actual and the forecasted value. The lower the number—the better.

- **Root Mean Squared Error**: It is similar to Mean Absolute Error but is based on a square root of the squared difference between the predicted and the actual values. This metric helps to identify large individual errors, as having a large number squared will produce a large average number.

Regression and recommendation

These tasks have the same set of metrics, which we will have a look at now:

- **R-Squared**: The value ranges from 0 to 1. The closer the value to 1—the better. However, the value of 1 may indicate an overfitted model. And a value of 0.5 is usually acceptable.

- **Absolute-loss**: The values are positive. The closer the value to 0—the better.

- **Squared-loss**: The values are positive. The closer the value to 0—the better. However, a relatively large value does not necessarily indicate a problem.

- **RMB-loss**: The values are positive. As with any type of loss, the closer the value to 0—the better.

Clustering metrics

The accuracy of a clustering model can be assessed by looking at the following metrics:

- **Average distance**: The closer the value is to 0—the better the model. A value closer to 0 correlates with more clustered data.

- **Davies Bouldin index**: The closer the value is to 0—the better. More dispersed data will result in a better score.

- **Normalized mutual information**: The value is between 0 and 1. The closer the value is to 1—the better.

Anomaly detection metrics

When we are interested in evaluating the performance of our anomaly detection algorithm, here are the metrics we should be looking at:

- **Area Under ROC Curve**: The value ranges from 0 to 1. The closer the value is to 1—the better. However, values lower than 0.5 means that the model is useless.

- **Detection Rate at false positive count**: The value ranges from 0 to 1. The closer the value is to 1—the better. This means that there are fewer false positives being detected.

Ranking metrics

Ranking ML models can be evaluated by looking at the following metrics:

- **Discounted Cumulative gains**: The numeric value is unbounded. The higher the value - the better.

- **Normalized Discounted cumulative gains**: The numeric value can range from 0 to 1. The closer the value is to 1—the better.

This summarizes the main metrics for each model type. So far, we have used a combination of CLI and code to build our model. But if you are a Windows user, you can build your ML.NET models in a low-code fashion by using GUI. This is what we will have a look at next.

Using a low-code model builder

To see how we can build a machine-learning model entirely by using GUI, we need to first enable the ML.NET workload via Visual Studio Installer as have been described previously. We can then create a console application project in Visual Studio. Then, we can right-click on this project, click on **Add** option and then click on **Machine Learning Model**, as *figure 10.3* demonstrates:

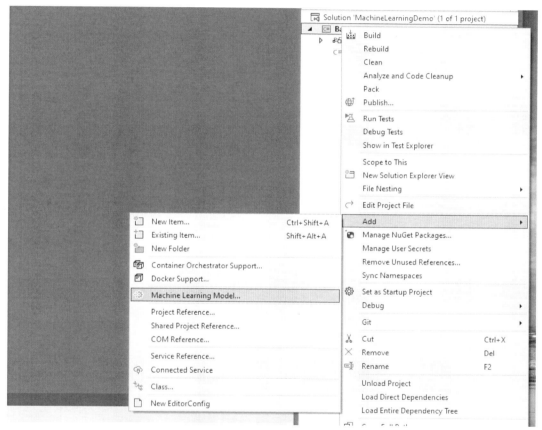

Figure 10.3: Adding a machine learning model to a console application

In the dialog that appears, we will then select the **Machine Learning Model (ML.NET)** template, as shown in *figure 10.4*:

Figure 10.4: *Selecting ML.NET template*

This will then take us to the screen where we will be able to select our ML **Scenario**, as *figure 10.5* demonstrates:

Figure 10.5: ML scenario selection

We can then select whether to run the ML training locally or in Azure. Some tasks only support one option, whereas others support both. When we select the right option and click **Next**, we are taken to the next screen, where we can select the dataset either from an SQL database or from a file. Once the dataset is loaded, we can preview it and select the label column, as *figure 10.6* demonstrates:

Add data

In order to build a model, you must add data and choose your column to predict.
How do I get sample datasets and learn more?

Input

Data source type
◉ File (.csv, .tsv, .txt)
◯ SQL Server

C:\Repos\a-complete-guide-to-implementing-csharp11-and-dotnet7\Chapter-10\MachineLearningDemo\yelp_labelled.txt   Browse...

Column to predict (Label): ⓘ

col1   ▾

Advanced data options...

Data Preview

10 of 1,000 rows, and all 2 columns (including 0 columns that are ignored).

col0	col1
Wow... Loved this place.	1
Crust is not good.	0
Not tasty and the texture was just nasty.	0
Stopped by during the late May bank holiday off Rick Steve recommendation and loved it.	1
The selection on the menu was great and so were the prices.	1
Now I am getting angry and I want my damn pho.	0
Honeslty it didn't taste THAT fresh.)	0
The potatoes were like rubber and you could tell they had been made up ahead of time being kept under a warmer.	0
The fries were great too.	1
A great touch.	1

Next step

Figure 10.6: previewing the dataset and selecting the label column

On the next screen, we can configure the training parameters and start training our model. Once the training is completed, we can see how accurate our model is. We can also evaluate it by passing arbitrary input data to it and checking whether it returns the right answers. Then, once we are happy with our model, we can consume or deploy it. We can also either retrain or improve our model if we are not fully happy with it.

Behind the scene, this process would have created the same kind of code as we had looked at when we used the command line. Also, while the training is running, the terminal in Visual Studio would have produced the same kind of output as would have been produced in the command terminal by the CLI tool. Both tools would produce similar code that can then be modified directly.

Conclusion

In this chapter, we have covered the fundamentals of ML that should be known by anyone who wants to apply ML in practice or analyze the accuracy of an ML model. We went through the types of learning that ML can do and the types of tasks that each type of learning can address.

We have also covered the usage of ML.NET, which is a tool that allows the generation of ML model code just by running an intuitive command with a simple set of parameters. We have learned how to use this tool both from the CLI and a visual editor perspective.

We went through all the tasks that ML.NET supports, and we looked at all algorithms that can be used in each of these tasks. We now know how ML.NET supports a variety of supervised and unsupervised learning tasks out of the box. Although reinforcement learning is not supported by ML.NET by default, we briefly had a look at how such tasks can be addressed by ML.NET by either writing some additional extension methods or by inserting additional functionality into the generated code.

In the upcoming chapter, we will have a look at the process of running .NET apps inside containers, so they can be deployed anywhere together with their execution environment.

Points to remember

- ML.NET is a .NET-based tool that can build ML models from either the CLI or a graphical user interface.

- There are three types of ML learning activities: supervised learning, unsupervised learning, and reinforcement learning. ML.NET supports the former two out of the box.

- ML.NET will generate the code for the model that it builds to address the task specified for the specified set of data.

- The accuracy of the model will depend on the algorithm used and the input parameters specified, such as the number of learning iterations and the depth of the neural network used if the selected algorithms use one.

- ML.NET can evaluate multiple algorithms and select the one that produces the best results.

Multiple choice questions

1. **What types of learning can be used in ML?**

   a. Supervised learning

   b. Unsupervised learning

   c. Reinforcement learning

   d. All of the above

2. **What is the role of MLContext class in ML.NET?**

   a. It provides access to most of the ML functionality

   b. It stores the data that has been loaded into the model

   c. It stores transformed data

   d. It stores the evaluation results of the model

3. **What is multiclass classification?**

   a. The process of predicting whether an input object has a particular property

   b. Assigning input data to one of two categories

   c. Assigning input data to one of any arbitrary number of categories

   d. Determining whether a particular image belongs within a specific category

4. **Which of the following tasks ML.NET does not support us out of the box?**

   a. Regression

   b. Ranking

   c. Natural language processing

   d. All of the above are supported

Answers

1. d

2. a

3. c

4. c

Key terms

- **ML.NET**: .NET-based tool that allows to build an ML model represented by C# code.

- **Supervised learning**: A type of ML where raw input data is given alongside the expected outputs.

- **Unsupervised learning**: A type of ML that looks for common patterns in the data without any expected input provided.

- **Reinforcement learning**: A type of ML where the model is encouraged to perform specific activities via a reward/punishment mechanism.

- **Binary classification**: An ML task that determines whether a particular record belongs in one of two categories.

- **Multiclass classification**: An ML task that determines whether a record belongs in one of several categories.

- **Regression**: An attempt to predict a value from a set of related values.

- **Clustering**: An unsupervised learning task that palaces various records into different groups based on similar features.

- **Anomaly detection**: An unsupervised learning task that detects values that do not fit an established pattern.

- **Ranking**: A task that assigns ranks to various data points based on some examples.

- **Recommendations**: An ML task that attempts to make a recommendation to users based on their historic behavior.

- **Forecasting**: An ML task that attempts to come up with a feature value based on the historic set of values.

- **Image classification**: An attempt to determine what category an image belongs to, which is often the same as attempting to determine what is shown on an image.

Join our book's Discord space

Join the book's Discord Workspace for Latest updates, Offers, Tech happenings around the world, New Release and Sessions with the Authors:

https://discord.bpbonline.com

CHAPTER 11

Microservices and Containerization on .NET 7

Introduction

Many popular Web applications have to deal with a large amount of data; for example, an application such as Facebook and Twitter deals with huge volumes of traffic at the time. They have to support millions of users simultaneously engaging in live interactions while keeping the performance high.

The Web applications that have to deal with large-scale usage are typically built as a collection of distributed microservices rather than a single monolithic application. Each microservice is responsible only for a specific functionality or a collection of related functionalities. This way, each part of the system can be scaled independently, and the load can be distributed among as many separate components as needed.

Normally, high-performance applications use two different types of scaling: vertical scaling (scaling up) and horizontal scaling (scaling out). The process of vertical scaling involves adding more hardware resources, such as RAM and CPU, to make the machine faster. This works, but it has its limits. Horizontal scaling, on the other hand, is about distributing the load among many instances of an application. With a well-implemented architecture, this process has virtually no limits. This is where microservices show their usefulness.

To make microservices even more effective, containerization was invented. This process allows each application to be deployed together with its runtime environment. The application would be completely isolated from the outside world, except for some of its parts, which can be intentionally configured. This would ensure that the application behaves consistently in any environment, as none of the processing happening on the host machine can cause any unintentional side effects to the application. This also ensures that the application can run on absolutely any machine that supports a specific containerization technology, regardless of what operating system runs on that machine and what system-level dependencies are installed on it.

The main containerization technology used in the IT industry is Docker. Although alternatives exist, Docker is the de facto standard containerization technology. It is also well-integrated with the .NET SDK. This is what we will cover in this chapter.

Structure

In this chapter, we will go through the fundamentals of Docker containers and their usage in the context of .NET. We will cover the following topics:

- Docker container fundamentals
- Base Docker image for .NET 7
- Orchestrating applications with Docker Swarm
- Orchestrating applications with Kubernetes

Objectives

By the end of this chapter, you will have learned how to publish a .NET application inside a container and how to orchestrate a distributed containerized application via Docker Swarm and Kubernetes.

Prerequisites

To follow this chapter, you will need the following:

- A machine running either Windows, MacOS, or Linux operating system
- .NET 7 SDK
- A suitable IDE or a code editor
- Being familiar with C# fundamentals

If you do not have any of the preceding listed dependencies installed already, you can use the setup instruction provided in *Chapter 1: Getting Familiar with .NET 7 Application Structure*, which also provides a recap of C# fundamentals.

Docker container fundamentals

A Docker container can be thought of as a lightweight **virtual machine** (**VM**). An ordinary VM would be a virtual version of a computer that runs inside an operating system or a physical computer and shares its resources. It would normally be a fully functioning computer that happens to be isolated from its host environment. It would have a fully functioning operating system, be accessible via a user interface, and otherwise be usable as a normal computer.

These characteristics of a VM make it heavyweight. Even though it is possible to limit the amount of hardware it can access, it would still require a reasonable amount of resources just to perform the most basic operations. It would also occupy a significant amount of storage on the disk due to its need to have a complete operating system of its own. This also makes the process of moving a VM to a different hardware somewhat difficult and time-consuming.

Docker has changed all of this. A Docker container is still an isolated environment that can run applications inside of it, just like a VM. But it does not have the full OS. Typically, a container would have a very lightweight version of the OS that only has the core components necessary for it to function. If the application that needs to be deployed into the container needs any specific tools, drivers, or utilities, these can be added to the container before the application is placed in it. This way, the size of the container might not be much bigger than the size of the application that runs inside it. This is what makes the containers easy to replicate, deploy, and move between physical machines.

Containers and container images

A Docker container refers to an active unit that is running in the system. Before a container can be built and launched, a container image must be created. The container image represents all the data container has. But it is not in an active state. In fact, it can be thought of as a file that can be downloaded and uploaded; even though it is not exactly a file, but it is conceptually similar. When an image is built, it can be *pushed* into an image registry, which is equivalent to uploading a file to storage. The image can then be *pulled* from the registry, which is analogous to downloading a file. Once an image has been pulled, a container can be launched from it.

Private Docker image registries can be created to host container images specific to a concrete system and/or a concrete organization. By default, Docker is connected to the Docker Hub registry, which is available publicly. Any image on it can normally be pulled onto any machine running Docker. Docker Hub is available via the following URL:

https://hub.docker.com/

Base images and layers

Every Docker container image is built on top of base images. Each base image will probably be based on base images of its own. The only exception is the so-called *scratch* image, which is empty.

A base image provides a reusable set of dependencies. For example, if we want to run a .NET application inside a container, we could create our image based on the standard .NET base image. This image will have all the necessary SDK components and tools that allow us to build and run our application.

To build an image, Docker uses the so-called **Dockerfile** script. Dockerfile is a standard name of a file that contains all commands necessary to add all the required components to the image. We can copy files, build applications, expose certain ports, download, install any missing OS components, and so on.

Typically, every time a command gets executed inside Dockerfile, an image layer gets created and cached in the local Docker instance. This makes subsequent builds a lot faster. If a sequence of the commands has not changed and the results of these commands are deterministic, Docker will not necessarily execute all these commands again when an image needs to be rebuilt. Instead, it will just pull an image layer that was created by executing these commands previously. Only subsequent commands will be executed if any new commands are added or if the target of any given command has changed (for example, there were code changes in the application that is being built).

Network isolation and port mapping

By default, a Docker container is completely isolated from any other applications running in the same environment. It can be accessed from within the inner Docker network, but nothing else can communicate with it. However, the applications inside a container can communicate and send requests to the outside world. So, by default, an application inside a Docker container can act as a client but not as a server.

To make an application inside a Docker container act as a server, a port mapping can be used. To make it work, a specific port is marked as *exposed* by a command inside the Dockerfile while the image is built. Then, a port mapping is added to the command that launches the container. The exposed container port is mapped to a specific port on the host machine. This makes the application accessible to anything on the network that the host machine is connected to, including the Internet.

File system isolation and bind mounts

By default, the file system inside a Docker container is fully isolated. It can be accessed by Docker and by executing specific Docker commands. But nothing else on the host machine can access the files inside the container.

Sometimes, however, there is a need to enable easy file sharing between a Docker container and its host machine. It might be convenient to expose log files this way. If it happens in a development environment, it would be convenient to see what is happening inside the container in real-time. Docker has the ability to map portions of the internal file systems of the containers to specific folders on the host OS. There are multiple ways of achieving it, but bind mount is perhaps the most popular technique.

A bind mount is a process of establishing a two-way mapping between a specific file or folder inside a Docker container and an equivalent file or folder on the host machine. Making changes to the mapped content on the host machine makes the same changes happen inside the container. The same is true the other way around.

Now, we will move on to the installation of Docker. The process will vary depending on what operating system you use.

Installing Docker on Linux

Docker was originally developed for Linux only before it became available on Windows and Mac OS. There are multiple ways of installing it. It can be done purely via a command line interface or via a fully managed Docker Desktop. There are also some differences in installing it depending on the exact Linux distro that is being used.

Because the ways of installing Docker on Linux vary depending on your personal preferences and the distro that you use, the best course of action is to follow the official installation instruction for Linux. This can be found via the following link:

https://docs.docker.com/desktop/install/linux-install/

Installing Docker on Mac

Mac will also have some variations of installing Docker depending on whether a specific machine uses Intel or Apple Silicon. The most up-to-date installation instruction can be found here:

https://docs.docker.com/desktop/install/mac-install/

Installing Docker on Windows

Windows installation of Docker Desktop requires Hyper-V, which is only available on 64-bit versions of Windows 10 or 11 Pro, Enterprise, and Education. Therefore, the only way to install Docker on the Home edition of Windows is to do it in a VM.

The detailed installation instruction for Windows is available via the following link:

https://docs.docker.com/desktop/install/windows-install/

Once we have Docker installed on our development machine, we can start looking at its integration with .NET 7 SDK. We will also look at some basic Docker commands, both the ones that are used inside a Dockerfile to build an image and the ones used by the CLI.

Base Docker image for .NET 7

Since .NET 7, Docker functionality is fully integrated with the SDK, the simplest way of creating a Docker image with your application inside of it is to publish it as a Docker image. This is what we will do next.

We can use any .NET application type but will use an ASP.NET Core Razor Pages application as an example. We can create such an application by executing the following command:

```
dotnet new web -o BasicContainerApp
```

Then, we can open the terminal inside the folder of the newly created project and execute the following command to add a temporary NuGet package to the project that is required for the seamless creation of a Docker image:

```
dotnet add package Microsoft.NET.Build.Containers
```

Next, we will execute the following command to create a Docker image:

```
dotnet publish --os linux --arch x64 -c Release
-p:PublishProfile=DefaultContainer
```

The **--os** parameter indicates what operating system Docker is configured to run. It is not the same as the operating system of the host machine, as Docker Desktop for Windows can still be configured to rung Linux containers. The **--arch** parameter indicates the CPU architecture that is being used, which can either be ×64 or arm64. This refers to the CPU architecture of the host machine. The **-c** parameter indicates that the configuration of the published application is **Release**. The **-p** parameter can be used to supply any other custom parameters to the .NET compiler. In our case, we are setting up a publish profile that allows us to automatically build an image.

By default, the Docker image that gets created by this process has the lower-case version of the project name and the semantic software version of 1.0.0. Therefore, assuming that our original project was called **BasicContainerApp**, the full name of the resulting image would be **basiccontainerapp:1.0.0**.

To start a container based on this image, we can execute the following command:

```
docker run -it --rm -p 5010:80 basiccontainerapp:1.0.0
```

docker run is the command that is used for launching a Docker container based on a specific image. The **-it** flag indicates that we are running it in the interactive mode, so the console will display the output from inside the container while it is running. We can also use **-d** if we want to run it in a detached mode. The **--rm** flag indicates that we remove the container and all the data associated with it once it stops. The **-p** attribute is the port mapping. The first number is the port on the host machine. The second number is the port in the container that it maps to. The latter needs to be exposed by the container for the mapping to work. Port 80 is exposed by default if we use this particular way of building a container. Finally, we have the image name at the end of this command, which is **basiccontainerapp:1.0.0**.

When we launch the container, the console will start displaying the output of the application. Because the Web application inside the container is listening on port 80, which is mapped to port 5010 of the host machine, we can navigate to the application in the browser by typing the following URL:

http://localhost:5010/

But this is not the only way to add Docker support to a .NET application. A traditional way would be to add a Dockerfile to the application and get Docker CLI rather than .NET CLI to build the image. If we are using Windows with Visual Studio as our IDE, we do not have to add the Dockerfile manually. We can add Docker support while creating the application project from the GUI.

Creating an application with Docker support

While creating a new .NET application from Visual Studio, we can select the **Enable Docker** option. This will also prompt us to select the **Docker OS**, which can be either Windows or Linux, as *figure 11.1* demonstrates:

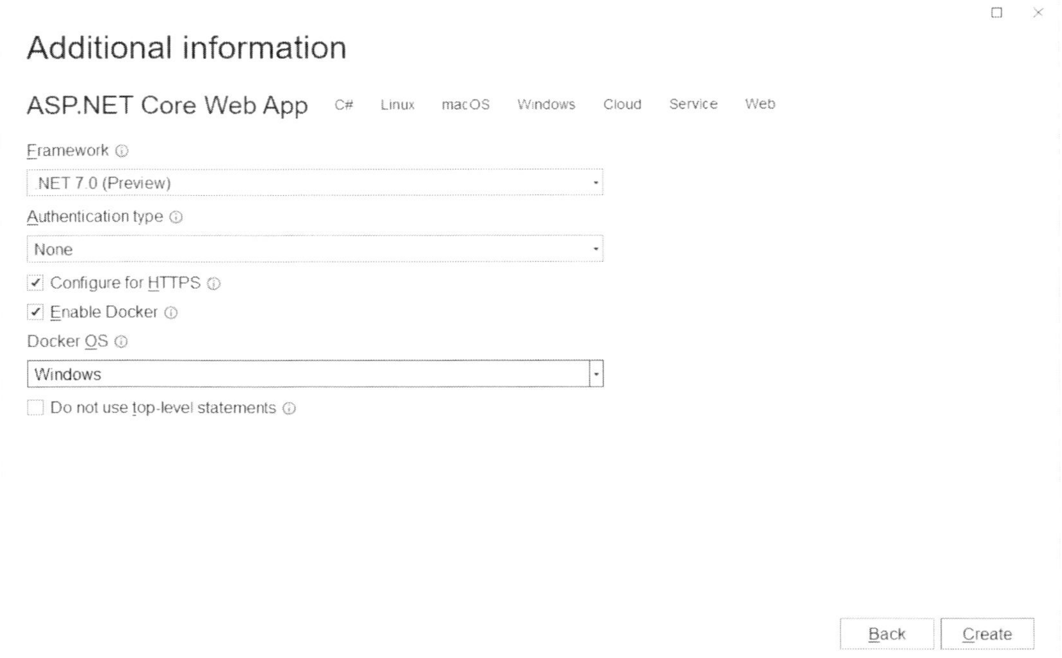

Figure 11.1: *Creating an application with Docker support*

Once the application project is created, a file with the name of Dockerfile will be placed inside the project folder. Its content will be similar to the following:

```
FROM mcr.microsoft.com/dotnet/aspnet:7.0 AS base
WORKDIR /app
EXPOSE 80
EXPOSE 443


FROM mcr.microsoft.com/dotnet/sdk:7.0 AS build
WORKDIR /src
COPY ["WindowsContainerExample/WindowsContainerExample.csproj",
"WindowsContainerExample/"]
RUN dotnet restore "WindowsContainerExample/WindowsContainerExample.
csproj"
```

```
COPY . .
WORKDIR "/src/WindowsContainerExample"
RUN dotnet build "WindowsContainerExample.csproj" -c Release -o /app/
build

FROM build AS publish
RUN dotnet publish "WindowsContainerExample.csproj" -c Release -o /app/
publish /p:UseAppHost=false

FROM base AS final
WORKDIR /app
COPY --from=publish /app/publish .
ENTRYPOINT ["dotnet", "WindowsContainerExample.dll"]
```

The content of this file will be the same regardless of which Docker OS we have chosen. The only differences will be the project and solution names. In the preceding example, we assume that the project is called **WindowsContainerExample**.

In addition to this, the following element will be added to the **.csproj** file:

```
<DockerDefaultTargetOS>Windows</DockerDefaultTargetOS>
```

This element is not strictly necessary. A Docker image can be built without it. But if we choose to use this element, we need to set our Docker instance to run the OS that is specified here. Otherwise, Docker will just build the image for whichever OS is set as the OS of the local Docker instance.

Visual Studio users can also add Docker support to an existing application. This is what we will have a look at next.

Adding Docker support to an existing application

If we have a .NET project open in Visual Studio that does not already have Docker support, we can right-click on the project and click on **Docker Support**, as *figure 11.2* demonstrates:

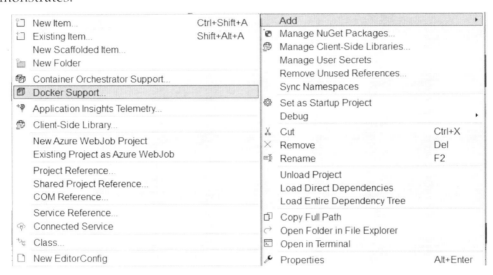

Figure 11.2: *Adding Docker support to an existing application*

If you do not use Visual Studio, then you would have to create a Dockerfile manually. Now, we will examine its structure more closely.

Dockerfile structure

Let us assume that we have an ASP.NET Core application project called **LinuxContainerExample**. It has the following content, which is based on what Visual Studio produces:

```
FROM mcr.microsoft.com/dotnet/aspnet:7.0 AS base
WORKDIR /app
EXPOSE 80
EXPOSE 443


FROM mcr.microsoft.com/dotnet/sdk:7.0 AS build
WORKDIR /src
COPY ["LinuxContainerExample/LinuxContainerExample.csproj",
```

```
"LinuxContainerExample/"]
RUN dotnet restore "LinuxContainerExample/LinuxContainerExample.csproj"
COPY . .
WORKDIR "/src/LinuxContainerExample"
RUN dotnet build "LinuxContainerExample.csproj" -c Release -o /app/build

FROM build AS publish
RUN dotnet publish "LinuxContainerExample.csproj" -c Release -o /app/
publish /p:UseAppHost=false

FROM base AS final
WORKDIR /app
COPY --from=publish /app/publish .
ENTRYPOINT ["dotnet", "LinuxContainerExample.dll"]
```

Let us examine it line-by-line. The first line is the following:

```
FROM mcr.microsoft.com/dotnet/aspnet:7.0 AS base
```

This is where we are telling Docker to use **mcr.microsoft.com/dotnet/aspnet:7.0** as the base image of our container. This is the standard runtime image for ASP.NET Core 7. Runtime image only has runtime components and no SDK, so it can be used to run an application but cannot be used to build it. We will use an intermediate image shortly. The next lines are as follows:

```
WORKDIR /app
EXPOSE 80
EXPOSE 443
```

This is where we set the **app** directory in the root of the container folder structure as our working directory and expose ports **80** and **443** to the outside world. Port **80** is the default HTTP port, whereas port **443** is the default HTTPS port.

In the next two lines, we are setting the official .NET SDK image as the base image of an intermediate image and are setting the **src** folder in the root of this image as the working directory:

```
FROM mcr.microsoft.com/dotnet/sdk:7.0 AS build
WORKDIR /src
```

Then, we copy the project file into the **LinuxContainerExample** folder inside the working directory:

```
COPY ["LinuxContainerExample/LinuxContainerExample.csproj",
"LinuxContainerExample/"]
```

The original path for the **COPY** command is either an absolute path on the host machine or the path relative to where the **docker build** command is being executed from. In our case, we assume that the **docker build** command is being executed from a folder immediately above the project folder.

The following two commands restore NuGet dependencies from the project inside the image and copy content from the current folder on the host machine to the working directory:

```
RUN dotnet restore "LinuxContainerExample/LinuxContainerExample.csproj"
COPY . .
```

This copies the remaining project files into the image. In the next two commands, we set the project directory inside the image as the working directory and compile the application from the project:

```
WORKDIR "/src/LinuxContainerExample"
RUN dotnet build "LinuxContainerExample.csproj" -c Release -o /app/build
```

The next lines would create another intermediate image from the build image and create a publishable executable application:

```
FROM build AS publish
RUN dotnet publish "LinuxContainerExample.csproj" -c Release -o /app/publish /p:UseAppHost=false
```

Finally, we copy the published application from the publish image into the final image and launch the application via the dotnet CLI:

```
FROM base AS final
WORKDIR /app
COPY --from=publish /app/publish .
ENTRYPOINT ["dotnet", "LinuxContainerExample.dll"]
```

In the final image, only the published application exists. We only have the .NET runtime and the application running inside of it. The intermediate images with .NET SDK and various build artefacts have been discarded.

This is the basic structure of a Dockerfile. Now, we will have a look at how we can build an image from it and launch a container from the image.

Building and running a Docker container

To build a Docker container image, we can execute a command similar to the following:

```
docker build -t basicapp:1.0.0 .
```

`docker build` is the base command that is used for building images. The **-t** parameter represents an image tag. We could choose any name, as long as it is not already taken by an existing image made by someone else. The part after the colon can be anything, but it is typically used for the version number. The last part of the command indicates the working directory on the host machine. If we use a dot at the end of the command statement, as in the preceding example, the directory we are running the command from is the working directory. This means that the current directory is the place where the command will look for all the necessary files.

The preceding example assumes that we have the Dockerfile in the directory from which we are executing the command. However, we could have the Dockerfile anywhere and point to it via either an absolute or a relative path by adding an **-f** or **--file** parameter followed by the file path.

In the preceding example, we have created an image with the full tag name of **basicapp:1.0.0**. We can launch a container from this image by executing a command similar to the following:

```
docker run -it --rm -p 5010:80 basicapp:1.0.0
```

This concludes an overview of how to build and run a single Docker container. In a real-life scenario, we often have to run multiple containers as parts of a single distributed application. We also want to make sure that the containers can be restarted when they encounter problems and that they can be scaled as needed. This is where orchestration comes from.

Orchestrating applications with Docker Swarm

As the name suggests, the process of orchestration is analogous to getting an orchestra to work as a single unit. In an orchestra, there are many people playing a diverse range of musical instruments. But they work together in a coordinated manner to create a pre-defined piece of music.

The process of orchestrating a distributed application is the same. The application consists of individual microservices. But these microservices work as a single distributed application. The orchestration ensures that everything inside the application works seamlessly. The microservices that were forced to stop are restarted. If there is a specific microservice that experiences an increased load, it is scaled out. If the hardware on a specific machine fails, the services deployed on this machine are removed and re-created on a different machine in the cluster.

There are multiple ways of orchestrating Docker containers. A production-grade orchestration system available with Docker is called Docker Swarm. We will have a look at it shortly. But first, we will look at a more basic orchestration-like functionality that can be achieved by using Docker Compose.

Basic orchestration with Docker compose

Docker Compose is a tool that is included with Docker. It uses YAML files to launch multiple Docker containers together. There are some other orchestration capabilities, such as the ability to launch the containers in a specific order and pre-configure individual containers to restart if they are stopped due to an error. But these are the limits of Docker Compose.

To use Docker Compose, we will need to create a YAML file. By convention, the file is called **docker-compose.yml**. But we can give it any name. If we do that, we will have to explicitly specify it in the Docker Compose commands.

If you are working on a Windows machine and using Visual Studio as your IDE, you can add the Docker Compose orchestration support to your application simply by right-clicking on your project, clicking **Add | Container Orchestration Support**, as shown in *figure 11.3*:

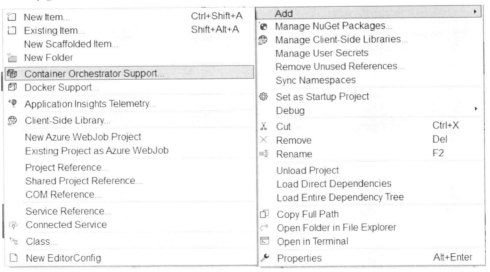

Figure 11.3: Adding Docker Swarm orchestration to a .NET app

This will create some files in the root of the solution. The main file used by Docker Compose is the **docker-compose.yml**, which will have content similar to the following:

```
version: '3.4'

services:
  linuxcontainerexample:
```

```
image: ${DOCKER_REGISTRY-}linuxcontainerexample
build:
  context: .
  dockerfile: LinuxContainerExample/Dockerfile
```

This file may contain multiple services, but in the preceding example, it contains only one service. Each service in the `services` section has its name. In the preceding example, our service is called **linuxcontainerexample**.

Then, we provide some instructions to either build an image for the container or pull an existing one. In our example, we are building a new image from a Dockerfile located under a specific relative path. The image field allows us to set the name of the image. We can also use environment variables, like the **${DOCKER_REGISTRY-}** value in the image name, as shown in the preceding example.

Now, to launch a distributed application and create all the required containers, we can run the following command in the directory of our YAML file:

docker-compose up -d

In this example, we are running all the containers in the detached mode by specifying the **-d** flag. But we could also run them in an interactive mode by omitting this flag. To bring down the containers, we could execute the following command:

docker-compose down

This concludes the overview of the basic Docker Compose orchestration. This orchestration mechanism is very limited and is only suitable for either very basic applications or a temporary development setup. Now, we will have a look at a more advanced Docker Swarm orchestration mechanism.

Starting Docker Swarm

Just like Docker Compose, Docker Swarm comes with Docker. But it is way more advanced as an orchestration mechanism than Docker Compose. It is suitable for production-grade deployment of scalable distributed applications, as it is capable of running across multiple machines, automatically distributing containers between machines, detecting and reacting to hardware failures, and scaling individual microservices by replicating them.

Docker Swarm is a cluster of coordinated nodes, which can be represented as either physical or virtual machines. To start a Docker Swarm, we will need to execute the following command, which will create a master VM that will serve the role of an orchestrator:

docker swarm init

The output of this command will show the command that needs to be executed to join the Swarm. It will be unique to a specific Swarm instance, as a unique join token needs to be generated. It will look similar to the following:

```
docker swarm join --token SWMTKN-1-1bj2ltc44eb9c45zq7482vt6f1ryx3ghrwe2z
xqlcakht7ui5x-csqtvblydg7h9ge5mw0qixuz0 192.168.65.3:2377
```

If we ever need to remind ourselves what the command is, we can execute the following command on the machine hosting the Swarm:

```
docker swarm join-token worker
```

Once we execute the **docker swarm join** command, we can start adding services to the Swarm. We can also dictate how many replicas of each service we want to add. For example, the following command adds three replicas of a container based on the **basiccontainerapp:1.0.** image and gives this service the name of **basic-service**:

```
docker service create --replicas 3 --name basic-service
basiccontainerapp:1.0.0
```

If we want to see what services are present in our Swarm instance, we can execute the following command:

```
docker service ls
```

The output of this command should be similar to the following:

```
ID      NAME   MODE   REPLICAS      IMAGE          PORTS
kgd33x72ae31 basic-servicereplicated   3/3      basiccontainerapp:1.0.0
```

We can also remove all instances of a specific service by executing the following command:

```
docker service rm basic-service
```

If the specified service was the only service present in the Swarm, the output of the **docker service ls** command should be as follows:

```
ID        NAME       MODE       REPLICAS   IMAGE     PORTS
```

If we want a specific node to be removed from the Swarm, we can execute the following command:

```
docker swarm leave
```

If we want to dissolve the Swarm, we can execute this command on the main node and add the **--force** flag to it.

Docker Swarm is not the only way of orchestrating Docker containers in production. Another popular platform is Kubernetes, which we will have a look at next.

Orchestrating applications with Kubernetes

Kubernetes is a popular container orchestration platform that was originally created by Google. It is more suited for large-scale distributed applications than Docker Swarm. This is because it has many additional features that make such a process easy. For example, groups of related containers can be organized into the so-called "pods". Also, Helm charts allows us to quickly build a distributed application based on a pre-defined pattern.

We can install Kubernetes on our development machine. The process will vary depending on what OS and CPU architecture we use. In both cases, we will need to install the server component and the command line client to manage it. The latter can be represented by a tool called **kubectl**.

Installing Kubernetes on Linux

On a Linux machine, we can install the **minikube** tool that will represent a development version of the Kubernetes server. If we have a machine with x64 CPU architecture, the commands will be as follows:

```
curl -LO https://storage.googleapis.com/minikube/releases/latest/minikube-linux-amd64
sudo install minikube-linux-amd64 /usr/local/bin/minikube
```

For an ARM64 machine, the commands will be as follows:

```
curl -LO https://storage.googleapis.com/minikube/releases/latest/minikube-linux-arm64
sudo install minikube-linux-arm64 /usr/local/bin/minikube
```

Then, we will need to install the **kubectl** tool that will allow us to interact with the cluster. The download command will be as follows on an ×64 machine. We will need to replace the **amd64** part with **amd64** on an AMD machine:

```
curl -LO "https://dl.k8s.io/release/$(curl -L -s https://dl.k8s.io/release/stable.txt)/bin/linux/amd64/kubectl"
```

Then, we will need to install it, which we can do by executing the following command:

```
sudo install -o root -g root -m 0755 kubectl /usr/local/bin/kubectl
```

Installing Kubernetes on Mac

Mac OS can also use **minikube** as the Kubernetes server in the development environment. The download and installation commands will be as follows for a Mac with an Intel CPU chip:

```
curl -LO https://storage.googleapis.com/minikube/releases/latest/
minikube-darwin-amd64

sudo install minikube-darwin-amd64 /usr/local/bin/minikube
```

The commands will be as follows for a device with an Apple Silicon chip:

```
curl -LO https://storage.googleapis.com/minikube/releases/latest/
minikube-darwin-arm64

sudo install minikube-darwin-arm64 /usr/local/bin/minikube
```

We can then download the **kubectl** tool by executing the following command, where **amd64** option in the path is used for the Intel chip device version, and **arm64** is used for the Apple Silicon version.

```
curl -LO "https://dl.k8s.io/release/$(curl -L -s https://dl.k8s.io/
release/stable.txt)/bin/darwin/amd64/kubectl"
```

Next, we will need to execute the following commands to make the **kubectl** available in the terminal:

```
chmod +x ./kubectl

sudo mv ./kubectl /usr/local/bin/kubectl

sudo chown root: /usr/local/bin/kubectl

Installing Kubernetes on Windows
```

On Windows, the simplest way to install Kubernetes is via Docker Desktop. We can do so by right-clicking on the Docker Desktop icon in the taskbar tray, selecting **Settings**, navigating to the **Kubernetes** section, and checking the **Enable Kubernetes** option, as shown in *figure 11.4*:

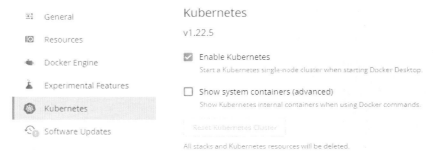

Figure 11.4: *Enabling Kubernetes on Docker Desktop on Windows*

Once we save the settings, all the required Kubernetes components will be installed, including **kubectl**.

Adding services to a Kubernetes cluster

Once our local Kubernetes cluster has been installed, we can verify it by executing the following command in the terminal:

```
kubectl --help
```

If there is no error, we can start deploying containers in our Kubernetes cluster. First, we can deploy a specific Docker container by executing the **kubectl** create **deploymen** command. The following example deploys a service with the name of **basic-service** from the Docker image with the name of **basiccontainerapp:1.0.0.**

```
kubectl create deployment basic-service --image basiccontainerapp:1.0.0
```

Next, we can execute the following command to expose port **80** of the service:

```
kubectl expose deployment basic-service --type=NodePort --port=80
```

We can view the information about any given service by executing the following command:

```
kubectl get services basic-service
```

The output of this command should look similar to this:

```
NAME            TYPE        CLUSTER-IP       EXTERNAL-IP    PORT(S)
AGE

basic-service   NodePort    10.109.141.219   <none>         80:31546/TCP
50s
```

To make the service accessible from the outside, we need to forward its internally exposed port to a port on the host machine. We can forward the previously exposed port **80** of the service to port **7080** of the host machine by executing the following command:

```
kubectl port-forward service/basic-service 7080:80
```

Now, we can test our setup by navigating to the following address in the browser:

```
http://localhost:7080
```

If we want to remove our Kubernetes cluster, we can just uncheck the Enable Kubernetes option in Docker Desktop on Windows and save the settings. If we are on either Mac or Linux, we can do so by executing the following command to stop all services in the cluster:

```
minikube stop
```

Then we can execute the following command to delete all the services.

```
minikube delete --all
```

This concludes the overview of building and orchestrating Docker containers. Let us summarize what we have learned.

Conclusion

In this chapter, we have covered the process of containerizing a .NET application. We have learned that the main containerization tool used for this purpose is Docker and that .NET 7 SDK has inbuilt support for it.

We have learned how to install Docker, write Dockerfile script, and how to build .NET applications into Docker containers. We have covered this process with a variety of GUI tools and the command line interface.

We have also covered the process of orchestrating a distributed application that consists of containerized microservices. We had a look at three industry-standard tools to do so: Docker Compose, which allows us to run containers together; Docker Swarm, which allows us to scale individual services; and Kubernetes, which comes with many advanced orchestration features. For each of these tools, we have a look at how to run it in a development environment.

This concludes the book about the core features of C# 11 and .NET 7.

Points to remember

- Docker is a technology that allows to deploy applications in containers.

- Each container would include the application and its most fundamental OS dependencies.

- The application inside a container is normally inaccessible from the outside unless it has port mappings and bind-mounting its internal folders to the specific folders on the host machine.

- Containerization is especially useful in distributed applications, which can be orchestrated via Docker Swarm or Kubernetes.

Multiple choice questions

1. **What is the difference between a Docker container and a Docker image?**

    a. They are interchangeable

    b. Container is a repository of Docker images

    c. Image represents container's data in a passive state, whereas a container represents a running application

    d. Container represents image's data in a passive state, whereas an image represents a running application

2. **What system can be used for orchestrating Docker containers?**

    a. Docker Swarm

    b. Kubernetes

    c. Either of the above

    d. Cron

3. **What are the benefits of using containerization?**

    a. Consistent behavior on all environments

    b. Isolation of an application from any potential sources of unintentional side-effects

    c. Application is easy to deploy and orchestrate

    d. All of the above

4. **What is the main benefit of using multi-stage image-building process in Docker?**

    a. Separating runtime from build SDK and build-specific dependencies

    b. Readability improvement

    c. Adherence to common standards

    d. There is no tangible benefit of doing it

Answers

1. c
2. c
3. d
4. a

Key terms

- **Docker**: A system that allows packing applications into isolated environments known as containers.

- **Docker container image**: A pre-build piece of software that contains an application and its OS dependencies that can be launched as a container.

- **Docker container**: An executable that includes the main application and the core OS components that allow the application to function.

- **Docker image registry**: A system that stores Docker container images that can be pulled.

- **Dockerfile**: A file that dictates how a Docker image is built.

- **Bind mount**: A process of mapping files and folders inside a Docker container to files and folders inside the host machine.

- **Orchestration**: The process of coordinating components of a distributed application to work as one unit.

- **Docker Swarm**: A group of physical or virtual machines that work together as a single cluster and can orchestrate a collection of Docker containers.

- **Kubernetes**: A heavyweight container orchestration system that is suitable for large-scale production deployments of distributed applications.

Join our book's Discord space

Join the book's Discord Workspace for Latest updates, Offers, Tech happenings around the world, New Release and Sessions with the Authors:

https://discord.bpbonline.com

Index